VOLUME 4

...*THAT THE WORLD MAY KNOW*
that Thou hast sent Me, and hast
loved them, as Thou hast loved Me.

John 17:23

THAT THE WORLD MAY KNOW

Volume 4

THE MUSLIM WORLD

The Muslim World

By
FREDK. A. TATFORD, Litt.D.

in association with
the Editors of Echoes of Service

with Appendix by

HAROLD MACKAY

1983
ECHOES OF SERVICE
1 WIDCOMBE CRESCENT, BATH, AVON BA2 6AQ

ISBN 0 946214 03 4

Photoset in 11/12 Plantin
Designed and produced by
PETER WHATLEY (Trowbridge)
for the publishers, Echoes of Service, Bath, Avon

Printed and bound in Great Britain by
Redwood Burn Limited, Trowbridge, Wiltshire

Contents

Acknowledgments

It goes without saying that the books in this series could not possibly be the work of one person. A certain amount of personal research has naturally been necessary, but the bulk of the information has been supplied by missionaries and very sincere thanks are due to them for their willingness to sacrifice time and effort in order to assist in this project. Without the details they have so readily furnished, the task could never have been accomplished.

A special debt is also due to Mr. S. F. Warren, whose energy and resourcefulness have been invaluable. The contribution he has made, particularly in securing information, is incalculable, and his patience in reading and re-reading drafts (often in the most illegible calligraphy) and in suggesting improvements and amendments deserves respect. We are also grateful to Mr. A. Pulleng, who with his wealth of knowledge of the mission field has so carefully examined every detail and whose encouragement in the project has been unwavering.

So many of the staff at *Echoes* office have been involved in one way or another in research, in planning and in typing that it would be invidious to mention anyone by name.

Mrs. M. V. Stockdale deserves special mention for her willingness to convert illegible manuscripts into legible typescripts, and David Restall of Shipham has given immense help in preparing the many photographs for publication.

If permission has not been obtained for some of the quotations included in the books, we tender apologies and trust that the sin of omission will be forgiven.

To ensure a measure of consistency the population figures quoted have been taken from the 1982/83 *Statesmen's Year Book* and the spelling of place names from the sixth edition (1980) of *The Times Atlas* (except in colour maps). Where appropriate, earlier spellings are shown in parentheses. Dates have been confirmed from latest available sources. The information is, as far as possible, up to date as at February 1983.

List of Illustrations

List of Maps

Preface

On the occasion of the centenary of the magazine, *Echoes of Service*, it was decided to produce a history of the work of assembly missionaries in the foreign field up to that time, and a fully illustrated volume, *Turning the World Upside Down*, accordingly made its appearance in 1972. The first edition in cloth boards rapidly sold out, and a paperback edition, still selling, is obtainable from Echoes Publications, 1 Widcombe Crescent, Bath, Avon BA2 6AQ.

Limited space made it impossible for the full story of the world-wide missionary effort to be told: even with the curtailment of detailed accounts and the restriction to missionaries commended from the U.K., the book reached 671 pages.

As a further eleven years have elapsed, it seems desirable to supplement the book with a series of others, dealing with the different fields of service and including a fuller reference to missionaries from the U.S.A., Canada, Australia and New Zealand.

Our colleagues in the Missionary Service Groups in those countries and the U.K. have co-operated fully in this new project. It is obviously not practicable to trace the complete story of missionary endeavour and, largely of necessity, the account has been restricted to workers from brethren assemblies. (An explanation of the term 'brethren' is given in Appendix I.)

When *Turning the World Upside Down* was compiled, it was prepared for the press and seen through to the stage of final production by Dr. Fredk. A. Tatford. When the new project was contemplated, therefore, we naturally turned to Dr. Tatford, who has always been interested in missionaries and their work and has visited many of them overseas. He willingly agreed to undertake the task of writing the books.

The complete series envisaged, under the general title of 'THAT THE WORLD MAY KNOW . . .', is as follows:

The research entailed in examining the source material covering many decades has been a rewarding exercise in which two earlier convictions have been confirmed and deepened. Firstly, that the work developed from small beginnings. Not infrequently it has involved the spirit of a pioneer constrained by love for Christ and those He came to save. Secondly, that New Testament principles of evangelism and church planting are timeless in their relevance and universal in their scope. From continent to continent and country to country the gospel has been preached, men and women have been converted and assemblies planted.

It is our hope and expectation that readers will find this account of practical help as a book of reference informing their minds about missionary personnel and the place, duration and nature of their service. If, additionally, the record increases devotion to the Lord Jesus and commitment to Him in the worldwide spread of the gospel, it will have well served its intended purpose.

A. PULLENG
S. F. WARREN

Countries Whose Population is More Than 40% Muslim

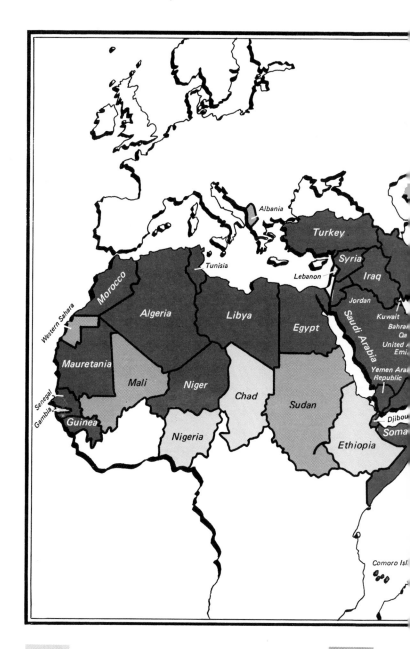

40 - 59% of country's population is Muslim

60 -

1

The Church's Failure

The evangelistic fervour of the early church was unparalleled in history. With the words of our Lord's commission (Matthew 28:19, 20) ringing in their ears, Christians 'went forth and preached everywhere' (Mark 16:20). There was plainly a realization of the Divine design and intention, which had never apparently been appreciated by Israel in an earlier economy, and the power of the Holy Spirit burst upon men as possibly never before. The sense of urgency and purpose drove the early Christian missionaries eastward as far as India and beyond, and westward along the north coast of Africa and through Europe to Spain. The flaming evangel of the Cross seemed destined to reach the whole of the civilized world.

Yet, by the third and fourth centuries, the fiery flame had become a smoking torch and, in some cases, the clear light of the gospel had been practically obscured. The burning zeal and dynamic evangelism of the first two centuries had diminished in force and intensity. There were, of course, many contributory factors. There is always a tendency for pristine enthusiasm to wane with the years: it is ever extremely difficult to maintain a consistent level of interest and determination over a long period. Moreover, the active opposition, which was evidenced from the very commencement of the Christian era, grew in volume and bitterness as time went on. But there were other tangible reasons for the lethargic condition of the church in those later days.

The simple form of church government, introduced initially by

El Jem – the colosseum   (Tunisian National Tourist Office)

Casablanca – Grand Mosque (R. Turpin, M.E.Ph.A.)

Rabat — minaret   (R. Turpin, M.E.Ph.A.)

the apostles and the apostolic delegates, had been superseded by an ecclesiastical hierarchy which exercised a sacerdotal authority over all church activities and outreach. At the same time, the spirituality inspired originally by a purity of faith and practice, common to all believers, had been dampened by the displacement of simple belief and practice by a new and completely organized sacramental system. The freedom of the individual to act at the dictate of the Spirit of God no longer existed. Personal witness was replaced by the official voice of the church.

Serious doctrinal controversies and the fratricidal conflicts which they provoked further weakened the power and testimony of the church. So far as the theologians were concerned – and, to a great extent, the rank and file of the church also – as one writer remarks, 'They were more interested in defending the purity of the gospel than in demonstrating its power.'

Perhaps the most important factor was the alleged conversion of Constantine in 323, and the consequent alliance of church and state. Thousands of heathen embraced the faith; many gave no

Sbeitla – a baptistry
(Tunisian National Tourist Office)

evidence of true conversion, and their pagan beliefs and practices accompanied them into the church; while not a few actually secured positions of influence and authority in the church. The emperor's patronage conferred status and respectability on the church and ended the 'reproach' of Christianity. But the material prosperity and official recognition now enjoyed provided no incentive to spiritual activity or evangelistic endeavour. As J. H. Kane pertinently remarks in *A Global View of Christian Missions*, p. 34, 'The alliance between the church and the state brought a measure of prosperity and prestige, but it hardly enhanced the spiritual stature or strengthened the moral fibre of the Christian community.'

Constantine assumed an authority in the ecclesiastical realm as well as in the political. It was he, for example, who summoned the Council of Nicea, and held it in the imperial palace, and himself presided over the proceedings. With Byzantium (or Constantinople) as his imperial capital, he became the head of the eastern church. Over the centuries since, the church has not infrequently been influenced and, in some measure, supported (and sometimes controlled) by the state. Where this has occurred, as has been aptly remarked, the wedding of ecclesiastical power to political power has always been to the detriment of spiritual power.

By the date of Constantine's death, the evangelistic impetus had gone and the church generally was in a condition of lethargic sloth and spiritual inertia. Historians frequently claim that, from the time of Muḥammad in the seventh century, the great Byzantine Empire was a bulwark against the inroads of Islām in eastern Europe. Politically, Byzantium was an obstacle to the Islāmic advance, but it is doubtful whether the same could be said of her religiously, and her influence certainly ceased with the fall of Constantinople in 1453. Long before that, the influence of the Christian church had seriously diminished.

For several centuries Christianity had been flowing in two streams, one emanating from Constantinople and the other from Rome. As regards eastern Europe and the Middle East, Basil Matthews says, in *Forward Through the Ages*, p. 50, 'It flows mainly from Constantinople, not from Rome. Its mother language in its Bible, and in its worship services is Greek, not Latin. It is more interested in abstract theology and less in its practical application than the western arm of the church: it can claim fewer missionary conquests. The heads of the eastern church, called patriarchs, were generally controlled by the emperor in Constantinople, the emperor being the head of the eastern church, as the pope was the head of the western branch. The civilization that grew up in connection with the eastern church was called Byzantine, because Byzantium was the earlier name of the city that the emperor Constantine later named Constantinople after himself.'

In north Africa the reasons for the change of attitude of the church were somewhat more complicated, although theological controversies were still a contributory factor. We can do little better than quote J. C. Thiessen. He writes in *A Survey of World Missions*, p. 174, 'All of north Africa was at one time considered Christian territory, but a decadent church and an unsound theology were unable to stand against the powerful influence of the new religion of Islām. One difficulty was that the Bible had

Making Berber pottery   (Tunisian National Tourist Office)

Fort Génois, Tabarka – off the North African coast
(Tunisian National Tourist Office)

not been translated into the language of the people. Another, that the church failed to become indigenous and missionary-minded.'

It should be appreciated also that the Reformation of the sixteenth century did nothing to retrieve the lost ground. Instead of reviving missionary endeavour and enthusiasm, the Reformers took the view that our Lord's commission of Matthew 28:19, 20 was not applicable to the present day. They maintained that the commission was given to the apostles and that they fulfilled it in their own day by carrying the gospel to every part of the civilized world of their day. If subsequent generations did not hear the gospel, it was because Divine judgment rested upon them for some reason, and it was not the responsibility of Christians to carry the gospel to them. If God desired to provide the heathen with the opportunity of repentance and salvation, He would undertake that in His own way. Others had neither the authority nor the responsibility to send missionaries to the heathen. Strangely enough, the same view is shared by some inactive Christians today, and has possibly acted as a disincentive to not a few young people.

From the seventh century to at least the sixteenth century, therefore, the influence of the church had largely evaporated. Its spiritual power and vitality had seriously deteriorated, its representation of Christ was pathetically restricted, and its missionary endeavour had practically ended. It was obsessed with irrelevancies and immersed in controversies, and it showed no trace of concern for the world in which it was found. It must have seemed without life or light.

The church was in a state of complete disunity. As W. H. T. Gairdner writes in *The Reproach of Islām*, p. 34, regarding the seventh to the eleventh centuries, 'the seamless robe of the church has been rent; throughout the Christian world, Christians are bitterly divided among themselves. In Rome and in Constantinople there are already ominous signs of the division which actually took place in 1054 into the "Catholic" and "Orthodox", or Roman Catholic and Greek Churches of the present day; while in the east, the Nestorian Christians, and in Egypt the Copts hate and are hated by the Established or Melchite Church of Byzantium.' Respect for the church had gone and the vast ecclesiastical body no longer stood as a bulwark against the foe.

Despite all the witness for Christ which there had been in Arabia, the church seemed no longer interested in the peninsula. Politically, Rome had failed to administer it, and Byzantium was concerned only to avoid any conflict with the hot-blooded nomadic tribes. The country was a tangle of tribes and clans with no real cohesion. Socially, 'the nation was divided into tribes, the tribes into clans, the clans into families. The conception of the blood feud tyrannized' them all. There was no strong central ruler with civil and military power. The tribal unit was virtually headless and justice was, in practice, in the hands of a vague number of elders. There was no education; reading and writing were practically unknown. Many of the tribes were almost irreligious and there was scarcely anything to satisfy the spiritual need of the people. They had no real religious leaders or teachers, no priesthood and no evangelists. And the church, which should have met the need, had utterly failed.

It was into conditions of this character that a new religion suddenly burst with the irresistible force of a militant, missionary zeal. It was a religion with a new vitality and a new morality and with a monotheistic faith. In place of the lifeless organization of the church, with its formalism and ritualism, and the mass of traditions in which the Divine revelation seemed to have been buried, the new religion appeared to be a living faith, with a simple, comprehensible message of God, and all its members were active participants and not merely subjects of ecclesiastical functionaries. It is no wonder that Islām swept across north Africa and intruded into Europe. 'The explosion of the Arabian peninsula into the conquest and conversion of half the Mediterranean world is the most extraordinary phenomenon in medieval history,' says W. Durrant in *The Age of Faith*, p. 155. But the explanation is only too sadly evident. Possibly the amazing expansion of Islām today is due to the current failure of the church.

Dougga – where Christians once were numerous

(Tunisian National Tourist Office)

2

The Prophet of Arabia

The origin of Islām was, of course, in the unattractive peninsula of Arabia. Centuries ago, Arabia was, it is thought, a land of great fertility. 'Through the millennia,' to quote Bernard Lewis in *The Arabs in History*, p. 23, 'it has been undergoing a process of steady desiccation, a drying up of wealth and waterways and a spread of the desert at the expense of the cultivable land. The declining productivity of the peninsula, together with the increase in the number of the inhabitants, led to a series of crises of over-population and consequently to a recurring cycle of invasions of the neighbouring countries by the Semitic people of the peninsula.'

The people immediately prior to the rise of Islām were mainly Bedouin nomads, who held together in tribes with a very rudimentary organization. The sheikh, or leader of the tribe, was elected by the elders, and he was advised by the *Majlis*, or council of elders. The religion was a form of polydemonism, but certain god classes were recognized as well, the principal ones being Manāt ('Fate'), Al-'Uzzā ('Strong') and Al-Lāt (the Goddess), but these three were subordinate to a higher deity named Allāh. There was no priesthood and the tribal faith centred in a tribal god, symbolized by a stone. In a few cases, the nomadic tribes settled down and established towns, the most important of which was Mecca, in the Hijāz. Each clan in a town retained its deity and its symbolic stone, but the stones were brought together to make a central shrine. In Mecca the shrine – a cube-shaped building –

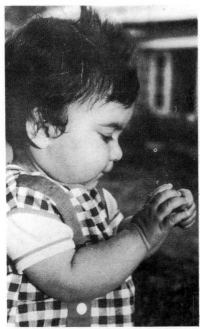 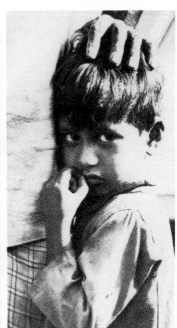

Tomorrow's Muslims?   (Wiedenest)

was known as the Ka'abah and the deities of all the clans were
enshrined there. Apparently, hundreds of minor deities were
worshipped there. A holy black stone (doubtless a meteorite) was
lodged in the wall and was the main object of interest. It was
claimed that the Ka'abah was originally constructed, not by the
Bedouin clans, but by Adam, that it was damaged during the
Noahic flood, and later repaired by Abraham and Ishmael. When
Arab traders came to Mecca, particularly at the annual fairs, they
made a pilgrimage to the Ka'abah, walking round the building
seven times and kissing the black stone. The shrine of Mecca was
an object of special reverence throughout Arabia.

Mecca stood on the old Arabian spice road to Syria and the
north, but it was also at the junction of the principal caravan
routes, not only to the Mediterranean in the north, but to the
Yemen in the south, to the Persian Gulf in the east and to Jeddah
on the Red Sea and to the sea lane to Africa. It was controlled by
the north Arabian tribe of Quraysh, who had become a pros-

I. de Jerba – North African jeweller   (Tunisian National Tourist Office)

perous trading community. 'The merchants of Quaraysh had trading agreements with the Byzantine, Abyssinian and Persian border authorities and conducted an extensive trade.' Twice every year they despatched great caravans to the north and south and smaller ones at other times of the year, as well as those to Jeddah and Africa. 'The commercial experience and mentality of the Meccan bourgeoisie gave them powers of co-operation, organization and self-control which were rare among the Arabs and of unique importance in administering the vast empire which was later to fall under their rule.' Mecca is described by Lammens as a merchant republic, governed by a syndicate of wealthy business men.

This was the milieu into which was born Muḥammad, the
founder of Islām. He was born in 570 into the family of the Banū
Hāshim, members of the Quaraysh tribe. His father, 'Abd-Allāh,
died before Muḥammad's birth, and his mother, Āminah, died
when he was six years old. His name, which means 'praised', may
have been regarded as inappropriate to him in his boyhood, but he
was cared for by his grandfather until the latter's death. The
young orphan was then taken by his uncle, 'Abū-Ṭālib, who
apparently showed him considerable kindness. Muslim tradition
says that Muḥammad was illiterate, but there is no confirmation
of this, although it may be true.

For centuries, Jews had lived in Arabia and some lived at Mecca
at this time. W. M. Miller claims that there were also 'three large
tribes of Jews, with their synagogues and their Scriptures' at
Medina, 280 miles north of Mecca. He says in *A Christian's
Response to Islām*, p. 16, 'They had prospered materially; they
owned camels and houses and lands, and largely controlled the
commerce of the city. Their education and standard of living were
higher than those of the pagan Arabs around them.' There can be
little doubt that Muḥammad came into contact with some of these
Jews and that he became acquainted with their teaching and
beliefs and the contents of their Scriptures.

At the same time there were Christians in Arabia. 'In the north,'
says Miller, 'there were several Arab tribes which had become
Christian. In the south in Najrān were many Christians who had
their bishops and priests, and their Scriptures in the Syriac
language.' Muḥammad evidently came into contact with these
Nestorian Christians. He was certainly well acquainted with a
Nestorian monk named Bahira and discussed the Bible with him.
His versions of Biblical stories, however, may possible indicate
that some of his knowledge was not acquired directly, but from
traders who were influenced by midrashic and apocryphal
renderings.

He may also have been affected by the pagan Ḥanīfs, who were
dissatisfied with the prevailing idolatry, but were not prepared to
accept either Judaism or Christianity. One fact emerges very
clearly – that he was for a long time a sincere seeker after the truth.
Whether he deliberately rejected Christianity or was never fully
acquainted with it, we will probably never know.

As a boy, Muḥammad was employed for a time as a shepherd in

the desert and this may have played a part in shaping his life and mentality at a later stage. As a youth, he probably participated in the desultory fighting by which blood feuds were settled. When he was twelve years old, however, his uncle, 'Abū-Ṭālib, took him with him as a camel-driver when he went with a trading caravan to Syria. This presumably continued and apparently at some point the young man was entrusted with the personal charge of the caravan. He quite early demonstrated his ability and business acumen and his complete integrity and reliability. So much so, in fact, that, at the age of 25, he was employed by a wealthy widow in Mecca, named Khadījah, to accompany her own caravan to Jerusalem, Damascus, etc. He was so successful in his trading on her behalf that Khadījah, although 40 years of age, proposed marriage to him. She was an influential and well-placed woman and the young man accepted the offer unhesitatingly. The marriage turned out well and they were very happy together. Two sons (both of whom died in infancy) and four daughters (the best known being Fāṭimah) were born to them. One of Khadījah's relatives, Waraqa, was a Ḥanīf who had become a Christian, and it is sometimes claimed that she also accepted the Christian faith, but there is no evidence to confirm this; in view of her reaction to her husband's subsequent teachings, it is doubtful. Almost undoubtedly, however, Muḥammad discussed the tenets of her relative's faith with him. By virtue of his wife's status, he also associated with the leading members of the city and gradually acquired a fairly full knowledge of the religious and political situation. He enjoyed 25 years of marital bliss and apparently had no desire to take another wife until after Khadījah's death. He

In the Sahara   (Tunisian National Tourist Office)

continued to worship at the Ka'abah, with its 365 deities, although evidently dissatisfied with the religious faith of his fore-fathers. Now that he was a wealthy man, he had time for thought and meditation and for discussion with others of the problems of life and of the role of the individual in life. At this time, he was clearly seeking the truth – as he may well have been at a much younger age – but for years it seemed to elude him.

As C. G. Fry and J. R. King remark in *Islām, A Survey of the Muslim Faith*, p. 40, he 'became increasingly reflective and intro-spective. He was overwhelmed by a sense of finitude and by the questions about personal guilt that all human beings share. He also questioned seriously the values of the city in which he lived, for he was deeply disturbed by what he perceived to be a breakdown of traditional Arab values in the expanding urban context, the break-up of families, infanticide and abortion, and the exploitation of the unfortunate. If issues like these troubled Muḥammad the husband and father, it was rampant profiteering, the sufferings of the poor, and all kinds of social injustice that troubled Muḥammad the public-spirited business-man.' Waraqa and his other Jewish and Christian contacts had evidently instilled in him ideas of monotheism and revelation which were foreign to Arab tradition. Altogether his mind must have been in a turmoil.

In common with others, he made his way from time to time to a cave about three miles outside Mecca in order to give himself to meditation, and it was here that he claimed to receive his call. It was one night, in the month of Ramaḍān, in the year 610, when he was 40 years of age, that he and his family were at this cave. He claimed that he heard bell-like sounds and that a voice (sub-sequently identified as that of the angel Gabriel) spoke to him. It is perhaps not insignificant that it was the angel Gabriel who an-nounced to the Virgin Mary the miraculous conception and virgin birth of our Lord Jesus (Luke 1:26–37). Muḥammad declared that Gabriel said to him, 'Recite in the name of the Lord, who created man from a clot of sperm. Recite! Your Lord is most munificent, who taught with the pen, who taught man what he did not know' (*Sūrah* 96 of the Qur'ān).

When he awoke, Muḥammad was completely overwhelmed. Was it an hallucination? Had he really heard a voice and, if so, did it really convey a message from God, or was it the voice of an evil spirit – one of the *jinns* who inspired the soothsayers? And, if the

Traditional musicians   (Tunisian National Tourist Office)

message came from God, which of the hundreds of deities of his
people had spoken to him? His mind was full of doubt and
anxiety, and the confused man turned to his wife for advice.
Khadījah consulted her cousin, Waraqa, who, surprisingly for a
Christian, assured her that her husband had obviously heard the
voice of God and had been appointed as God's spokesman or
prophet to his nation. Although, for a long time, Muhammad was
doubtful and depressed, he ultimately accepted that this must be
so. It seems quite clear that he had no intention of deceiving
anyone and that he was extremely reluctant to accept the responsibility which he thought was being thrust upon him.

It is usually claimed by the sceptical that the voice he heard was
that of his own inner conscience. The remarkable similarity of
some of his messages and some of the passages of the Bible is
probably explicable by the fact that he was familiar with the
Scriptural passages and that they were obviously retained in his

unconscious mind. Whatever explanation is proposed, it is clear that the 'call' effected a fundamental transformation in his own life. He had experienced a conversion of some kind, 'a radical reorientation of his life and his values.' And his messages concerning morality, idolatry, social responsibility and justice, came to the polytheistic and amoral society of his day as the words of a prophet indeed.

It was about two years after the first experience that further revelations came to him. According to his own account, he sometimes saw the angel Gabriel, at other times he merely heard a voice or the sound of a bell through which the words came to him. Sometimes a revelation came to him by means of a dream, but at others it was by the thoughts of his mind. The messages were always in the Arabic language and they were recorded by others when he repeated the words to them. He did not personally put anything into writing. After his death the messages were gathered together into the Qur'ān (i.e. 'recitation'). He consistently maintained that the words were the words of God and not his own, that he was only the 'reciter'. This is still the Muslim belief today. They have never regarded Muḥammad as divine: he was only the prophet of God and spoke the words of God. It must be admitted, however, that many claim that he embodied 'the Divine Word' and, in *Mystic Quest*, pp. 10, 11, L. Bakhtiar quotes Muḥammad as saying, 'I was the Logos when Adam was between water and clay.'

As the messages came to him, Muḥammad proclaimed them fervently to the people of Mecca, seeking to bring them to repentance and to faith in Allāh. At first, very few people believed him. His wife, Khadījah, was the first and she was followed by his adopted son, Zaid, and a young cousin, 'Alī. Subsequently a merchant named 'Abū Bakr and some of the humbler people of Mecca, joined the number of 'believers'. The majority in the city rejected him and his message. In particular, there was strong opposition to his monotheistic teaching and the implicit attack upon the 365 deities of the Ka'abah and the thousands of the country as a whole.

In 619 he lost his beloved wife, Khadījah, and also his uncle 'Abū-Ṭālib, and the opposition of his fellow-citizens became stronger. There was strong objection, not only to his monotheism and the consequent denigration of the other deities, but also to his

A Muslim woman   (Tunisian National Tourist Office)

egalitarian teaching that all men are equal in God's eyes. Other features of his messages were regarded as having dangerous political and social implications. The hostility displayed was so bitter that some of his followers moved to Abyssinia, and eventually Muḥammad decided to leave Mecca. The citizens of Yathrib, an oasis 280 miles to the north, pledged him their support and in 622 Muḥammad and his followers migrated to Yathrib (Medina). The flight (*hijrah*) was regarded as marking the commencement of a new age, and a new calendar started with the designation 'A.H.' – 'after the Hijrah'. The Islāmic year is one of twelve months of 29½ days, so that 100 Islāmic years equal 97 Gregorian years and A.D. 1982 is regarded as 1402 A.H.

Prior to the Hijrah, Muḥammad had a vision in which he saw himself carried from Mecca to Jerusalem and from thence to heaven, where he talked to the apostles and prophets of the past and was attested by them. This 'Night Journey' was later described as a literal physical ascension to heaven, although the prophet's young wife, 'Ā'ishah (the seven-year-old daughter of 'Abū Bakr), declared that he did not leave his bed that night.

Initially Muḥammad found some sympathizers (although not adherents) among the Jews. Some, in fact, rather thoughtlessly suggested that he might possibly be the prophet referred to in Deuteronomy 18:15 – a view which many Muslims still endorse. (They also claim that our Lord foretold his coming when He spoke of the future Paraclete in John 16:7.) But this was soon rejected and the Jews also made it clear that he could not possibly be identified with the Messiah for whom they waited. Up to that time, Muḥammad and his followers had endeavoured to conciliate the Jews, and they had observed the Jewish Day of Atonement, and had always faced north to Jerusalem in their prayers. Muḥammad now substituted a fast in the month of Ramaḍān and directed that prayer should be made facing south to Mecca. As his first sermon after the flight was delivered on a Friday, this became the day for congregational worship in place of the Jewish Saturday and the Christian Sunday.

His teaching was reasonably clear. A belief was inculcated in God, angels, creation, resurrection, judgment, blessing, heaven and hell. To quote W. M. Miller, op. cit., pp. 20, 21, Muḥammad taught that 'there is no god but Allāh, the one true God, who created heaven and earth and everything in them. Man is God's slave, and it is his first duty to submit to God and obey Him. God's goodness and mercy are seen in His provision for all the needs of men, and men must be grateful. A great and terrible day is coming, when the earth will be shaken, and God will raise all the dead to life, and will judge them. He will reward with the pleasures of a sensual paradise those who worship Him and do good deeds, and will condemn to the fires of hell those who do evil deeds, the worst of which is associating other gods with God.' There is little doubt that the principal concepts of his message were derived from the teachings of Judaism and Christianity.

At Yathrib, Muḥammad's life entered a new phase. The oasis had no political organization or rule. Because of the citizens'

Muslim lacquer work (P. Grainger, Wycliffe Bible Translators)

22

Testour – mosque
(Tunisian National Tourist Office)

Decorated Muslim pottery   (P. Grainger, Wycliffe Bible Translators)

A Tunisian market   (Tunisian National Tourist Office)

respect for his wisdom and sound judgment, he was invited to act as arbitrator in the many local disputes and, before long, he became both civil and religious ruler of the city. Many in Yathrib realized the advantages to be gained from acknowledging the new faith and became Muslims. The Jews refused to accept him, and Muḥammad's followers drove them from their homes and confiscated their property. Yathrib became known as Medina al-Nabi, i.e. 'the city of the Prophet', or later merely as Medina. The new faith became known as Islām, or 'submission', and its adherents as Muslims, or 'those who submit' (i.e. to God).

The Meccan oligarchy were not content to leave Muḥammad alone and an army of a thousand men was sent from Mecca to destroy him and his new headquarters. They met the Muslim army at Uḥud, near Medina, and soundly defeated them and wounded Muḥammad. In the fifth year of the Hijira, a further attack was made by the Meccans with an army of 10,000, but they were unsuccessful. In 628, however, a treaty was entered into and the following year the Muslims were allowed to enter Mecca and to make their pilgrimage to the House of Allāh or the Ka'abah.

Despite the treaty, Muḥammad marched on the city with a force of 10,000, but the Meccans surrendered and he took over the rule of the city and destroyed the images at the Ka'abah. In the next two years many tribes submitted to the Muslims since they were not strong enough to resist them.

In 632 Muḥammad, with 100,000 people, made his last pilgrimage to Mecca. On his return to Medina he died and was buried there. Later a mosque was built at the site and became a place of pilgrimage. At his death, he had twelve wives and two concubines. He had made no provision for any succession and had not even created a council similar to the tribal Majlīs to exercise authority during the transitional period. Not unnaturally difficulties arose immediately. Some claimed that Muḥammad had nominated his son-in-law, 'Alī. Others proposed to follow the tribal practice for the election of a tribal chief. 'The crisis was met,' says Prof. Lewis, 'by the resolute action of three men: 'Abū Bakr, 'Umar, and 'Abū-'Ubaida, who by a kind of *coup d'état* imposed 'Abū Bakr on the community as sole successor of the Prophet.' He was given the title of Caliph (or Deputy). The people had been beside themselves in their grief, but 'Abū Bakr calmly declared, 'Muḥammad is dead: the Faith lives,' and as soon as the mourning ceremonies were over, he ordered the army to invade Syria.

Muḥammad taught that he was the last and the greatest of the

Teaching the Koran   (Miss S. M. Dudgeon)

prophets of God, who included Adam, Noah, Abraham, Moses and Jesus. All the great prophets, he declared, were sinless. (Adam, it is said, repented and was forgiven.) Jesus was a great prophet, but was not divine and certainly not the Son of God. He was not crucified, but raptured to heaven, another – possibly Judas Iscariot – being crucified in His place. Each of the prophets had a written message, e.g. the Torah of Moses, but these were all superseded by the Qur'ān. Its message is final and completely comprehensive. Islām believes in one God, in angels and four archangels (Gabriel, Michael, Izraīl the angel of death, and Israfīl the angel of resurrection), in Satan and, as already mentioned, in a resurrection and final judgment, and in heaven and hell.

The Qur'ān is the sacred book of Islām. It is composed of 114 chapters or *sūrahs*, which were brought together after Muḥammad's death. The prophet's words were written by his companions on parchments, palm leaves, fragments of bone, flat stones, etc. It contains quotations and misquotations from the Bible, the Apocrypha and the Talmud. Its text was revised and standardized in the seventh century by order of the Caliph 'Uthmān and all variant texts were then destroyed.

It is frequently maintained that Muḥammad deliberately distorted the Biblical teaching in his teachings as recorded in the Qur'ān, but this is not a justifiable conclusion. A large number of the references to Old Testament history, which are found in the Qur'ān, may be traced quite clearly to a Talmudic origin and to the fanciful Jewish theology which was current at the time. Similarly, the mass of references to New Testament statements, are traceable to the apocryphal beliefs and documents which were current among the Christians with whom he came into contact. Even his teaching that our Lord was not personally crucified was to be found in the teachings of the gnostics. The heresies of the church were a contributory factor to the false teaching of Islām. Had the teaching of the Scriptures been presented to Muḥammad in their purity, it is at least possible – if not probable – that Islām would never have developed.

In addition to the Qur'ān, the entire practices and utterances of Muḥammad are regarded as authoritative guidance. The records of these are preserved in *ḥadīths*, or traditions, recounted by people who knew him. There are, however, quite a number of spurious *ḥadīths* extant and Muslim scholarship is faced with the constant task of determining the validity and authenticity of some of them. The Qur'ān and the *hadīths* together form the basis for traditional Islāmic law.

The Qur'ān opens with the *sūrah* known as Fātiheh: 'In the name of God, the merciful, the compassionate, Praise belongs to God, the Lord of all being, the all-merciful, the all-compassionate, the Master of the day of doom. Thee only we serve, to Thee only we pray for succour. Guide us in the straight path, the path of those whom Thou hast blessed, not of those against whom Thou art wrathful, nor of those who are astray.' The collection of stories, poetry, laws, moral principles, exhortations and warnings is disjointed and not easily readable, but this is Islām's sacred book.

The character of the revelations changed over the years. As W. H. T. Gairdner says, op. cit., pp. 48, 49, 'From speaking of the broadest and most general religious truths, God, the Resurrection, the Judgment, and After, he began to expand and give detail to his themes. Then, as his contact with the hard realities of life at Mecca produced ever altering circumstances, it seemed that a *sūrah* or *āyah* (verse) came to meet every circumstance. Later on, after the death of Khadījah, the fitness of the revelation to the circumstances increased, until it seemed to degenerate into sanctions for his personal needs and notions and policies and, saddest of all, his revenges and his personal desires. The style of the Qur'ān shows the change for the worse. As its sincerity, in the deepest sense of the word, seems to diminish, its subject-matter gets more and more mundane and prosaic; and with that the fire, the terseness, the rhymed beauty of the style gradually fades away into prolixity, tameness, obscurity, wearying repetitiousness.'

Islām has also five 'pillars'. First is the Kalima or Chehada, the Muslim creed or confession, which is, of course, unitarian. 'There is no god but Allāh, and Muhammad is the prophet of Allāh.' This must be repeated aloud at least once in a lifetime. Its meaning must be fully understood. It must be believed in by the heart. It must be professed until death. It must be recited correctly. It must always be professed and declared without hesitation.

The second 'pillar' is that of prayer. This service must be rendered to Allāh at least five times every day, the day being divided into five periods for the purpose, viz. El Fajr, dawn or daybreak; Zuhr, when the sun is in the centre of the heavens and shadows lengthen slightly; El'Aṣr, when the shadow on the sun-dial is twice the length of the gnomon or arm on the plate; El Maghrib, at sunset, when the sun has just disappeared below the horizon; and 'Ishā', when twilight has disappeared. The very devout add two other sessions in the evening. Prayer must be in Arabic; the clothes and body must be ceremonially clean; and the place where prayer is made must be free from all impurity. It must always be preceded by Wudzū', or ablutions on the body, mouth, ears and hands. The words of the prayer consist of the first *sūrah* of the Qur'ān and must be uttered facing the east for Mecca. Various bodily movements are prescribed, including prostration (*sujud*) and bowing (*rukū'*), standing, bending, raising the arms, kneeling, and complete prostration.

In Ramaḍān, the ninth month of the year, a strict fast must be observed from the dawn of the day to sunset each day in the month. After sunset the Muslim may feast, with the result that sleep suffers and tempers are frayed. It was during Ramaḍān that the Qur'ān allegedly began to be revealed to Muḥammad from heaven. Muḥammad declared that during Ramaḍān, 'the gates of paradise are open and the gates of hell are shut, and the devils are chained by the leg.'

The fourth pillar is the giving of alms. It takes two forms – Zakāt and Cadaqa. The former is similar to the Jewish tithe and, for the Muslim, it constitutes the legal alms or poor rate. Zakāt must be given annually and is related to property, money, cattle, grain, fruit and merchandise. The giving of Zakāt is to purify both the giver and the property from original sin. In addition, Cadaqa, or voluntary almsgiving, is practised with a view to increasing the blessing of sins forgiven. Almsgiving is a system of good works for salvation. Alms are given to pilgrims to Mecca who cannot de-fray their expenses, religious mendicants, debtors who cannot discharge their debts, beggars, poor travellers, and proselytes to Islām.

The fifth pillar is the pilgrimage to Mecca, the home of Muḥammad. On his death, it became the chief shrine of Islām and the object of pilgrimage (*el ḥaji*). The pilgrimage must be undertaken at least once in a lifetime. Every step in the direction of the Ka'abah blots out a sin, and he who dies on the road to

Preparing for prayer

(Wycliffe Bible Translators)

Mecca is enrolled in the list of martyrs. Pilgrimages to the Ka'abah took place long before Muḥammad's day, in order to pay homage to the idols in the building, but after he destroyed the idols and consecrated the Ka'abah entirely to the service of Allāh, the pilgrimage assumed a different guise and became part of Islām.

In Islām there is not the dichotomy of political and religious loyalties and rule. Islām is one and covers every aspect of life – social, political, religious and personal. Since man is deemed to be the slave of God, he must submit to the will of God. A kind of fatalism has consequently developed. Whatever happens, it is the will of Allāh and must be accepted: it cannot be questioned.

Islām is not without its schismatic tendencies. Almost from the start, there have been divisions on certain matters. The largest sect is the body known as Sunnites, who take their name from *sunnah*, i.e. 'norm'. They regard the *sunnah* embodied in the Qur'ān, the *ḥadīth* and in *sharī'ah* law as completely binding. They read the Qur'ān literally and accord it the central place in their faith. The Sunnites originated in the conflict over the succession to Muḥammad, and contend that the first four caliphs ('Abū Bakr, 'Umar, 'Uthmān and 'Alī) were rightly chosen and that their election was an expression of the will of Allāh. They have four orthodox sects, the Hanifīs, Shāfi'īs, Mālikīs and Hunbalīs, which are really schools of interpretation of the law.

The Shī'ites, on the other hand, argued that 'Alī, the husband of Muḥammad's daughter Fāṭimah, was the appropriate successor to the Prophet. 'Alī did eventually become caliph but, as one writer puts it, 'Shī'ism became essentially the expression in religious terms of opposition to the state and the established order, acceptance of which meant conformity to the Sunnī, or orthodox Islāmic doctrine.' They later found considerable support in the malcontents of the Mawālī (i.e. people of other races who had become Muslims), who were regarded by the Arab aristocracy – particularly during the Umayyad period – as inferior but who enjoyed the tolerance of the Muslim state in return for the payment of a higher rate of taxation and of certain social disabilities. There is also a difference of attitude regarding the *imāmati*. The Sunnites regard the imām as merely the leader of the Friday prayers. The Shī'ites, however, deem the imām to be a divinely appointed leader in social, cultural, religious and

Cairo – Islāmic buildings   (D. Frost, S.I.M. International)

political matters, in a direct line of succession from Muḥammad. In their view, the imām has the duty of preserving the divine message.

The Shī'ites have themselves split on the question whether there were seven or twelve imāms after the Prophet before occultation (i.e. a state in which the imāmate is hidden when no earthly man can be identified). Those who believe in the smaller number claim that Isma'īl was the last imām before occultation: as the Fāṭimids they later controlled Egypt and founded Cairo. Those who believe in the larger number are the dominant party in Iran.

The Zaydīs are an exclusive sect, who are hostile to the Sunnites and refuse all contact with non-Muslims. They are found primarily in Yemen.

The Khārijīs are opposed to compromise on many questions. They found their origin when Mu'āwiyah challenged 'Alī for the caliphate and the latter agreed to negotiate. The Khārijīs (the root means 'to leave') deserted 'Alī's party and one of their members later murdered him. They were divided and subdivided again and again.

The Mu'tazilites are a philosophical school, who form the Islāmic rationalists, and who reject the concept of a Qur'ān which has always existed in heavenly form. H. A. R. Gibb claims in *Mohammedanism*, pp. 113–14, that they were 'harshly dogmatic', but that their movement embodied a truly 'liberal' theology that enabled Islām to enter into dialogue with European philosophy. They were founded by Wasil in the ninth century and deny the Muslim doctrine of Fate and affirm freedom of will and action. They reject tradition and found their belief solely on the Qur'ān.

The Wahhābī movement (a Sunnite sect) began in the eighteenth century and is more puritanical than the other sects. It takes its name from Muḥammad ibn-'Abd al-Wahhāb, 'a lawyer and theologian who in the 1740's found support for a programme which involved a return to the original purity of Islām.' They destroyed shrines and eliminated certain idolatrous practices. Their principles are reflected particularly in Saudi Arabia. Their power was broken by the Turks in 1818. They hold that each man must judge for himself from his knowledge of the Qur'ān and tradition.

Ṣūfism grew up in the ninth century as a protest against the growing intellectualism of Islāmic thought in Baghdād and other places. It is anti-establishment and seeks enlightenment through which reality may be comprehended. It employs terms such as 'revealed truth' and 'ultimate reality'. The Ṣūfī aims at union with God, to be attained by absorption and loss of personality. Their teaching leads to the denial of any moral distinction between good and evil. It is very popular in America and Europe.

A sect, which has virtually become a separate religion, grew out of Shī'ism in 1844, when Mīrzā'Alī Muḥammad of Shīrāz claimed to be a Bāb, or gate, to the truth, and subsequently the Imām Mahdi, whose advent had long been anticipated by the Shī'ites. Although he attracted a number of supporters, there was strong opposition on the part of the faithful and he was eventually put to death in 1850. He was succeeded by Mīrzā Husayn 'Ali Nura, whose claims were even more outrageous, for he described himself as Bahā'Allāh, i.e. 'the Glory of God' and declared that he was the divine person foretold by the Bāb. His leadership was brief, for he was banished to Baghdād in 1852 and later to 'Akko (Acre) in Palestine.

His eldest son, Abdul Bahā' (i.e. 'the Servant of the Glory'),

Gabès – an Islāmic shrine   (Tunisian National Tourist Office)

systematized the new faith, which became known subsequently as Bahā'īsm. The basic claim was made that he and his two predecessors were all manifestations of the unknowable God, and their writings became the sacred literature of the Bahā'ī worshippers. The Bahā'īs believe in the unity of religions and of mankind. In their view, the founders of all the great religions have been manifestations of God and have been entrusted with part of the revelation of the divine plan for mankind. They believe in the brotherhood of man and have no ritual and no priesthood. The beautiful Bahā'ī Temple at Haifa is the shrine of the Bāb and is their headquarters.

The Bahā'ī literature has been translated into nearly 400 languages and centres of worship exist at Frankfurt (West Germany), Sydney (Australia), Kampala (Uganda) and Wilmette (U.S.A.).

Islām appeared at a time when the Christian church was in a

Kairouan – inside the Grande Mosque   (Tunisian National Tourist Office)

state of spiritual torpor. When Muḥammad died, to quote Bernard Lewis, op. cit., p. 47, 'he had brought a new religion which, with its monotheism and its ethical doctrines, stood on an incomparably higher level than the paganism it replaced. He had provided that religion with a revealed book which was to become in the centuries to follow the guide to thought and conduct of countless millions of believers. But he had done more than that; he had established a community and a state well organized and armed, the power and prestige of which made it a dominant factor in Arabia.' His death was followed by a burst of activity which demonstrated the inspiration he had provided. And a sleeping church was quite incapable and unready to meet the challenge.

Nevertheless, there is, on the other hand, some substance in Albert Schweitzer's words, 'Islām lacks spiritual originality and is not a religion with profound thoughts on God and the world. . . . It has preserved all the instincts of the primitive religious mind and is thus able to offer itself to the uncivilized and half-civilized peoples of Asia and Africa as the form of monotheism most easily accessible to them. . . . Islām can be called a world religion only in virtue of its wide extension.'

3

The Conquest by Islām

'From their very beginning,' writes Marius Baar in *The Unholy War*, pp. 27, 28, 'followers of Muḥammad sought to dominate other countries and conquer Europe, not by conversion but by force. In the sixth and seventh centuries the followers of Islām swept out of Arabia to claim the Holy Land and what is now the region of Turkey. They then spread westward across northern Africa, conquering the fertile Nile valley and seizing control of Africa's lucrative slave trade. They forced the Coptic church to accept Islām and all but destroyed the influence of Christianity on the African continent. In 711 the Moors (a militant clan of African Muslims) crossed the Strait of Gibraltar and took Spain. They pressed across the Pyrenees and would have taken France as well, had they not been turned back by Charles Martel's army at the battle of Tours in 732. The Moors fell back to make Spain their stronghold, establishing an Islāmic capital at Cordova.' How did it all happen? It was not until 1492 that Ferdinand and Isabelle were able to capture Granada, the last Moorish fortress in Spain, so firmly had the Moors entrenched themselves.

Before Muḥammad died, he had laid the foundation of an empire. He had not only become the civil ruler of Medina as well as its religious leader, but he had captured Mecca and had cleansed the Ka'abah of its idols and had converted it into a mosque. His followers had carried the message of Islām to every part of the peninsula of Arabia and, in all parts, the people had joined his ranks.

A typical North African village   (Tunisian National Tourist Office)

The treaties into which Muḥammad had entered with the various tribes of Arabia were terminated automatically by his death, and the new caliph's first task had been to subjugate them afresh by military action. Muḥammad had gathered together an army of 3,000 faithful young men to face the forces of the great Roman Empire. It seemed either sheer audacity or consummate folly. But the new caliph, 'Abū Bakr, with a vision of world conquest, sent forth two small armies, one to travel westwards to attack Syria, and the other to go eastwards to attack Persia. They were completely victorious and they carried away the booty of city after city.

Byzantium had become the capital of the Roman empire, but its power was slowly draining away. Constant fighting with Persia

had weakened both empires, and in 636 the Muslims smashed the
Roman army by the river Yarmuk in Palestine. Both Muslim
armies were successful and the whole of Syria, Palestine and the
east was open to them. Damascus, Antioch, Jerusalem fell and
then the army swept down upon Egypt. The Copts were
dissatisfied with their rulers and were prepared to help the
invaders. As T. W. Arnold says in *The Preaching of Islām*, 'the
rapid success of the Arab invaders was largely due to the welcome
they received from the native Christians, who hated the Byzantine
rule, not only for its oppressive administration, but also – and
chiefly – on account of the bitterness of theological rancour.'
When 'Amr ibn al-Āṣ invaded Egypt in 641, therefore, the
country was soon overrun.

Having routed the Persian forces, the second Muslim army tore
through Turkestan towards India and China. The western army,
instead of laying siege to Constantinople and forcing open the
gate to the whole of Europe, travelled along North Africa and
crossed into Spain at Gibraltar. The rapidity of conquest was
amazing. Gibbon pertinently remarks, 'In the ten years of the
administration of Omar, the Saracens reduced to obedience
36,000 cities and castles, destroyed 4,000 temples and churches of
the non-believers and erected 1,400 mosques for the exercise of
the religion of Muḥammad.' As already mentioned, the conquest
of Europe was halted, however, at the Pyrenees in 732, when the
Arabs were confronted with a determined Christian force under
Charles Martel of France and were completely routed between
Tours and Poitiers. Nevertheless, a hundred years after
Muḥammad's flight to Medina, his followers occupied territory
stretching from India to the Atlantic – no mean achievement in a
century. Had they not made the error of choosing the North
African route rather than the Balkans one, they might have
conquered most of Europe.

Even the conquest of Africa has had a permanent effect upon
the Dark Continent. R. J. H. Church pertinently remarks in
Africa and the Islands, p. 3, 'The seventh century penetration of
Africa by the Arabs, introducing Islām and Islāmic law, Arabic
architecture, decorative motifs, thought and culture, was of
profound significance to much of Africa, and has remained so.
Islām ultimately replaced Christianity in the Sudan and Egypt,
and became dominant in all North Africa, coastal East Africa, and

North African carpets   (Tunisian National Tourist Office)

The Sahara – camel caravans of traders   (Tunisian National Tourist Office)

Young Muslims (Tear Fund)

Pathan stronghold – Mazar-i-Sharif   (A. Hutt, M.E.Ph.A.)

in most of the dry lands immediately south of the Sahara, to which it was taken by camel caravans of traders and teachers. . . . Only small groups of peoples in inaccessible areas remained non-Islāmic, for example, the Coptic Christians protected by the fastnesses and steep seaward edges of the Ethiopian massif, the peoples of the Jos Plateau in Northern Nigeria, and those of the forests.' It cannot be too strongly emphasized, moreover, as the African countries have proved, that Islām is not merely a religion: it is a political force, a legal code, a mentor and arbiter in the arts, and a way of life in general. There is, in fact, no sphere of life into which it does not intrude and in which it does not claim complete submission.

In the eighth century the greater part of the known world was divided between Charlemagne in the west and Haroun al-Rāschid in the east. The two were on good terms with one another and Haroun actually gave Charlemagne the keys to the Church of the Holy Sepulchre at Jerusalem (built over the traditional site of Calvary).

With the death in 661 of Muḥammad's son-in-law, 'Alī, who had been the fourth caliph, the capital of the empire was moved from Medina to Damascus. To quote P. K. Hitti in *History of the Arabs*, pp. 183–4, when he died, 'the republican period of the caliphate, which began with 'Abū Bakr (632), came to an end. The four caliphs of this era are known to Arab historians as al-Rāshidūn (orthodox). The founder of the second caliphate, Mu'āwiyah the Umayyad, a man of the world, nominated his own son Yazīd as his successor and thus became the founder of a dynasty. The hereditary principle was thereby introduced into the caliphal succession, never thereafter to be entirely abandoned. The Umayyad caliphate was the first dynasty in the history of Islām. . . . The Umayyad caliphate (661–750) with its capital at Damascus was followed by the 'Abbāsid (750–1258) at Baghdād. The Fāṭimid caliphate (909–1171), whose main seat was Cairo, was the only Shī'ite one of primary importance. . . . The last great caliphate of Islām was non-Arab, that of the Ottoman Turks in Constantinople (1517–1924). . . . In March 1924 the caliphate was abolished.'

By the eleventh century the expansion of the Muslim empire was being effected, not by Arabs but by Turks, partly because the military and other demands made upon the former by the

Sfax – mosque
(Tunisian National Tourist
Office)

**London – Regents
Park Mosque**
(Red Sea Mission Team)

conditions of the previous four centuries had sapped their vitality and reduced their strength. The population of Turkestan had, to a great extent, embraced the new faith and the Turks were beginning to supersede the Arabs as leaders. The Seljuk Turks conquered Persia, Iraq, Syria, Palestine and Anatolia, and became the real rulers, even though the caliphs remained nominally so. As Gairdner says, op. cit., p. 107, 'The Turkish *Sultans* (as the monarchs were called who ruled in practical independence of the Caliph) became from 1050 the *de facto* rulers of the Muslim kingdom, from Egypt to Turkestan.' With this the second period of expansion commenced.

Subsequently, in 1255, Mongols from Central Asia swept across Asia into Russia. In Turkestan and South Russia they embraced Islām. Fugitives from Turkestan moved westwards and settled in Asia Minor. Two centuries later, in 1453, they captured and looted Constantinople and occupied part of eastern Europe and isolated Europe from the east. The Ottoman empire began to expand and eventually covered almost the whole Arabic-speaking world – Palestine, Syria, Egypt, Iraq, Arabia, the Barbary States, etc. were all subject to the Ottomans by the sixteenth century.

At the same time from 1096 to 1270 the Crusaders commenced their endeavours to liberate the Holy Land – and particularly Jerusalem – from Turkish control. The Arab empire was slowly crumbling and the influence of Islām was seriously waning. The First World War, however, ended Ottoman rule in Arab lands and in the following three decades, a number of Arab states (all Muslim) secured independence and recognition as republics or kingdoms.

In the last quarter of a century there has been a revival in the Islāmic world, due apparently to the economic strength of the petroleum-producing countries and their recognition of the fact that they can – to a great extent – hold the western world to ransom.

From the beginning, it has been the intention to bring the whole world under the sway of Islām, and from the seventh century onwards, Muslim hordes have swept over countries where Christianity once held sway, until today at least one-sixth of the population of the world is Muslim. In 40 countries, Islām now holds sway – or substantially so. A conservative estimate of Muḥammad's followers today is 720 million. The Evangelical

Missions Information Service reports that: 'An estimated twenty-four million Muslims live in Europe. Most have come in recent years from Pakistan and India. Many of them are showing a greater interest in a commitment to Islām than before. Most of the several hundred mosques in Britain are seriously overcrowded. In 1977, a seven million dollar mosque was dedicated in Regent's Park, London. The Queen was present for the dedication. Most of the funds came from Saudi Arabia, but nearly every Muslim country was involved in the project.' Muslims constitute the second largest religion in Britain.

Speaking in Germany in 1981, Eberhard Troeger, a gifted missionary strategist, said that soon one person in four of the world's population will be a Muslim. In 1900 Muslims numbered 100 million, compared with 500 million Christians. Now they number nearly 800 million, roughly the same number as that of nominal Christians. Yet only two per cent of missionaries work among Muslims.

A recent report stated that there are more Muslims in France than Christians, and that West Germany is rapidly approaching the same position. There are two million Muslims in North America. Mosques have ben built in Austria, Belgium, Britain, France, Germany, Italy, Spain, Switzerland and other European countries. A mosque costing eighteen million dollars was erected in Chicago and an even more expensive one is under construction in Rome, as a rival to the Church of St. Peter's.

As *The Wider Look* pointed out in 1981 also, Islām is significant for two reasons: (1) she equates politics with religion (a concept entirely foreign to the western mind), and (2) she has enormous financial backing in the oil reserves of the Muslim countries.

Islāmic Centres, for the dissemination of information about the Islāmic faith and with the object of the evangelization of the Christian community, have been set up all over the world, and millions of dollars or pounds are being spent in the effort to convert 'Christians' to the 'faith'. At a mission academy at Mecca, the Qur'ān has been translated into more than a hundred languages. A thousand Muslim missionaries are trained in Cairo each year, to go to every country in the world, but many are sent to Europe and North America. And all this goes on while the Church continues to sleep peacefully.

The Sudan Interior Mission states that 'two hundred and

Veiled lady
(Tunisian National Tourist Office)

thirteen of Africa's eight hundred tribes are either solidly Islāmic or so heavily Islāmicized that there is little or no opportunity for Christian evangelism.' Against that, one report says that the total number of Muslims converted to Christ in our present century is less than 30,000. Missionaries working among Muslims have said that the average number of Muslims won for Christ is one per missionary per lifetime. Does this constitute no challenge?

Muslim of the South
(Tunisian National Tourist Office)

The following countries have a high percentage of Muslims (from *The World of Figures* 1981):

Country	%	Vol.	Country	%	Vol.
Afghanistan	95	4	*Mali*	65	4
Albania	69	9	*Mauritania*	99	4
Algeria	98	4	*Morocco*	98	4
Bahrain	96	1	*Niger*	85	4
Bangladesh	85	4	Nigeria	55	6
Chad	45	4	Oman	100	1
Comoro Islands	99	4	*Pakistan*	97	4
Djibouti	90	4	Qatar	100	1
Egypt	94	1	Saudi Arabia	99	1
Ethiopia	40	6	*Senegal*	80	4
Gambia	58	4	*Somalia*	100	4
Guinea	85	4	*Sudan*	70	4
Indonesia	91	5	Syria	88	1
Iran	98	1	*Tunisia*	99	4
Iraq	96	1	Turkey	99	1
Jordan	94	1	United Arab Emirates	100	1
Kuwait	95	1	*Western (Spanish) Sahara*	78	4
Lebanon	50	1	Yemen Arab Republic	99	1
Libya	97	4	Yemen People's		
Malaysia	50	5	Democratic Republic	91	1
Maldive Islands	100	4			

N.B. The percentages shown in Volume One have been taken from different sources.

4

Pathan Stronghold

A landlocked country of 260,000 square miles to the north-east of
India, Afghanistan is bordered on the north by the U.S.S.R., on
the west by Iran, and on the south and east by Pakistan. With the
exception of desert lowland in the south, the country is almost
entirely mountainous. It is divided from the north-east to the
south-west by the towering Hindu Kush and Pamir ranges, and
some of the peaks rise to 23,000 feet. The mountains and arid
deserts are interspersed with small fertile valleys, which are
cultivated wherever practicable. Large forests, particularly of
conifers, grow on the main ranges at 6,000 to 10,000 feet, but yew,
hazel, juniper, walnut, wild peach and almond are found at lower
levels. So rich is the soil in the valleys that, in most parts of the
country, there are two harvests a year. The main products are
wheat, barley, lentils, rice, millet, maize, cotton, tobacco, beet and
turnips. Edible wild rhubarb is a local luxury, and mushrooms are
used as a substitute for meat. Tigers, leopards, wolves, jackals,
foxes and hyenas are found.

It is a poor, under-developed country and life is hard; the life
expectancy is only 40 years. Fifty-three per cent of the people
wrest a living from the soil. The few industries providing employment for a small percentage of the population are textiles, soap,
furniture, shoes, carpets, fertilizers and cement. Afghanistan has
long been famed for its carpets, and a considerable trade in these
has been conducted in the past, particularly with the U.S.S.R.
The country's natural resources include natural gas, oil, coal,

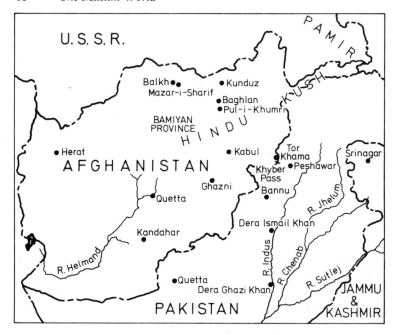

copper, zinc, iron, lead, antimony, talc, barites, sulphur, gold, silver, and precious and semi-precious stones.

The population is over fifteen and a half million, of whom 50 per cent are Pashtun (Pathan), who are of fair complexion and who usually have fine figures. The remainder derive their origin from conquered races and include Tajik, Uzbek, Ḥazāra, Aimeq and Turkoman. There are also a few Jews, Indians and Sikhs. The Ghilzai people claim to be of Persian origin, but the Afghan chroniclers term them 'children of Israel' and maintain that they descended from King Saul (whom they call Talui), through a son named Jeremiah, who is said to have had a son called Afghana. The similarity of the Afghan physiognomy to that of the Hebrews has often been commented upon in support of the theory. The people themselves claim that their ancestors were deported from Palestine to Media by Nebuchadnezzar, but there is no substantial historical support for the claim.

The Afghan is courteous, hospitable and friendly. He is a fearless mountaineer, a respecter of womanhood, a faithful friend but an unyielding foe. He still pays regard to the vendetta or blood feud.

The country is one of the most backward in the world. The literacy rate is under ten per cent and the average person has very little knowledge of the outside world. The government is, however, actively encouraging education and, some 30 years ago, invited Dr. Frank Laubach and Dr. J. Christy Wilson to undertake a literacy survey preparatory to an attempt to increase the rate of literacy. Streets of cities are narrow, crooked and dirty, with no water or sewage system, and typhoid, malaria and dysentery are naturally common diseases. Travel is mainly by horse, mule or camel or on foot, although there is an air service nowadays.

The largest city is Kabul, the capital, in the east, which has a population of over 900,000. Herat, near the Iranian border, has 150,000 and Mazar-i-Sharif, near the Soviet border, has 100,000. Other smaller towns, with modest industrial bases, include Kunduz, Baghlan and Pul-i-Khumri, but none is expanding very rapidly. Fewer than ten per cent of the people live in the cities.

Afghanistan is a strictly Muslim country. Eighty-five per cent of the population are Sunnī Muslims and ten per cent are Shī'a Muslims. There remain foreigners (e.g. doctors, nurses, business men) some of whom are Christians, but these are strictly forbidden to proselytize, and no Christian missionaries are permitted to enter the country. The profession of Christianity by an Afghan is (at least in theory) punishable by death. Islām pervades all aspects of life, and religious doctrine and codes provide the principal means of controlling conduct and settling legal disputes. The *mullahs* wield almost undisputed power over the people. They teach the principles of Islām, not only in the mosques, but in the schools as well.

Frequently described as the crossroads of Central Asia, Afghanistan has had a turbulent history. As Arnold J. Toynbee writes in *Between Oxus and Jumna*, p. 4, 'A huge procession of nomadic and ex-nomadic migrant peoples have passed through Afghanistan from Central Asia en route for the Indo-Pakistani sub-continent.' In the second half of the second millennium B.C., the Aryans poured through to bring the Sanskrit language to India and to supplant the pre-Aryan culture of the Indus Valley. In the seventh century B.C. there was an invasion of Iranian-speaking nomads, one of whose tribes (the Paetyes) were the ancestors of the Pathans who occupied the Helmand River basin. The second century B.C. saw a further swarm of Iranian-speaking invaders, the Sakas, who gave the name of Seistan to the area previously known as Sarangia. The Yüeh-chih soon afterwards settled in Bactria (the present-day Balkh) between the Oxus and the Hindu Kush, and in the first century A.D., the Kushāns, one of their tribes, established an empire which lasted for centuries.

While the country was part of the ancient Persian empire, it was invaded in 328 B.C. by Alexander the Great, who crossed the Helmand River and the Hindu Kush to capture Bactria. Later there came invasions by the Scythians and, in the fifth century A.D., by the White Huns whose ferocity was unparalleled. In A.D. 652 came the armies of the Arabs with the new religion of Islām and conquered the country, only to be displaced by the Persians, who controlled the area until 998.

Then the Turkie Ghaznavids swept in and the great empire builder, Maḥmūd (988–1030), established his capital Ghazni, as a great cultural centre and as a base for his frequent invasions of India. Following his short-lived dynasty, various princes attempted to rule sections of Afghanistan, until the coming of the Mongol scourge of Ghengis Khan (1155–1227), whose armies destroyed Herat, Ghazni, Balkh and other cities and laid waste fertile agricultural areas. If the Huns were ruthless and fierce, the Mongols were infinitely worse.

In the fourteenth century the country was once more devastated – this time by Timur Lang, or Tamerlane (1336–1404), who, in 1380, at the head of his Tartar hordes, initiated a series of campaigns through which he gained Afghanistan, Persia, Faris and Kurdistan, and incorporated them into his vast Asian empire. Tamerlane claimed to be a descendant of Ghengis Khan and, in the early sixteenth century, a descendant of both, named Bābur Shah (1483–1530), leading the Uzbegs of Western Siberia, became ruler of Afghanistan and also the founder of the Moghul dynasty of India (although some historians claim that the Timurids whom he expelled were the real founders of the Mogul Empire). Bābur was buried at Kabul, his favourite city.

A new phase of Afghan history was entered upon in 1747, when a Pashtun prince, named Aḥmad Shāh Durrānī, carved out a kingdom for himself by consolidating chieftainships, petty principalities, and fragmented provinces into one country, which became known as the Durrānī Empire. For over two centuries, the country was governed by rulers from branches of the Durrānī tribe and, from 1818, from the tribe's Moḥammadzai clan. Mohammad Daoud, who was President and Prime Minister during the 1973–78 Republic era, was also a member of the clan.

During the nineteenth century, as British power expanded and Russia moved into Central Asia, the history of Afghanistan was influenced significantly by European countries. In fact, British efforts to secure a stronger position in order to counter Russian influence in Iran and Central Asia led to the first Anglo-Afghan war from 1838 to 1842. Continued geopolitical concern over Russian advances in Central Asia and over Afghan dealing with Russia resulted subsequently in the second Anglo-Afghan war from 1878 to 1880. One outcome of this was that it brought the Amīr 'Abdor Raḥmān to the throne, and he agreed to British control of his country's foreign policy.

During the First World War, Afghanistan remained neutral, but a reaction began to set in against British control of Afghanistan's foreign affairs. In consequence of Habībullāh's assassination, his son Amānullāh acceded to the throne in 1919, and he sought more actively to put a stop to the British influence. The result was the third Anglo-Afghan war, which lasted only a few months. Eventually, Britain agreed on August 19th, 1919, to allow the country to conduct its own external affairs. This day was always celebrated subsequently as Independence Day, although the country had always been an independent state and had never been colonized by the British.

Almost immediately, Amānullāh began attempts to modernize the country. Leaving Afghanistan's traditional isolation, he entered into diplomatic relations with other nations. He abolished the traditional Muslim veil for women and was proceeding to take further steps, which alienated tribal and religious leaders. But his reformations, coupled with the depletion of the national treasury and the deterioration of the army, led to a rising tide of opposition. Eventually a brigand named Bacha-i-Saquas in 1929 captured Kabul and proclaimed himself king under the name Habībullāh II. A few months later, however, Nādir Shāh Khān defeated the usurper and regained the crown for the Durrānī tribe. A constitution, adopted in 1932, provided for an independent constitutional monarchy, with Islām as the state religion. The five major provinces were to be administered by governors and the four minor provinces by chief administrators.

Unfortunately Nādir Shāh Khān was assassinated in 1933 and his son, Mohammad Zahir Shah, succeeded to the throne. The new king's uncles occupied the office of Prime Minister until 1952 and then his cousins filled the office and that of Deputy Prime Minister until 1963, when he shook off their hold and asserted his rights. In 1964 he introducd a new constitution, providing for a more liberal parliamentary rule, with universal suffrage, a free press, an independent judiciary, and freedom of worship – although the last was honoured more in the breach than the observance.

The reformations did not satisfy the extremists, however, and in 1973 there was a virtually bloodless military coup, led by the king's cousin and former Prime Minister, Mohammad Daoud. The monarchy was abolished and the 1964 constitution was abrogated, and Afghanistan was declared a Republic with Mohammad Daoud as its first President and Prime Minister. A new constitution, which he proposed in 1977, however, was rejected and a revolution the following year resulted in the establishment of a Democratic Republic with a Revolutionary Council, headed by the President, Noor Mohammad Taraki. The coup in 1978 had brought a Marxist government to power, and this was not altered basically by eruptions which took place in 1979.

The U.S.S.R. signed a 'Treaty of Friendship, Good neighbourliness and Cooperation' with the new rulers in December, 1978, and proceeded to provide considerable military assistance to Afghanistan. In the spring of 1979 Soviet military involvement began to escalate dramatically until it culminated in December, 1979, with the Soviet invasion which installed the new régime. The party that controls the present régime is Marxist–Leninist orientated.

The U.S.S.R. is, of course, Afghanistan's major customer and it imports Afghan natural gas, cotton, wool and oilseed. In return, Russia supplies capital goods, petroleum products and sugar. Some 120 projects are being built or are under construction with Soviet assistance.

Occupation of Afghanistan has brought the Soviet nearer to

Iran and the Ābādān oilfields and also nearer to the Arabian Sea. It would not be difficult for Russian forces to sweep through Iran to close the Straits of Hormuz and to cut off supplies of Middle East oil to the West. But it is difficult to forecast the future.

The gospel reached Afghanistan at a fairly early date. According to tradition, the apostle Thomas travelled through Afghanistan and Pakistan about A.D. 50 on the way to South India. In reply to a question, he said his mission was to build up the Lord's work. This was embarrassingly misinterpreted as a statement that he had come to build a palace for the King, Gunda Pharos. He escaped punishment for not being able to do this when the King discovered that he gave money to the poor of the country in order to prepare the King 'a habitation'. Instead the monarch asked to hear the gospel message and allowed the apostle to continue his journey.

The story is an intriguing one but obviously quite apocryphal. Remains of Christian churches, dating form the 4th and 5th centuries, however, have been discovered in various parts of the country.

Nestorian Christians, despite their heretical view on the incarnation, were zealous missionaries to Central Asia and J. C. Thiessen says in *A Survey of World Missions*, p. 139, that in Afghanistan, 'flourishing Nestorian churches existed during the fifth and sixth centuries.' In fact, one writer states that 'By A.D. 424 a flourishing church had been established at Herat in the west, and others at a number of places in A.D. 585 a church is known to have existed at Quadis, presided over by Gabriel of Herat.'

Regrettably, when the Muslims began their conquests, it was not long before they had penetrated this mountainous country with their new faith. By A.D. 642 Herat had become a Muslim city and by the tenth century the Nestorian church had been completely dislodged from Afghanistan, and Islām was firmly entrenched in its place. It is claimed by the authorities that there is not a single national Christian in the country today, but that is perhaps open to doubt. One believer many years ago was Quazi Abdul Karim, who had been a judge in Quetta. He toured the country, preaching the gospel and selling Bibles and New Testaments. He was beaten, deprived of food, and on more than one occasion was poisoned. Finally, he was tortured, tied to a donkey and paraded through the streets of Kandahar. He died in prison in Kabul, as a result of torture and some reports said that he was skinned alive. It cost something – and still does – to be a Christian in Afghanistan.

Since the country is closed to missionaries, most attempts to reach the people with the gospel message have been by the establishment of stations near the frontiers, where contact has been possible with the limited number of Afghans crossing the borders. H. E. Rawlence writes, 'Just before the Indian Mutiny in 1857 some British administrators and generals recommended to the Church Missionary Society the establishment of mission hospitals all along the Indo-Afghan border. Such hospitals were accordingly established along the roads by which Afghan traders and pilgrims to Mecca entered India. Quetta, Dera Ismail Kahn, Dera Ghazi Khan, Bannu, Peshawar, Srinagar each had a mission hospital. . . . In these hospitals the Afghans received Gospels in Persian and Pushtu. They were taught the principal points in the life of Christ's teaching from one of the four Gospels.' The American Presbyterians commenced on the Iranian side of the border, and several other societies followed the same course.

Some doctors have been able to secure permission to conduct temporary clinics in various parts of the country, but they have had to enter as medical practitioners and not as missionaries, although most have naturally not hidden their faith from their patients. A large number of Afghans have been treated at the mission hospitals on the borders and some have evidently been affected by the Christian teaching to which they listened there. Some have also been educated at the mission schools in Pakistan close to the frontier, where again they have had to listen to the Scriptures and to the exposition of the gospel message. In addition, the gospel is beamed into the country by the Far Eastern Broadcasting Company from the Seychelles. So that the population are not entirely cut off from the gospel.

In 1832, a Jewish Christian, named Joseph Wolff, was allowed to visit the small Jewish communities in the country and to present the message of Christ to them, but this was very exceptional and may have been due to a misunderstanding by the authorities of Wolff's actual intentions.

Others have been able to enter the country for secular purposes and have witnessed to personal contacts during their visits. The

Bible has been translated into Pushtu and a large number of copies, as well as a considerable quantity of Christian literature, have found their way into Afghanistan.

In 1955 Daniel Herm was commended from Germany to work in Pakistan, but with the intention of contacting people in Afghanistan as practicable. He worked in association with the Afghan Border Crusade and was able to visit Kabul and other areas fairly regularly – as well as since his return home. Christians from different countries were considering the development of various projects and. schools, and in 1966 the International Assistance Mission came into being through the initiative of Dr. Christy Wilson. German assemblies built up their own aid programmes – a school for the blind, a hospital for eye diseases, and a medical assistance programme in the central highlands. Daniel Herm's service concluded because he was invited to take up an appointment at Wiedenest Bible School.

Martha Brauner from Berlin was commended in 1960 to the work in Pakistan and had acquired the Pushtu language during her eight years' service in that country. She transferred to the medical assistance programme for Afghanistan in 1968. Albecht Hausen and his family and several other workers from Germany joined the work in the succeeding years.

Dr. J. Christy Wilson went to Afghanistan some 30 years ago at the invitation of the government, and was for some years the principal of a boys' school of 2,000 students. In 1956, with official approval, he became pastor of a Christian church in Kabul – and later of others at Kandahar and Bost, but these three churches were restricted to members of the international community, and Afghans were not allowed to attend, except at Christmas and for funerals. Others have also been able to work among the expatriates, but the evangelization of nationals is strictly prohibited. Quite exceptionally, Youth for Christ International was able in 1969 to present a musical programme to 700 (including many of the nation's intelligentsia) at the Intercontinental Hotel, and to 450 local students, hippies and others at a public restaurant.

Dennis and Gladys Clark, who had earlier served the Lord in India and Pakistan, felt a strong urge to penetrate Afghanistan. To circumvent the prohibition on missionaries entering the country, he commenced a trading company in Peshawar, called

The Central Asian Trading Agency, the whole of the profits being used to found the Christian Publishing House (M.I.K.) at Lahore and also to assist the one (M.S.S.) at New Delhi. During their service at Peshawar, an assembly was formed, with which Miss Flora Davidson was associated, who gave her life for the Christian work in the North West Frontier Province and Afghanistan. In 1946, Dennis having visited Afghanistan as a tourist and tried to distribute Scriptures, was arrested and after a long trial was brought to the frontier in handcuffs and expelled for being in possession of a Persian New Testament, and for witnessing in Persian and Pushtu. Later in Peshawar in 1973, he wrote *The Life and Teaching of Jesus the Messiah* (a book specially slanted to Muslims), which is now circulating in twelve languages.

Mr. and Mrs. Graham Craig from New Zealand assemblies went to Afghanistan in 1968 to engage in building for a year or more, but were unable to engage in public evangelization.

Dr. and Mrs. Howard F. Harper, who had previously worked in Pakistan, spent a year in Kabul in 1966, setting up eye clinics and engaging in Christian witness, before returning to Pakistan. Later, from 1971 to 1973, they returned to Afghanistan, working among hippies and world travellers who came to that land. Howard was chairman of the committee to administer a World Vision £6,000 gift of milk powder and vitamins, as well as being associated with the Leprosy Mission's work. The Harpers' ophthalmological work continued to expand and to provide opportunities for witnessing to Christ, although conditions became increasingly difficult. In 1973 they were forced to leave Afghanistan and had a grim journey to Tehrān in Iran. They returned to Afghanistan on a temporary permit and Dr. Harper taught at the Medical School, but in 1974 they were again required to leave and after a short furlough, they returned to undertake hospital work in Iran.

It is estimated that 150,000 hippies and drug addicts come to Afghanistan because they are able to secure cheap drugs there. The problem they create is so serious that official approval was given to the setting up of Christian rehabilitation centres for them, so that, through this medium also, the Word of God is made known.

J. H. Kane says, 'There are no missionaries in Afghanistan, but there are three Christian congregations serving several hundred

Afghanistan – In Bamiyan Province (A. Hutt, M.E.Ph.A.)

Kabul – Shah Jehan Mosque   (A. Hutt, M.E.Ph.A.)

Christian expatriates. In addition, there are at least forty or fifty professional people, mostly medical personnel, who are in the country for the express purpose of serving the people of Afghanistan in the name and spirit of Jesus Christ.' With the Russian occupation, conditions are a little more difficult, but the need is tremendous, and it seems incredible that no assembly workers have felt exercised regarding this. At the Khyber Pass alone, there are countless opportunities of contacting the many Afghans passing in and out of their country, and medical and educational work still afford possible ways of reaching the people. Pathan tribesmen, who have never recognized the frontier between Afghanistan and Pakistan come and go as they please, and German, Japanese and other tourists are always to be found in numbers at Torkham in the Khyber. Do not all these constitute a challenge?

A recent report suggested that a tentative agreement had been reached between Russia and America to restore the exiled king, Mohammad Zahir Shah, to his throne, primarily to forestall a powerful Islāmic alliance between the Mujahideen groups of Afghanistan and their co-religionists in Pakistan and Iran – and possibly to allow Russia to embark on a measure of withdrawal without losing face. If that occurred – as is not impossible – there might conceivably be some lessening of the rigid opposition to all missionary work, but that is speculation. At least, Christian workers ought to be prepared for such eventualities.

Sixty years ago, W. Wilson Cash wrote in *The Moslem World in Revolution*, p. 121, 'Parts of Arabia and Afghanistan have been impossible spheres of missionary enterprise. In the areas surrounding Mecca and Medina in Arabia the missionary has been forbidden to enter. But the spread of the gospel does not depend on the missionary alone. The Bible, translated into Arabic, has found its way into the sacred place of the Prophet. Copies of the Scriptures have been sold in Mecca and Medina. Muslim Arabs have been treated by the missionary doctors at Amman and Salt, and they have carried back into the closed lands the message of a divine love.' Perhaps the opportunity will return!

5

Barbary Beauty

The Barbary States, as they were known in the seventeenth century, are really one homogeneous unit and were so regarded by the ancient Roman administration. There are no well-defined natural boundaries between them and the Arabs refer to the whole area as Jezīrat al-Maghrib, or the Island of the Sunset. The name, as Geoffrey Furlonge says in *The Lands of Barbary*, p. 2, 'is not only imaginative but apt; for the Maghrib is in effect a piece of land surrounded by seas – a 3,000 mile strip of cultivation, pasture, and mountain bounded on the north by the Mediterranean, on the west by the Atlantic, and on the south and east by the sand-seas of the Sahara and the "western desert" of Egypt respectively. Each of the four independent States between which this land is shared – Libya, Tunisia, Algeria, and Morocco – also includes a piece of the Sahara, which, with the discovery of oil, is actually or potentially of greater economic importance than all the non-desert areas.'

The area is a fascinating one. J. J. Cooksey's description in *The Land of the Vanished Church* is well worth quoting *in extenso*. He says, pp. v and vi, 'Their most outstanding feature is the great Atlas range of mountains, which, starting from a point north of Cape Juby in the west, lies across the heart of the land. It stretches away to the north and centre of Tunisia in the east, broken throughout its length and breadth, however, by the great system of the "Tell" – a series of high plateaux, fertilized by the northern Atlas watershed, and of high productivity for cereals. Here were

Constantine   (North Africa Mission)

grown those magnificent harvests, from whose superabundance
the Rome of the Caesars was fed. In the valleys which intersect
them lie the immensely rich grazing lands of the nomads. South of
the "Tell" the Saharan Atlas watershed forms a system of oases in
the desert. Stretching from Tafilet in the west, to Kufra and Siwa
in the extreme east, they run in an irregular chain across the
continent, more than fifteen in number. Emerald islands of
romantic beauty, set in seas of sand, whence set forth the fleets of
desert ships laden with rich merchandise for the teeming cities of
the Sudan. North again of the "Tell" country, declining gently
toward the sea, is the broad belt of the maritime plain, rich in
general agriculture; home of the palm, the vine and olive,
luxuriant in wheat and barley, and famed for its luscious fruit
gardens for more than two thousand years. Here were the gardens
of the Hesperides – daughters of Atlas and Hesperis – land of the
apples of gold, sung in story and in song by the poets of ancient
Greece.' In the north there is a magnificent stretch of over three
thousand miles of coast, from Cape Blanco to the Libyan border,
with some of the finest scenery in the world.

The physical conformation indicates that, in the past (probably in the Pleistocene Age), the area was joined to Europe, and this is confirmed by the similarity of flora and fauna and by the existence of the primitive, indigenous white race.

Algeria lies between Morocco and Tunisia, with the Sudan on the south and the Mediterranean on the north. Two Atlas Mountain ranges, covered with oak, pine and cedar trees, cross the country laterally, dividing it into three zones. A narrow coastal plain, which is quite fertile, lies between the Mediterranean and the Tellian Atlas Mountains. From the

Djidjelli

Tellian Atlas Mountains to the Saharan Atlas Mountains to the south is a high plateau, 3,000 feet above sea level and almost entirely barren. South of the Saharan Atlas Mountains is mainly desert. Altogether about 80 per cent of the land area is composed of desert, steppes, wasteland and mountains: the balance is cultivable land and pasture.

The total area is 918,497 square miles and there is a coastline of 620 miles. The total population is 18,250,000 of whom 54 per cent are under the age of eighteen. The majority of the population are Arabs and Berbers, although there are some Jews and a small number of Europeans (there were, of course, more before the French withdrew). The Berbers are Kabyles, a mountain people, who are shepherds and olive growers. 'Another important community,' says John Gunther in *Inside Africa*, p. 119, 'is that of the M'zabites, a people so peculiar that they have been called both the "Jews" and "Quakers" of the Muslim world. Their capital is the desert city Ghardaia: they are intensely puritanical and fiercely acute men of business. Many retail shops in Algiers are M'zabite. When a M'zabite dies, he is supposed to be buried at his birthplace, and the bodies are sometimes shipped down to Ghardaia by taxicab.'

Ninety-one per cent of the people live along the Mediterranean coast in an area which represents only twelve per cent of the total land area. But the south is desert, while the vineyards and terraced hills are to be found in the north. There are indications of petroleum deposits in the south, however, and these may transform the whole location of population – as well as the national economy.

The languages spoken are Arabic, Kabyle and French. The literacy rate is 46 per cent and it is tending to rise because of the educational system.

The principal occupation is agriculture, and wheat, barley, oats, olives, wine and vegetables are produced. Algerian industries include the production of petroleum and natural gas, the manufacture of petrochemicals and fertilizers, and the mining of iron, zinc, lead, mercury and coal.

The dominant religion of Algeria is Islām. Ninety-eight per cent of the population are Sunnī Muslims but, J. C. Thiessen remarks, op. cit., p. 179, 'The Islām of Algeria, mixed with animism and the worship of saints, rests upon a basis of social customs, traditional usages, the family and tribal ties, or the influence of the ruling people, rather than upon theological knowledge and conviction. The *Marabouts* or holy men, settled among the Berbers and attempted to teach them the Muslim faith.'

The country has a very long history. There are said to be traces of palaeolithic and neolithic man, dating back to prehistoric times. Certainly the land has since been invaded by Kabyles, Chaouis, Mozabites and Touaregs, but all of these except the last have been absorbed by the Berbers or Kabyles. The Chaouis, who probably originated in Europe, are semi-nomadic shepherds, who live in villages in the Aurès Mountains in the north-east. The Mozabites originated in the Sahara and are proud and exclusive; they belong to the Ibāḍīte sect of Islām.

The Touaregs are also of Saharan origin and are a warlike race, although occupied now mainly in the herding of sheep and camels. They live in the harsh Hoggar region of the Sahara. The macabre formation of the Hoggar has been described as savagely solid formations of cold red rock, thrown up centuries ago by the fires under the Sahara. The capital of the region is Tamanrasset, the principal Touareg centre, although these people are largely nomadic tent-dwellers. The Touaregs are Hamitic but their origin is unknown. They are a matriarchy and rank is transmitted through the female line. The men (not the women) wear blue veils and use blue eye paint.

There are fairly large numbers of negroes in the area, descendants of former slaves of the Touareg nobles, whose ancestors were set free by the French.

It has been said that Algeria was never a real country, a national entity, in the past. In fact, General Augustin Guillaume said, 'Algerians became French before they became Algerian.'

In Roman times Algeria formed part of Numidia, the rest being known as Mauritania. The country suffered repeatedly from invasions and fell into the hands successively of the Carthaginians, Romans, Vandals, Byzantines, Arabs, Turks and French. The Arabs poured into Algeria in the eighth century A.D., driving out the Byzantines and attempting to convert the Berbers to Islām. The Turks were invited by the Algerians. Large numbers of Spaniards had occupied a number of places on the coast and eventually Algeria sought the help of the Turks in

A town in the Sahara   (North Africa Mission)

expelling them. The Turks not only gave the necessary assistance, but then proceeded to occupy and rule Algeria. Liberation from the shackles of the Ottoman Empire came in 1830, however, but it meant the exchange of one ruler for another. The French troops landed, ostensibly in reprisal for piratical activity and to avenge an insult offered by the ruling dey Husayn to the French consul. Eighteen years later the country was declared French territory with its littoral as an integral part of France, and many French

Cherchell – Roman ruins   (North Africa Mission)

people settled there and occupied themselves in business and agriculture.

Inability to secure equal political rights led to an organized revolt in 1954. During the trouble (which continued until the signing of the Evian Accorde in 1962, when France declared Algeria to be independent), some 10,000 French officers and men and possibly as many as 250,000 Muslims lost their lives. Subsequently, the elected president was replaced, after a bloodless coup, by a Revolutionary Council. The National Assembly was dissolved and for eleven years the country was ruled by decrees. In 1976 a new constitution was approved by referendum and a stable government has ensued. The country is divided into 31 Wilāyas (regional administrative entities), which are further subdivided into districts and 676 communes, but there is still strong centralization of authority. The government espouses revolutionary socialism and applies this philosophy to the domestic and foreign policies.

Before independence, about twelve per cent of the population were Europeans, but in that year over a million fled to France within a few weeks, leaving behind them most of their possessions and bringing chaos to the commercial side of the country. Many deserted Algiers and the administration suffered in consequence. Today there is only a small European minority.

Christianity came to Algeria early in our present era and a large number of churches covered the country. Thiessen, op. cit., p. 180, says that 'The conquest of the Vandals in the fifth and sixth centuries did not succeed in crushing the Church, but did alter it to some extent. When Justinian in 533 reconquered this territory for Rome, the revived church discarded the adulterating Arian doctrines.' He claims that, at that time, Christianity was chiefly the religion of the Latin-speaking population and did not touch the native Algerians, but this is open to question, for many Berbers undoubtedly turned to Christ during that time. In the subsequent Byzantine period, attempts were made to evangelize the country, but the Muslim invasion violently swept out the Roman Catholic missionaries.

The devastation was complete. One writer remarks, 'One of the first things a missionary to North Africa regards with wondering eyes is the debris of magnificent Christian churches scattered over the face of the country from Morocco to Libya. And the Muslims he has come to teach are proudly conscious of the fact that they are the sons of the men who destroyed them. The implications of this mass of devastated Christian memorials cannot be escaped by the modern missionary. They constitute a ringing challenge to his Christian faith.'

Although Algeria is a Muslim country today, there is reasonable liberty for religious activity. The message of Christ was brought to the country in 1307 by Raymond Lull (see chapter 23), but he was deported in the following year and when he returned in 1314, he was stoned to death at Bougie. Nevertheless, French R.C.'s continued to work in Algeria from 1646 to 1827. The McCall Mission and the Basle Mission commenced Protestant work in 1830, but later withdrew. Missionaries of the French Reformed Church and of the Lutheran Church commenced work in 1832, but principally among European expatriates.

Glora M. Wysner says that 'the best known missionary, Archbishop (later Cardinal) Lavigerie, arrived in 1867. Soon 2,000 orphans came under his care owing to cholera and famine.

Tlemcen – Muslim ruins
(North Africa Mission)

He provided schools, religious instruction and farming. In 1868 he organized a society called the White Fathers, and later the White Sisters. Their habits resembled Arab dress, and they became known throughout Africa. Emphasis was placed on acquiring indigenous languages, living like the people, and ministering to their needs. The first work began in Kabylia in 1872. The first three White Fathers among the Touaregs were martyred in 1875. Charles de Foucauld, former French Trappist, worked among the Touaregs from 1901 to 1916, when he was murdered.'

Assembly witness began in 1880, when Mr. and Mrs. George Pearse, who had been engaged in literature distribution in Paris, moved to Algeria to work principally among the Kabyles. The Pearses discovered that the difficulties of evangelism were not so much from opposition on the part of Muslims themselves, as from the fear of the French authorities as to the effect of proselytization. The Pearses appreciated that medical missions would be of great value in Kabylia, as Muslims regarded Jesus as the great Healer. The influence of Christian women visiting houses and teaching women would be invaluable. George had been deeply disturbed to discover, when visiting Algeria in 1874, that no evangelistic work of any kind was being carried on among the nationals. He pleaded for others to meet the tremendous spiritual need of the country. His interest later led to his becoming one of the founders of the Kabyle Mission (later to become the North Africa Mission), the secretary of which was Edward H. Glenny of an assembly at Barking. Mr. Glenny himself visited Algeria in 1881 and encouraged the first missionaries of the Kabyle Mission to settle at Djamaa Sahridj, a large village in Kabylia.

The North Africa Mission also did excellent work among the many Kabyles employed in the city of Algiers, but not the least of its achievements was the translation of the Scriptures at an early date into the Kabyle language. It is understood that some of those involved in the first translation were from assembly circles.

From 1888 the Algiers Mission Band devoted its activities primarily to the service of Arabs, producing excellent evangelistic literature, conducting children's classes, and also classes to teach Braille to the blind, home visiting, colportage and a book depot. French members of the staff engaged in witnessing to French-speaking young people. The Band owed its existence primarily to the vision and determination of Miss I. Lilias Trotter, an English woman of outstanding artistic ability, who was a friend of John Ruskin. She went to Algeria in her middle thirties and spent the remainder of a long life in the Lord's service there. The Jewish population at one time exceeded 100,000 and the London Jews' Society made considerable efforts to reach them by means of literature and home visiting. From 1888, two English missionaries devoted themselves to personal work among the many Spanish people in the country.

Algiers, the capital of the country, often claims to be the Paris of North Africa. It is an attractive, colourful city, situated on the Mediterranean coast and, with all its variety of entertainments, is a very popular centre for tourists. It has a very large university, with faculties in law, medicine, arts, science, etc. Here is also the residence of the Roman Catholic Archbishop and of a number of Jewish rabbis. French missionaries care for the spiritual need of the diminishing French population, while Lutheran missionaries concern themselves with Alsatian colonists. The Y.M.C.A. and a number of other organizations provide guidance and protection for the thousands of young people faced with the temptations of the metropolis. Algiers is a city of challenge and potential, where one might expect to find a band of assembly missionaries, occupied in various parts of the city. In the whole of Algiers with its two and a half million needy souls, however, the only remaining missionary was Miss Irene R. Harris who returned home in 1982 although some former missionaries still make occasional visits.

Some years ago there were three assemblies in the city, but the work was confined almost entirely to Europeans. Mr. and Mrs. Thomas W. Speare commenced the flourishing assembly at Bab-el-Oued in 1904. The majority of the Christians were of Spanish extraction and in the early years this was the language used, but later French was more widely employed. Until her homecall in 1924, Mme. Lowitz worked for many years among the Spaniards in Algiers, and received and helped Thomas Speare on his arrival. She proved a devoted friend to the Speares and their work, and was much used of the Lord. Scarcely a year passed without baptisms, the Christians were well taught, and an autonomous assembly was formed, which continued after the homecall of Tom

Speare in 1947. After his death Mrs. Speare (the second) continued a work among the women, encouraging those engaged in their normal occupations to continue the spiritual work in the assembly.

For a few years from 1900 onwards, a French widow, Mme. V. Arnaud, held separate weekly meetings for Jewish and Spanish children. At that time there were numerous Jews in the city, and many Jewish parents asked Mme. Arnaud to open a school for their children. This work proved a happy ministry to teacher and pupil alike, and soon she extended her ministry to visiting Arab tribes in the vicinity of Algiers. For the brief time that she was there Mme. Arnaud was much valued by fellow-Christians.

Miss A. M. Isabelle Wordler, born in Paris, spent some of her life in England before setting out in 1911 for Algiers, where she laboured until her return to England in 1925.

Edmund T. R. Buckenham was brought to the Lord through

Algiers (North Africa Mission and F. L. Perkins)

this assembly. He speaks French and Arabic fluently. Edmund and Esther had met at the Bible Training Institute at Glasgow and, after marriage, had been led to Algeria to undertake work with the Algiers Mission Band. Later they resigned from A.M.B. to work with assemblies.

When they went to Mascara they had met only one person from the town and had no hope of securing any accommodation, but amazingly two rooms became available, which were sufficient for a start – and they were located right in the midst of the nationals. Subsequently, larger and more suitable accommodation was offered to them without any move on their part. Children's meetings started practically of their own accord and quickly grew in size until 170 were in attendance. Homes were opened and contacts established with a number of women and a few men. But the opposition started. The most influential Koranic school headmaster started a widespread campaign against them. Practically the whole of the population was aroused; attendance at the children's meetings dropped to a mere handful and contacts with adults became almost impossible. They transferred to France in 1957 to continue their missionary service there.

A small assembly was also formed at Hussein Dey, and this prospered considerably when Mr. and Mrs. Ralph H. Shallis went there in 1950. By 1956 some 100,000 people had been evangelized. Ralph is now working in France, devoting himself largely to the production of books in French for the benefit of believers in that country. A number of those who were converted in Hussein Dey are now in full-time service for the Lord in France. Some Algerians were members of the assembly, but the majority of the meetings were held in French or Spanish.

Another French-speaking assembly was formed in 1897 by H. G. Lamb and John Griffiths, and met for many years at Rue Drouillet. In the early days it was developed through the ministry of Allen Moore, James Hunter, James Robb and H. S. Mayor. This assembly did not grow to any extent numerically or spiritually. Mr. and Mme. Jules Dufey rendered valuable help there for many years, and he engaged in colportage work in the surrounding towns and villages and in holding meetings in some of the outlying suburbs. After a period of service at Tazmalt, Mr. and Mrs. Mungo E. Hepburn moved to Algiers, where they sought to be of help in the French-speaking assembly.

H. S. Mayor

Jules Dufey

In 1918 H. S. Mayor, who had served with the N.A.M. at Mokeniya and had been the first missionary in Kabylia, commenced advertising gospel meetings in the Algiers newspapers. This resulted in strangers attending. He then offered Scriptures by advertisement in the same newspapers. He then was agreeably surprised to receive many requests from persons of all classes of society, including representatives of the nobility. Even after he had left Algeria for Switzerland in 1931 he continued this ministry, which by this time had been extended to include advertisements in the newspapers of Morocco and Tunisia. Enquiries came in large numbers and not a few were saved.

James Robb went to Algeria in 1915, and worked for a short time at Jabarouth before going to Algiers, where he married Clare Mennell in 1919. From the capital he would often go on colportage tours, by bicycle to many villages and larger centres including Ténès, Théria, Boufarik, Bouïra and Orléansville. On one tour he covered a distance of 600 miles. In 1920 a new missionary venture was launched when Miss H. Freeman of the Algiers Mission Band offered a Gospel Van for the colportage work, and on occasions he was assisted by Henry G. Young and Thomas W. Speare. Children's services were held in the open air, and Bibles, New Testaments, Gospels, and tracts were placed in countless homes. There were many opportunities for conversation with the people at their doors. On one occasion a town cinema was used for meetings, 600 persons being present to hear the gospel.

Mr. and Mrs. Arthur H. Charters joined Mr. and Mrs. John Griffiths at Algiers in 1922 to study Kabyle and to help in the work, but in 1924 they moved to Tazmalt.

Writing in 1969 Charles R. Marsh said that the assembly hall in Algiers had been taken over by the Baptists and that a small mixed company now gathers twice weekly. Miss Irene Harris gave help here and had independent classes and a ministry among women and girls in and around the city. The halls at Bab-el-Oued and Hussein Dey have also closed, so that, for some time, there was no assembly in the capital.

Miss Irene Harris undertook some medical work in Algiers, and was able to help poorer families with gifts of clothes sent by friends in the U.K. Her principal sphere of service, however, was in personal work. Many women and girls visit her in her home, some of whom are believers. She had weekly women's meetings and for some years also had girls' classes. House visiting and monthly gatherings for those who are restricted in their movements have proved a blessing to many. Irene reports that there is again a growing assembly in Algiers, consisting of believers of several nationalities, although the majority are Algerians.

Muslim women

Barbary Beauty winter landscape   (North Africa Mission)

Bordjbou Arrèridj in Winter   (F. L. Perkins)

Children of the Bengal Nation (Tear Fund)

Djibouti – Tadjoura (Red Sea Mission Team)

Algerian brethren are taking increasing responsibility in the assembly.

The difficulty of working among Muslim women is accentuated by their domestic situation. In *Missionary Romance in Morocco,* p. 57, James Haldane writes, 'The Arab is an inveterate polygamist. He sees no more sense or convenience in being bound for a lifetime to one woman than he sees in being kept on one diet. He claims that Allāh, who created him, understands his desires and propensities, and has made generous provision to satisfy these, having allowed him four wives at one time, and as many concubines as he pleases. His wives are bought in the same way as his cows or donkeys. He bids for them, haggles over the price, and having made his purchase, brings them home as his absolute property. If at the end of a week, or later, he has reason to be dissatisfied with a wife, he can divorce her with little or no trouble.'

What Haldane says applies, of course, to any Arab country and not merely to Morocco, about which he was writing. Jealousy and resentment are often present in the home. Older wives, finding themselves displaced by younger ones, will attempt to adorn themselves and to make themselves more attractive to their lord and master. When they are eventually discarded – as so many are – there is sometimes nowhere to go and nothing is left in life. What answer can the Christian faith give? It is easy for the westerner to voice the glib statement that Christ is sufficient for every need, but it is more difficult for the missionary to convince the rejected and hopeless wife with no future before her that the solution to all her problems is to be found in the Saviour.

Oran, at the head of the gulf of the same name, was founded in 903 by Muhammad Ben Abdun. The city was burnt to the ground in 1055, but rose again to attain considerable prosperity. In 1509, however, it was captured by the Spaniards under Cardinal Ximenes, and over a third of the Muslim population was put to death and the majority of those left were deported to Spain. After an earthquake in 1790 had destroyed most of the city, it was taken the following year by the Bey of Morrocco. Occupied by the French in 1831, it was later ceded to the Bey of Tunis, but subsequently reverted once more to France.

After service first in Uruguay and the Argentine and then in Spain, Percy M. and A. Ellen Moore commended from U.K.

arrived in Algeria in 1908, but she died within four years. An assembly was established at Oran and the work prospered for many years. Percy Moore spent a lot of time in Sidi-bel-Abbès, where much invaluable work was done. Later a Spanish brother from Algiers, Don Armengol Felip, joined him. Most of those who were converted and baptised in Oran were Spaniards. Gospel meetings were also held in various parts of the city (which has a population of three-quarters of a million) and in private houses, and there were promising results.

Not so encouraging, however, was the work amongst the Jews. Together with Mr. Moraine, a colporteur of the B.F.B.S., Allen Moore visited the city and his description in 1906 *Echoes* of their efforts affords an example of the kind of opposition that Christian workers encountered: 'After a day's run by train we reached the city of Oran, where we spent nine days moving among the people, giving the greater part of our attention to the Jews. Our reception day by day was not pleasant, for we received constant insults. We were usually treated as Russian or German Jews who had fallen so low as to turn traitors to their religion. On one occasion we were surrounded, hands were thrust into our sacks and pockets, and numbers dragged at the books we were holding. The same day a Jew pretended to be looking at a book, when he suddenly spat into it, gave it back, and ran away.' For a few years Percy Moore was ably assisted by Miss Marie E. Gieser, whose work amongst children often proved very difficult, however, not least because of the persistent, sometimes cruel opposition of Roman Catholic priests and adherents.

The assembly subsequently divided in order to meet the need more effectively. Mr. and Mrs. John Moore continued the work until they returned to England just eight months prior to the outbreak of the national uprising. The assembly was taken over by the Baptists, and several Spanish believers and a number of Arabs still attend meetings. But there is now no assembly in this, the second largest city in the country.

At the turn of the century Allen Moore-Davis, commended from U.K. having arrived in Algeria in 1891 and served the Lord at Azeffoun (Port Gueydon) and Tabarouth, made visits to Sidi-bel-Abbès, Tlemcen, Aïn Témouchent, Saida, Mostaganem and Relizane. Thousands of portions of God's Word were distributed, many meetings were well-attended, and innumerable households

Oran

were visited. As often as not the general reception given to Allen and his helpers was most encouraging, but the Jewish populations in these towns also proved very hard and bitter towards these attempts at evangelization.

With the help of an antiquated type of Ford car (which gave ten years' service), John Moore (the son of Percy) commended from U.K. in 1933 was able to travel extensively in the interior. Much tract distribution was done in Oued Trélat, Tiaret and Hamman-Bou-Hadjar, for instance. On the road from Oran to Aïn Témouchent a string of large villages and the town of Bou Tlélis received gospel literature on a number of occasions and, at the small mining town of Sidi-Safi, a fine group of Christians was formed, having weekly meetings independent of outside help save for rather rare visits from John Moore. To the east of Oran, Arzew was systematically evangelized, and the town of St. Leu, a short distance further on, was occasionally visited.

Some 40 miles south-west of Oran is located the village of Ain-El-Arba, where a Spanish widow was raised up to full-time service. A staunch witness to all around and a true shepherdess, of the small Christian group there, she also had a shop. Because her house was used for breaking of bread meetings, she eventually closed her shop on Sunday mornings. This was no small achievement in a country where it was the custom for people to pay at that time for what they had taken on credit during the week. Others tried to emulate this sister's example, but yielded under pressure. She later removed to Oran and there too proved to be a most valiant servant of the Lord.

Assembly work in Algeria has been concentrated very largely on Kabylia, an area running from Dellys to Djidjelli and extending inland from the Mediterranean about 50 miles. It is a mountainous region and the villages in which the people live are often built on the crest of the hills and are accessible only by steep narrow paths. The area is divided in two by the river Soummam, the western section being known as Greater Kabylia and the eastern as Lesser Kabylia. In his excellent book, *Too Hard for God?*, p. 6, Charles R. Marsh says that Prof. A. H. Sayce 'traces the Kabyles to the Amorites of the Old Testament. They are a white-skinned race with European characteristics. Their mountain strongholds were never fully subdued by the Romans. Successive invasions of Arabs, Turks and French failed to assimilate them. They have retained their Berber language with the dialects of Greater and Lesser Kabylia. Missionaries and others have reduced these to writing, but the language varies from tribe to tribe and often from village to village.'

He says that 'the people can be divided into two classes, Kabyles and Marabouts, but all speak Kabyle and are ardent Muslims. The Marabout families claim to be the direct racial descendants of Muhammad, but probably came into the country from Morocco through religious pioneers of Islām. They are the upper class, men and women of character, genteel and polite, even though they may be desperately poor. They live in different villages from the Kabyles, or in a separate part of the same village. A Marabout may take a Kabyle girl in marriage, but a Marabout girl may not be given to a Kabyle man.'

The first assembly missionary to the Kabyles was Miss Elizabeth A. Gillard. She was living in Algiers but in 1883 heard of the very great spiritual and physical needs of the Kabyles from a man of Taaroost. She regarded this as a Divine call and travelled

Kabyle village   (Miss S. M. Dudgeon)

up-country by stage coach and then by horse until she reached the isolated village of Taaroost, far away from any civilized centre. For some months, although used to all the refinements of civilization, she lived in a rough straw house with walls of unhewn stone. She hung sheets round the walls to exclude some of the draughts that penetrated between the stones, used a rush hurdle to cross the gap that formed the entrance, and cooked on a smoky open fire with no chimney. She learned the language of the people and won their love and confidence.

In 1888 she was joined by Miss Una Tighe and Miss Emmie M. Merralls. They purchased a plot of ground near the market and in front of the mosque, and on this they erected a three-roomed house and commenced presenting the gospel message to the women and children in the area. The house was later enlarged to provide accommodation for a number of of orphans. Despite Emmie Merralls' few years on the field during which she suffered double bereavement she, as well as her missionary colleagues, were much loved by the Kabyles. When she left, one of them said, 'Poor thing! You have no brother or sister now, stay with us and we will be your sisters and bothers.'

After the two English missionaries had left, Miss Gillard was joined in 1901 and 1911 respectively by two devoted Swiss workers, Mlle. Laura Briggen and Mlle. Ruth Squire, who assisted in the work for many years. They conducted large children's classes, ran a small dispensary, and engaged in visiting the women and children in the surrounding villages and presenting the gospel to them. In some villages they were even able to hold regular meetings, attendances at which were sometimes so good that there was insufficient room in the houses in which the people congregated. For many years they had several orphan girls living with them and at least two of these were baptised. For a few years Miss Gillard was ably assisted by Miss Frances Handford (U.K. 1894) in the work at Azeffoun and together they ran separate classes for children and women, while Miss Gillard also used her medical skills to create opportunities for spreading the Word. Miss Handford helped also in class work at Tabarouth.

About a mile above Taaroost is the large Kabyle village of Tabarouth, where a work was started by Mr. and Mrs. Allen Moore in 1896. Shortly before they left to work in Algiers, they were joined in 1897 by Henry G. Lamb. The latter married Miss Mary A. Watling in 1899 and they continued in the work in this centre until 1945, when ill-health compelled their retirement to England, where he died in 1947. Mary returned to Algeria later that year and engaged in visiting amongst the Kabyle women of Lafayette, as well as serving for a period at Taaroost, at a time when Mlle. Laura Briggen was extremely frail and unable to pursue her work effectively. Mary Lamb eventually left the field for England in 1949.

In the course of a tour of the mission stations in Algeria, Prof. A. Rendle Short and his daughter spent some days in 1935 at Tabarouth and were particularly interested in the dispensary. Dr. Rendle Short's concern for Mr. Lamb's health led him to appeal for help on his return home. As a result, Kenneth W. Scott, a young man in the same assembly (Bethesda, Bristol) responded to the appeal and he was there for two years when, being taken for a British spy, he was sent to Tizi Ouzou and there placed under house arrest at an orphanage run by a French missionary. After the Allies liberated Algeria, Kenneth joined the British Red Cross Commission before coming to England in 1944, where he married Grace W. Pavey (U.K.). They returned to Tabarouth in 1946. Miss N. Jones subsequently helped in the work there and were

INSET A

Alger(Algiers)
Hussein Dey
Guyotville
Dellys
Azeffoun (Port Guedon)
Taaroost
Tabarouth
Mokeniya
Ikherbane
Taaroost
Bejaia (Bougie)
Jijel (Djidjelli)
Thénia (Menerville)
Tizi Ouzou
Azazga
Yakouren
GRAN DE KABYLIE
R. Soummam
El Kseur
PETITE KABYLIE
Draa el Mizan
Tizi Reniffe
Djemaa Sahridj
Akbou
Seddouk
Kherrata
Boufarik
DJURDJURA
Ighil Kerare
Beni Ourtilane
Bouïra
MTS.
Tazmalt
Bougaâ (Lafayette)
Maillot
Beni Mansour
Hammam
Sour el Ghozlane (Aumale)
Sétif
Bordjbou Arrèridj
Sidi Aïssa (Sidi Aich)

SPAIN

ALGERIA

SAHARA

Alger
Oran
Cherchell
A
Constantine
B
Bou Saâda
C
Souk Ahras
ATLAS SAHARIEN
Tolga
TAFILALT
Touggourt
Ghardaia
Ouargla
MOROCCO
TUNISIA
LIBYA
SPANISH SAHARA
MAURITANIA
MALI
Tamanrasset
HOGGAR

MEDITERRANEAN SEA

El Bayadh (Ténès)
El Asnam (Orléansville)
Arzew
Mostaganem
Oran
St Leu
Relizane
Bou Tlélis
Oued Trélat
Beni-Saf
Hammam bou Hadjar
Aïn Témouchent
Mascara
Tiaret
Sidi-Safi
Sidi-bel-Abbès
Tlemcen
Saïda
INSET B

Constantine
Sétif
Batna
Barika
Tazoult
Timgad
Lambèse
Aïn Touta
Medina
El Kantara
AURÈS
Arris
Biskra
INSET C

joined later by Miss Lilian E. Castle (U.K.) who continued devotedly at Tabarouth for many years.

This village is situated in the wildest part of the mountains of Kabylia. The rough peasants were ignorant, fanatical Muslims and in the early years, they bitterly opposed the work in every possible way, not only boycotting the meetings but imposing heavy fines on all who went near the mission premises. On one occasion they attempted to burn down the house, which was built partly of wood. They piled straw and wood around it on every side, while the missionaries watched from within, realizing that any attempt to escape would be met by the combined brutal force of the entire Muslim population. They were obviously doomed, and committed themselves to the Lord. But God miraculously intervened and a totally unexpected sub-tropical downpour of rain made it impossible for their tormentors to ignite the straw.

On a later occasion, when the missionaries attempted to help the poor widows by distributing a small ration of wheat, the religious leaders in Tabarouth collected all the grain from the recipients and threw it into the gospel hall. Again, a plan was set afoot to kidnap and bind one of the missionaries with ropes and then to kill him, but the ringleader was suddenly afflicted with raging toothache and was forced to come and plead for the tooth to be extracted – so the plans went awry.

Another time, a forest fire threatened to burn down the whole station; the flames devoured the tinder-dry cork-oak trees and rushed on at an alarming rate to engulf all the buildings. It seemed clear that the whole of the buildings were doomed. But Mr. Lamb stood on a stone pillar and cried out confidently, 'Our help is in the name of the Lord who made heaven and earth.' The wind suddenly changed direction and the property was miraculously saved.

Through happenings of this character, the people gradually realized that God was with the missionaries and slowly the confidence of these fierce mountaineers was won. At the same time, any attempt by Muslims, who had been converted, to break away from Islām was fanatically thwarted. A man and his wife, who had broken the fast of Ramaḍān, together with their baby, were eliminated by poison.

A modern hall and a large dispensary were erected later and the needs of thousands of patients were met every year. When Sir

Converts from Islām
to Christ
(Miss S. M. Dudgeon)

John Laing and Alec Pulleng visited the dispensary 30 years ago, there was no doctor and they found Kenneth Scott dealing with a variety of cases – a thumb nearly completely severed by an axe, pneumonia, tuberculosis, etc. – 65 cases in all in one morning. And before treatment the patients listened quietly to a gospel talk, illustrated by flannelgraph.

Miss Castle had classes for children and meetings for men and women were well attended. Mr. Lamb used to travel to surrounding villages by mule, caring for the sick and preaching the gospel, while over the years, the sisters visited the women and children in their homes. Work was carried on in several neighbouring villages, when Mr. Henry G. Young joined the team in 1910, marrying Violet E. Hare in 1914. Miss Catharine A. Clark arrived in 1922. She sometimes accompanied Mr. and Mrs. Lamb on their journeys to distant villages, in which many doors had been opened through the medical work at Tabarouth. Miss Clark on one occasion observed no less than 162 people, representing many villages, receiving medical treatment, and related that each day large crowds would listen well to the gospel. As for believers, she noticed that even deep snow and the most

Mary A. Lamb and Lilian E. Castle in a Kabyle home   (*Echoes*, 1953)

inclement weather did not dissuade them from attending
meetings. In 1946 Kenneth and Grace Scott took over the work.
Miss Castle and Mrs. Scott were fully occupied in children's work
and in the evangelization of the women. Kenneth continued the
work alone during the early years of the fight for Algerian
independence. His life was frequently in danger from both sides,
but he proceeded on his lonely journeys until the authorities
compelled him to leave. On one occasion the medical work nearly
came to an end because supplies were exhausted. But when they
were on holiday in Algiers, Kenneth was offered the whole of the
remaining stocks of the British hospital in Algiers, provided he
cleared the hospital completely. He did! And there was enough to
share with his delighted fellow-missionaries. On another occasion
the doctors ordered him to fly to England for an investigation.
The consul offered to pay the fare, but Grace told him the Lord
always met their needs. She had the joy of 'phoning him the next
day to say that the Lord had sent the cheque (unexpectedly) that
day.
   A nurse was badly needed to assist in the medical work at

Mr. and Mrs. John Griffiths

Tabarouth and in 1954 Miss Irene R. Harris of Cheltenham was
called to this particular field. Fighting had broken out in various
parts of the country just prior to her arrival, so she and the Scotts
stayed for a brief period with Miss Jessie A. E. C. Sinclair at
Yakouren, which is also in the mountains of Kabylia, until they
were given official permission to go on to Tabarouth. Here Irene
was soon immersed in the work and in learning the language.

Miss Elizabeth A. Gillard and girls' sewing class   (*Echoes*, 1907)

Lilian Castle had to return home in 1956 to care for her elderly mother, leaving the children's and women's work to Grace Scott and Irene Harris. Because of the unsettled conditions, the Scotts decided in 1956 to return to England with their family, while Irene moved to Algiers to continue language study and to help in medical work and in visiting. The mission house at Tabarouth was destroyed and it was impossible to return there later.

In 1899 Mr. and Mrs. John Griffiths took up work in Tazmalt, a small French village on the river Soumman. Both were excellent linguists and many young missionaries went to them for language study, while helping in the work, preparatory to commencing in other centres. Miss Edith A. Crabtree, Mr. Ernest A. Wall, Miss Ellen M. Davis, Misses Dorothea K. and Suzanne M. Dudgeon, Miss Violet E. Hare, Mr. and Mrs. Mungo E. Hepburn, Mr. and Mrs. Stuart J. Sears, Miss Harriet O. Dobbs, Miss Louisa O'Connor and others were among those who spent some time in Tazmalt in this fashion.

John Griffiths, as did the Misses Dudgeon and Miss Crabtree, regularly visited the surrounding villages with the gospel and spent many hours in chatting to people over the Word. Whereas in most places a gospel message was given before medical treatment, at Tazmalt John preferred to talk personally to people waiting at the dispensary.

For a few years Mr. and Mrs. Henry J. Pomeroy served here, and also regularly visited a nearby village called Magourra. Here Miss Elizabeth Gillard had started classes for boys and girls, and these were recommenced with some success. Frances Pomeroy described how the inhabitants of Magourra would come in crowds to welcome them, afterwards following them until they were out of the village.

Associated for a few years in the work at Tazmalt was Josiah T. C. Blackmore (U.K. 1905), who was distinguished by his arduous tours into the difficult and sometimes dangerous territory along the north side of the Djurdjura mountains. In attempting to evangelize the many unreached tribes of the area, unimaginably steep and rough mountain paths had to be traversed, and often Mr. Blackmore would arrive at a village physically exhausted. It is impossible to know to what extent Josiah Blackmore's labours were lastingly fruitful.

Stuart J. Sears was another itinerant, who did so much to spread the gospel amongst the Chaouis who, as already mentioned, had their habitation in the Aurès mountains. Though fanatically Muslim, each was distinctly marked in the forehead with a small blue cross, thought by some to be an indication of earlier Christian influence. Mr. Sears' aim was to reach the towns and markets, some at the edge of the Sahara Desert. The markets were of enormous size, thronged by thousands of traders who came from many miles around, so that Scriptures distributed would reach hundreds of neighbouring villages.

Miss Dorothea Dudgeon had been called to serve the Lord in Algeria, but in 1923 her sister, Miss Suzanne Monica Dudgeon, who was a trained nurse and midwife, joined the Griffiths at Tazmalt and commenced helping in the dispensary and in sick visiting. The village had few amenities and the nearest doctor was twelve miles away, so that over 100 villages and several tribes were dependent upon the dispensary.

Tazmalt is 900 feet above sea level and some of the villages visited were at 2,000 feet. In places the roads were steep and narrow, often with a ravine on one side and a precipice on the other, and the only means of travel was by mule or donkey or on foot. The villages, dotted over the mountainside, were picturesque with their red-tiled roofs and rough stone walls. After a few years, the Misses Dudgeon acquired a plot of ground and

Ighil Kerare – the Dudgeons' bungalow   (Miss S. M. Dudgeon)

built a bungalow at Ighil Kerare, as an outstation from Tazmalt, and lived among the people from 1931, working among women and children. Miss Suzanne Dudgeon had three dispensary mornings each week, other mornings being devoted to treatment. Miss Dorothea Dudgeon was responsible for the women's classes. A room was rented in another village, where the sisters ran classes for women and children. A number were blessed and joined the assembly at Tazmalt.

For a few years they enjoyed very happy fellowship with Mlle. Marguerite Steiner, who, commended by Swiss assemblies, had intended to join them in 1940 but had been prevented by war conditions. Arriving at Ighil Kerare in 1946, she soon proved an excellent worker with the chldren and quickly gained the loving regard of those for whom she laboured. In 1951, however, Mlle. Steiner returned to Switzerland after having contracted typhoid.

Miss Florence R. J. Wicks was trained at Bermondsey Medical Mission Hospital and was called to Algeria and went out with Miss Dorothea Dudgeon in 1950, the latter having just spent a furlough in England. She found the work at Ighil Kerare extremely varied and soon threw herself into all the activities. The rebellion from 1954 to 1962 brought many changes and dangers. They never knew when they would be visited by officials. They were accused of hiding people and eventually, in 1956, it became necessary to leave the village for the safety of those connected with the mission station. They accordingly moved to Guyotville (a suburb of Algiers), where they were still able to engage in visiting and literature distribution, as well as holding classes for girls. When they eventually returned to Ighil Kerare, it was to find the house badly damaged and everything of value stolen. The Misses Dudgeon returned to England in 1964, but Miss Wicks continued for another nine years. She was joined in 1969 by Miss Christine Hook who gave valuable help for three years, particularly in the dispensary work. The mission station at Tazmalt closed and Florence's position became increasingly difficult and she eventually returned to England in 1973. Miss Gillian G. Barker spent 1952 to 1953 with the Misses Dudgeon, but had to return home because of ill-health.

Amzian and Muhammad Zarour and his wife Zizine helped in the evangelistic work of the station for many years. When Mr. and Mrs. Henry J. Pomeroy transferred to Nigeria, the orphan boys for whom they had been caring went to live at Tazmalt. The Griffiths retired in 1952 and Mr. and Mrs. Henry G. Young then took over the work for some years. Although there were doubtless many secret believers, only 23 persons were baptised at Tazmalt during the whole of the half century of the Griffiths' service there – an indication of the extreme difficulty of winning Muslims for Christ.

Mr. and Mrs. Arthur H. Charters joined the work at Tazmalt in 1934 but later started a work at Akbou, about ten miles from Tazmalt. Arthur Charters also engaged later in visiting ships and in colportage work in isolated European villages and farms. Because of the difficulties in the country, the Charters left in 1955 and took up work in France. Miss E. A. Crabtree carried on the work at Akbou for some time, before moving to Sidi Aich and finally to a small town near Algiers, and in each of these centres worked amongst women and girls, besides adopting a small number of orphans.

For some years Mr. Charters was ably assisted by Mr. C. Leslie Phillis, who was commended from Malta where he had been stationed as a sergeant in the Army. Using Akbou as their base, they proclaimed the gospel in many surrounding villages, particularly in the region of Maillot and Beni Mansour.

Miss Daisy M. Marsh, who had been born in Algeria, had a narrow escape from death when her father Charles discovered a poisonous snake curled up about to strike beside the pram in which she slept. The snake was decapitated only just in time. Daisy's first months were spent in a small bug-infested cottage in Lafayette, and rats would occasionally run over her cot and lick the cup from which her mother had just drunk. As Daisy grew she became well-acquainted with the missionary work in the country, and was trained as a nurse in England. She was called to the mission field through addresses given by Stephen F. Olford and Douglas G. Broughton (of Mongolia). Contrary to expectation, she did not join her parents in their work at Lafayette, but in 1953 was led to Tazmalt, where a helper was then urgently needed for the medical work. The first eight years were extremely difficult because of the conflict and the work was greatly curtailed. The French suspected the missionaries of conspiracy because their work was so closely identified with the Kabyle people. Over 100 were killed in Tazmalt alone, and the cries of tortured people

Miss Daisy M. Marsh
broadcasting to
Kabyles

could constantly be heard in the nearby army camp. For weeks a military guard prevented anyone approaching the missionaries.

When independence came in 1962 the Youngs had to return to England for health reasons, but the floodgates opened. The French doctors had fled from the country and Daisy was left to cope with hundreds of women and children in the dispensary. The grateful parents allowed their children to attend the Bible classes and 150 boys and girls did so every week. In 1963 Daisy was joined by Miss Irene Harris, and they continued the dispensary and also the visiting and class work. After over two years, however, Irene's health failed and, after operations and

Mali – people of the Lion Prince   (T. Sanders, M.E.Ph.A.)

Market in the Desert Land

Nouakchott

periods of sickness, she moved to Algiers to work with Mrs. Catharine Speare.

For five years Daisy was the only European in Tazmalt and the local assembly was under the guidance of an Algerian brother. Although two nurses and a school teacher from England visited her, and for a brief time her mother Pearl helped by taking two of her five classes for children and in sharing the Bible talks in the homes and women's meetings, no one felt the call to share in the work permanently. The burden of the medical work was increasing to such an extent that there was a risk of the spiritual work suffering. It became clear that a change was essential if a physical breakdown was to be avoided. But there was another and still sadder reason. Before leaving, Daisy went round to every home and told the occupants why she was going. Year after year they had needed her for material help, but they had made no response whatsoever to the gospel. After eighteen years, therefore, the mission property was sold and a small house built for the faithful Algerian workers. Following a period at Bethnal Green Medical Mission and then in France, she commenced broadcasting in the Kabyle language with Trans World Radio from Monte Carlo. These broadcasts have continued for ten years, and families and groups listen regularly to the message. One result is an increasing demand for literature. But occasionally she is reminded of the intolerant fanatacism that impeded her ministry whilst still in Algeria. One listener wrote, 'You are no true Kabyler, only filthy Jews seeking to force your religion on us. For Jesus to say "I am the only way," is wicked and shameful! Go to the Devil!' And from another correspondent, 'I followed the correspondence course with joy for a time, but my father found the lessons and burnt them all.'

An extract from Miss Marsh's report of her last visit to Tazmalt in 1976 may give a picture of conditions. 'Being the guest of a Kabyle family had its advantages as well as disadvantages. My comfort seemed to be their primary concern, but it was necessary to be up at 4 a.m. each morning so as to be out of the living room by the time the family appeared. Myriads of flies and very little privacy caused me to appreciate the kind of life to which I had become accustomed in Europe. By 7 a.m. each day, I was already in the homes of the people, being called from one house to another, where large groups of women, children and youths gathered eagerly to hear again a gospel message. At midday I would return to my hostess, laden with bottles of olive oil, eggs, cakes, bread, fruit and vegetables which I had received as gifts. By the last day, having drunk so much strong black coffee, I was sure that had I shed tears, they would have been of coffee. The poverty struck me after the affluence of Europe, yet how generous and open-hearted were these simple folk. It seemed that the poorer they were, the more they gave. At 4.30 a.m. I set off for a trek to the mountain villages in the company of a young Christian lad. By 6.30 a.m. we had arrived at Ighil Kerare where the Misses Dudgeon and Miss Wicks worked for so many years. As news spread of a visitor's arrival, women began preparations to receive me. Coffee, cakes and other Kabyle specialities were set before me as I went from house to house. By the end of the day I had given eight gospel addresses to groups of between five and fifteen people, who seemed hungry for the message they had heard for so many years and now missed so much.'

In 1911 Mr. and Mrs. Henry J. Pomeroy started a home for orphans at Draa el Mizan, another French village. A family of four left destitute at their door was their first care and others were added later. They also engaged in visiting in the mountainous Snana district just two hours' journey from Draa el Mizan. A house was hired in a village which itself was in the centre of nine others, scattered within a short distance of each other. Weekly visits were made to hold a children's class and other meetings. In each village men, women and children readily heard the message. During the First World War they distributed Testaments and Gospels to young men on leave or going to the front, and corresponded with them, a heavy task that earned the Pomeroys the very real gratitude of relatives. In 1922, however, the Pomeroys transferred to Nigeria, and, for some time, the work was in the hands of Mr. and Mrs. Ernest A. Wall. Working from Tizi Reniffe, Mr. and Mrs. Henry G. Young also continued this particular activity.

At the same location the Walls began separate classes for girls, women, boys, and young men, but toward the close of their service in Algeria they encountered great opposition from a Muslim society and the local R.C. priest. Along with Mr. Henry Young, Mr. Wall also used Draa el Mizan as a base to evangelize towns to the south, including Aurnale, Sidi Aich, and the large

Mr. and Mrs. Henry J. Pomeroy and orphans   (*Echoes*, 1917)

oasis town of Bou Saâda, to and from which armed caravans of camels went. Many conversations were had with Kabyles, Arabs and Jews, with some of whom contact was established and to whom Christian literature was later forwarded.

Henry Young was an inveterate traveller, and much of his time at Draa el Mizan was used in spreading the gospel to neglected parts of Kabylia, visiting towns and villages rarely touched, and occasionally being allowed the use of the mosque or cinema to preach the Word. Often accompanied by other missionaries, like Arthur H. Charters, Stuart J. Sears and Thomas W. Speare, his scope of operations covered territory as far apart as Tiaret and villages on the slopes of the Djurdjura mountains. Of one of these trips, we quote from *Echoes* August 1930.

'Native villages are rarely visited by Europeans, unless by missionaries, and curiosity is immediately aroused. Women's heads shoot out from courtyard doorways, to be quickly withdrawn again. A side glance in passing reveals eyes here and there, peering through the badly-fitting doors to get a glimpse of the "Iroumien" (Europeans) as they pass by. Just as we reached a village gathering-place, a wedding procession passed. The bride, heavily veiled and mounted on a mule, was followed by the friends of the bridegroom, who were firing guns. The men soon made us feel at home in their midst, and three of us told forth the story of God's great love. When the last speaker had finished, they applauded, a most unusual thing for Moslems to do. One felt much helped of the Lord in speaking to this particular company of men. When the children were inclined to be restless, their elders sent them off, so that none of our words should be lost. We left the

Draa el Mizan – a village of the Mechtras tribe

village with thankful hearts and with the conviction that the Lord's voice had been heard.'

It was also Mr. Young's privilege to spend some time with the Mechtras tribe, situated some distance east of Draa el Mizan. It is interesting to note the frequency and pleasure with which Muslims accepted gospel literature.

Bougie is the port of Kabylia from which crude oil is exported. At one time a Carthaginian post and later the Saldae of the Romans, Bougie subsequently fell into the hands of the Vandals. In the eleventh century it was peopled by Berbers, who raised it to considerable prominence under the name Bedjaïa, of which 'Bougie' is a corruption. It was captured by Algerian forces in 1553 and became a piratical harbour, but the French occupied it in 1833 and bestowed a more respectable character on it. It was here that the first attempt was made to evangelize the Muslims by Raymond Lull (a Roman Catholic), who was martyred on the sea-shore outside the gate of the city in 1316. Raymond Lull was well aware that he would almost undoubtedly be killed because of his witness for Christ and, long before, he had written, 'Men die of old age; die owing to the want of natural warmth and to excess of cold; and, therefore, may Thy servant, if it please Thee, not die such a death. I have often shivered from great cold and fright, but when will that day and hour be, when my body will tremble, owing to the great glow of love, and its great desire to die for its Saviour?'

Two French ladies started a work among Algerians in Bougie in 1903. Mr. and Mrs. Henry G. Young settled here in 1914 and commenced working among Kabyles. Over the years a number professed conversion and were baptised.

Miss Harriett Pearse, who had served the Lord for eight years in Algiers among French people, moved to Bougie, and purchased a piece of land in an excellent position overlooking the harbour. She erected a hall with living accommodation above and helped to establish an assembly here, composed, however, entirely of Europeans.

Miss L. Amelia L. Murdoch spent her first eight years of service in Bougie before moving on to Djidjelli in 1930. She was of considerable assistance to Miss Pearse, especially in the difficult task of witnessing to the Jews. One sad episode that both ladies experienced while at Bougie was the murder of a converted police inspector. A few years after Miss Murdoch's departure from Bougie, Miss Anna Müller, who had been associated with Miss Pearse for some time, was commended to the work by Swiss assemblies and proved herself a most efficient helper. When Miss Pearse was obliged to retire because of ill-health, Mr. and Mrs. Stuart J. Sears, who had spent a few years in the Kabyle village of Ikherbane, took over the work amongst the French population. With independence, most of the Europeans left Algeria, and the small assembly came to an end. During the Second World War many servicemen passed through Bougie and numbers were helped at special meetings held for them by Mr. Sears. He also had an excellent class of educated young people, such as school teachers.

Miss Harriet O. Dobbs and Miss Louisa O'Conor served for some time in Seddouk and then at El Kseur. At the latter there was a doctor in residence, and the medical work was consequently on a much smaller scale than at Seddouk. The two ladies did not depend so much on Muslims for an opening, for the inhabitants of El Kseur were less fanatical and more ready to listen to the gospel than those of Seddouk. After more than a year's prayer, Harriet and Louisa were able to rent a house for classes in the nearby village of Thakhleigh. Here, more than 80 children regularly attended classes (compared with under twenty in Seddouk) and many parents gave them a hospitable reception.

Whilst most of these centres were occupied for a few years only, the work at Ighil Kerare, as already indicated, has been more sustained. After the retirement of the Misses Dudgeon, Miss Joyce Wicks carried on as much of the work as possible, but ultimately had to retire.

Yakouren, on the main road from Algiers to Tabarouth, was an offshoot of the work at Tabarouth. Before her marriage to Thomas W. Speare, Miss K. Clark opened up this small French hamlet, with work also in the nearly Kabyle village. Yakouren is 2,300 feet above sea level and is a favourite summer resort; it is set in a very picturesque situation in the midst of an extensive forest. Miss Jessie A. E. C. Sinclair joined Miss Catharine A. Clark and a work amongst children and a gospel meeting for Europeans were continued for many years. Part of Miss Sinclair's small house was used as a hall in which a variety of meetings were held. Mr. Arthur of Azazga conducted regular gospel meetings here. At that

Bougie workers' conference 1949. *Left to right: Back row:* Arthur H. Charters; Miss Jessie A. E. C. Sinclair; Miss Elsie Sills; Miss Lilian E. Castle; Miss L. Amelia L. Murdoch. *Middle row:* Stuart J. Sears; Jules Dufey; John Moore; Henry G. Young; Charles R. Marsh. *Front row:* Mrs. Speare; Dorothy Sears; Ruth P. Marsh (sister to Daisy); Pearl M. Marsh; Suzanne M. Dudgeon

time, the native women were not allowed to visit the European section of the town where Miss Sinclair lived, and she, therefore, visited them in their homes. Sir John Laing told of a visit he and Alec Pulleng paid to a friend's farmhouse. 'Seven married sons and their families all lived under the same roof. The lower part of the house provided shelter for the cows, lambs and innumerable chickens. Our gaze was arrested by what appeared to be huge store pots. Actually they were made of cow-dung and earth, and were used to store figs and lentils; primitive, but secure from vermin. In this home an old man lay on a bed before a fire with no outlet for the smoke. He informed us he was suffering from *la grippe* (influenza). Thus appraised, our interest in the house vanished and we bade them farewell.'

To the east of the river Soumman on the Mediterranean coast is the town of Djidjelli, the route to which is through wonderful mountain scenery, including the celebrated gorges of Kherrata. At the latter a huge dam has been constructed in connection with a hydroelectric scheme to supply power for a large area of North Africa. The small assembly at Djidjelli was established through

Yakouren 1962 – in front of Miss Jessie A. E. C. Sinclair's house

the witness of Miss Amelia Murdoch and Miss Elsie Sills, in fellowship with local believers of Spanish extraction. There was considerable blessing amongst the large European community, but the majority of the Europeans left the country when independence was secured. Miss Murdoch and Miss Sills also engaged in work among Arab girls, but found much Muslim opposition in this fanatical town.

Indeed, for some time Miss Sills allowed one of her pupils to live with her, since the girl's father nearly killed her and threatened to try again. Even so there were refreshing exceptions, as when one day Miss Murdoch noticed an Arab wielding a stick as he tried to hasten his unwilling daughter into one of the classes. That same girl became a regular attender. Others came eagerly for the classes.

Mr. Charles R. Marsh gave a good deal of help in teaching the new converts, but there were unfortunately no local brethren to assume responsibility in the assembly.

The Lord spoke to Charles R. Marsh through Henry G. Lamb (see *The Challenge of Islām*, pp. 10–12) and he subsequently married the latter's daughter, Pearl. Pearl Marsh had spent her childhood at Tabarouth and was acquainted with the conditions as well as with both the French and Kabyle languages. They served initially with the North Africa Mission, with which George Goodman and other brethren were associated, and commenced work at Sétif, where only Arabic is spoken. They

Miss Elsie Sill's pupils

could find no accommodation, but visited the Guergour tribes about 60 miles away before returning to Azazga. The road rose to a height of 4,000 feet and, as far as the eye could see, there were hundreds of unevangelized villages, while in the distance the majestic snow-clad Djurdjura mountains rose in splendour. They were convinced that this was to be their part of the great world field.

Djurdjura mountains   (Miss S. M. Dudgeon)

They returned to Lafayette, the nearest French centre and, within half an hour, had found and rented a small house. Pearl got into many Muslim homes. Classes and meetings rapidly increased in numbers. Gospel meetings in French attracted many Europeans and, among others, their landlord's wife was converted. Then their house was sold and they had to move to Hammam, a thermal centre renowned for its hot springs in Roman days, where only Arabic was spoken. In 1944 they severed their connection with the N.A.M. and were commended by their home assemblies.

It was evident that, to reach 500 villages effectively, an outstation was needed. Ground was accordingly purchased at Beni Ourtilan, very near a large weekly market, and this provided an excellent centre from which they continued to radiate with the gospel, but to which people also came to them. So the work continued at Lafayette, Hammam and Beni Ourtilan. Market day brought crowds of men and boys; regular classes and meetings were established. Dispensaries were opened at Hammam and Beni Ourtilan and as many as 150 were treated in a morning.

Charles translated the four Gospels into Kabyle and then assisted in the revision of the New Testament and also in a translation of the whole Bible into Arabic. At the same time he was covering a wide area of Lesser Kabylia in his ministry. Opposition was usually intense and he was often driven from a village by a shower of stones. Pearl was greatly beloved by the Muslim women and was very busily occupied in the Master's service. Charles was the only speaker at meetings for ten years.

The area was evacuated during the war for independence and the gospel hall fell into the hands of the Muslims. When the French forces returned, they destroyed the hall and the living accommodation. In 1958 the bridge leading to the hall at Hammam was washed away by the torrent during a terrific storm and the hall was also carried away in the swirling flood. In 1962 Charles and Pearl withdrew and subsequently went to the Chad for a time making a brief visit to Algeria. Pearl returned from the field in 1969 and was called home in 1981. Charles continues in active service for the Lord – especially in encouraging Operation Mobilization teams.

The most recent centre to be occupied is Bordj-bou-Arreridj, a small town at an altitude of 5,000 feet on the main railway line

Handicrafts for boys (F. L. Perkins)

between Constantine and Algiers. The population is mainly Arab, although many Kabyles are also to be found there. After a brief initial period with a senior missionary in village evangelism in 1950, Fred L. Perkins felt led to the townships where the population was predominantly Arabic-speaking. He met and married Madge Hutchinson and eventually heard from Charles R. Marsh of a small flat at Bordj-bou-Arreridj. When war broke out, the French authorities imposed travel restrictions, which limited the missionaries' outreach. Conditions worsened and murders in the town became a frequent occurrence. Even so, Mr. Perkins had the opportunity, along with two helpers, to constitute the team to take over the B.F.B.S.'s stand at the 1960 Sahara Travelling Trade Fair. Quargla, Touggourt, Tolga and Biskra were reached, and in these oasis towns there was a distinct sowing of the seed, by word of mouth as well as in book sales. Even after independence, there was considerable civil disorder, but there was a tolerant attitude to missionaries until the Muslim upsurge in 1965.

After spending three years in Lafayette to learn Arabic and to assist Pearl Marsh, Miss Audrey Mee (U.K. 1952) joined the Perkins at Bordj-bou-Arreridj in 1955. Her awareness that she was to serve God in a foreign country dates back to her childhood when, at the age of nine, her unconverted father took Audrey to

1982: Baptism in the desert   (F. L. Perkins)

see a film in a local church concerning the life of David
Livingstone. At that time the population of Bordj-bou-Arreridj
was 40,000; today the Europeans have gone but the population
has doubled. There was an atmosphere of insecurity, but by
visiting and medical work, the opportunities came to sow the good
seed. In 1962 Audrey was joined by Mlle. Martha Daniel,
commended by the assembly at Lille in France. By then the
uncertainties had gone and opportunities for witness increased
tremendously. They had the joy of seeing some converted and
baptised.

In 1970 the government expelled 50 per cent of missionaries on
various pretexts, but did not bring pressure to bear upon Audrey
and Martha, although they and the Perkins were interrogated.
Some of those converted and baptised left to secure employment.
For the next three or four years remaining missionaries and
national believers alike were continually subjected to police
harassment. The then Minister for Religion in the Algerian
Government tried hard to get rid of all Christian missionaries and
stamp out national Christian groupings. But, partly due no doubt
to earnest prayer, the general position remained intact and the
Minister was dismissed from his post! Then in 1976 the Perkins
returned to England for the sake of their family. Others, however,

were saved and one brother started regional conferences for the better educated young Christians. In 1980 a French lady, who had been converted, opened her home for the believers to meet, and two other homes have been opened since.

Audrey and Martha have moved to France to work among Arabic people there and to make periodic visits to Algeria. There are now no assembly missionaries resident in Algeria. It seems incredible that no one is apparently concerned about this strategically placed country. A. Pulleng raises the question 'whether, in view of the continued sterility of this field, it is justifiable to continue existing work by replacement, and still more to extend it. In recent years it has often been suggested by reputable authorities that the impact of the European mode of life, by means of education, the cinema, radio and television, and the contact of many North Africans with France as they go there to work for a period of years, are bound to lessen the fanaticism of Islām and evoke a more tolerant attitude towards the Christian message.' But, as he says, 'there is no indication of this taking place. Indeed,

Miss Audrey P. Mee

the spirit of nationalism particularly, and to a lesser degree the spirit of materialism, is not tending to produce more converts. Any new workers proceeding to the Muslim field should not assume that the work will be more productive of results in the near future than in the past.'

Should we then ignore the spiritual needs of the country and concentrate on easier and more productive fields? to quote the title of Charles R. Marsh's book, *Too Hard for God?*

6

Bengal Nation

The People's Republic of Bangladesh (literally 'Bengal Nation') was formerly known as East Bengal. It is 55,598 square miles in size and is virtually an enclave into India. In the south it is bounded by the Bay of Bengal and in the south-east by Burma, but otherwise is surrounded by Indian territory. It is a low-lying country, principally a deltaic, alluvial plain formed by the confluence of the Ganges and Brahmaputra rivers, the Meghna and their many tributaries. Hills rise above the plain in the Chittagong in the south-east and the Sylhet district in the north-east. It has a long marshy coastline of 370 miles. It has one of the world's highest rainfalls, averaging 85 inches a year. Since much of the country is partially submerged or subject to flooding during the rainy season, land travel is very difficult, and transport is mainly by boat.

When India was granted independence in 1947, two nations emerged – India which was predominantly Hindu, and Pakistan which was mainly Muslim. Punjab and Bengal were both divided into two parts to form West and East Pakistan. With the exchange of populations that ensued, there were considerable upheavals for some weeks. Administration of the new state of Pakistan was difficult with a thousand miles of Indian territory between the two sections. Furthermore, the inequality in economic development as well as cultural and linguistic differences led to agitation in the early 1950's for coequal status for East Pakistan.

By the mid-1960's, seeming disparities between the East's and

To Chalna Bazaar by boat   (Tear Fund)

West's share of development expenditures and representation in
the armed forces and civil service had caused still greater
resentment and gave impetus to a movement in the East for
provincial autonomy. In 1966 Sheikh Mujibur (or Mujib)
Rahman, who was president of the East Pakistan Krisha Starnik
Awami (People's) League, emerged as a leader, but he was
subsequently arrested for his political activities. In 1971 Bengali
nationalists declared an independent People's Republic of
Bangladesh and, in the following year, the government was
reconstituted with Mujibur Rahman as prime minister. In 1975
he assumed the presidency, but was killed a few months later in
a military coup. Gen. Ziaur Rahman (or Zia), who became
president subsequently, was assassinated in 1981 and was
succeeded by the vice-president. The country has taken a long
time to settle down, but is gradually adjusting to its responsibilities as a sovereign state.

After acquiring independence in 1971, Bangladesh faced an

Fès – Bab Bou Jeloud　　　　　　　　　　　(R. Turpin, M.E.Ph.A.)

Fès – a souk   (R. Turpin, M.E.Ph.A.)

immense task in establishing its own economy and, at the same time, trying to recover from the ravages of war, as well as the disastrous effects of a cyclone in 1970. Nationalization of the most important industries, a serious famine in 1974, and hyper-inflation compounded its problems. Since 1975, the economy has begun to recover as a result of successful financial stabilization measures, a larger role for the private sector, and improved national policies in industry and development, but there are still serious problems to be solved. Electricity is, however, produced by hydroelectric power at Kaptai on the Karnafuli river.

The population is 89 million, of whom 98 per cent are Bengalis. Eighty-five per cent are Muslims, sixteen per cent Hindus, and the remainder are Christians, Buddhists and others. The official language is Bengali, but English is still widely spoken. The capital, Dacca, has a population of three million, Chittagong has 388,000, Kulna over 600,000 and Narayanganj about 360,000.

Bangladesh is an extremely poor country. It suffers from pressures caused by a dense and rapidly growing population, low agricultural productivity, and chronic food deficits which result in widespread malnutrition. Its monsoon climate is erratic, and the great rivers which traverse the country are subject to periodical uncontrolled flooding. Except for natural gas, the country has practically no natural resources, and its industrial base is weak and inefficient. There are coal deposits at Jamalput

Near Faridpur – digging a canal   (Bangladesh High Commission)

and Rajshahi but they are difficult to exploit because of the depth at which they lie.

The principal industry is agriculture and approximately 90 per cent of the population derive their livelihood from this, either directly or indirectly. Rice, jute, tea, sugar and wheat are among the main products. Unfortunately the land is fragmented into small, inefficient plots, and half of the rural families are landless. Industries are largely nationalized and badly organized. Jute products, cotton spinning, fertilizers, pharmaceuticals, paper and leather goods represent the major industries.

Considerable financial assistance has been received from the U.S.S.R. and China and there are extremely friendly relations with the latter. It will be appreciated that a poor country like Bangladesh is the type which most readily responds to the philosophy of communism.

Fewer than 0.25 per cent of the total population profess to be Christians. The Bihar people of Dacca and Chittagong are Muslims. The tribal population of two per cent is divided into 28 groups, only four of which have their language reduced to writing. They are more receptive to the gospel than the Bengalis and a number of missions have been established among them.

It has been said sometimes that the effects of the apostle Thomas's teaching at Lahore reached as far as to what is now Bangladesh, but that is extremely improbable. Nor is there much evidence that the Nestorian Christians affected this area. The effect of William Carey's preaching two centuries ago still remains, however. In addition, as professor of Indian languages at Fort William College in Calcutta, he undoubtedly influenced many of the young men who entered the civil service in Bengal.

English Presbyterians and other churches have reached the Santalis through schools and dispensaries, and the Oxford Mission has workers among the Gāros. Other bodies have seen conversions among the Khāsis, Lushais and Tipperahs. Operation Mobilization (the teams of which include a number of assembly workers) has engaged in literature distribution and personal evangelism. The O.M. ship *Logos* visited the ports of Chalna and Chittagong in 1972 and 1973 and further activities are planned.

The assembly missionary effort in Bangladesh has always been small. The total number of assembly commended workers who

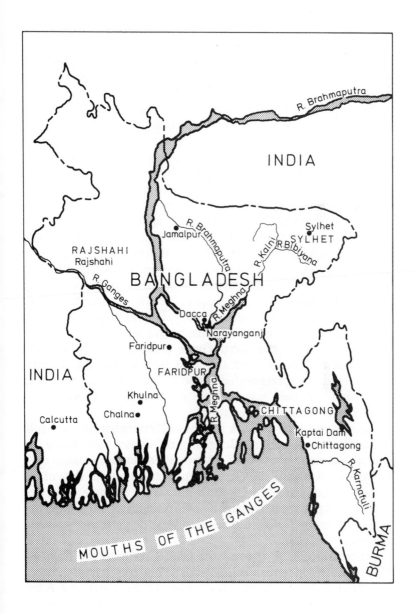

have served here is only five and it continued latterly with only one couple – and this in a country the population of which will be over 100 million by the end of the century.

In 1961 Stewart and Gillian McKenzie went to Bangladesh, but after four years they had not seen a convert and had not been able to found an assembly.

Few who were present at the London Missionary Meetings in 1965 can forget the poignant report that Stewart gave. In 1961 when he went to East Pakistan there was no assembly and there was none at the time that he spoke. In the four years of their service, there had been no baptisms, and none had accepted Jesus Christ. The work was hard and unrewarding. He would go to the market to sell Gospels. The Muslims would sometimes tread them underfoot and spit in his face. The children in Gillian's class were antagonistic. 'Jesus,' said one little girl, 'He is nothing at all.'

They sought confirmation of their call from God and, in reply to their prayers, had the joy of seeing a young man converted from Islām. This new convert suffered much for his profession, being disowned by his father, turned out of his lodgings and thrown out of his job. But he is still standing today. He was the only one saved out of hundreds of correspondence course students.

In 1967 Philip and Avril Game (commended from U.K.) arrived in the country, working first with Stewart and Gillian. They found unprecedented opportunities for advance and expansion; all that was lacking was workers. There was a tremendous hunger for literature.

They were joined by Ruth Bourne of Birmingham in 1969 and, while Ruth was learning Bengali, girls' classes were started at Dacca and many house-bound Muslim women were visited with the gospel. Ruth and the Games returned home at the time of the Indo-Pakistan war in 1971. Ruth has found a sphere of service among Bengali-speaking people in Birmingham and Dudley, of whom there are 22,000, and has seen blessing particularly among children.

On returning after the war the Games resumed the Emmaus Bible Correspondence Course work. This grew rapidly after a distribution campaign by a team from Delhi. Barry and Anne Mackey (Canada) were a great help in this. In 1976 follow-up meetings involved considerable travel but proved to be a time of blessing but they were hampered by lack of national brethren to

Dacca – girls' class   (R. Bourne)

help. Avril was involved in girls' classes in English and Bengali, but visiting became difficult and there was no other woman worker. For some months in 1973 help was given by a couple from Britain, but they felt unable to remain permanently and Avril ultimately had to carry on the girls' work unaided and consequently had to turn many away who had been prepared to listen to the gospel. Philip and Avril Game left the country in 1980 and there is now no assembly missionary there.

In 1970 over 500,000 died as a result of the severe cyclone and assemblies and Christian groups poured relief funds into the country. But no one apparently felt sufficiently exercised about the spiritual need of the people to go there to work among them.

Since 1971 the government has required all persons engaged in missionary work to register with the policy department on arrival. Registration imposes restrictions on movement; for example, prior approval must be obtained to spend more than seven days outside the area of registration. New missionaries are allowed only as replacements for missionaries who have left and will not be returning. Visas specify the localities in which the missionary is allowed to work. Despite fears to the contrary, legislation introduced in 1978 has not led to the expulsion of missionaries or

Chittagong – selling Christian literature   (S.G.M.)

to any curtailment of their activities. The subsequent military take-over has brought some changes, however.

A recent report on Bangladesh says that the outstanding ministry carried on in the country is the Bible correspondence school programme. Emmaus courses were translated in 1963 and are available in Bengali as well as in English. At one time 15,000 students had enrolled and 1,100 lessons were graded on a monthly basis, but there is now no one to deal with this work.

There is a great demand for Bengali Bibles, New Testaments and Gospels and the United Bible Societies have been able to distribute large numbers, but the demand is greater than the supply.

7

Sao's Lost Kingdoms

The fifth largest country in Africa, the Republic of Chad has an area of 495,750 square miles. It is completely landlocked, being surrounded by Libya, Sudan, Central African Empire, Cameroon, Nigeria and Niger. It is shaped rather like a shallow basin, which rises gradually from 750 feet above sea level at Lake Chad in the west to over 12,000 feet in the Tibesti Mountains in the north. A number of rivers from the south run into Lake Chad.

The country is composed of three regions. In the north, the Sahara desert extends deeply into Chad and the small number of

N'Djamena – confluence of the Shari and Lagone river

nomadic inhabitants there tends to congregate almost entirely around the oases. In the dry season, the scorching *harmattan* dries up all vegetation and there is only a sandy waste. Vast plateaux rise to peaks of a considerable height, Emi Koussi, for example, being 11,203 feet.

The centre and a great deal of the south is mainly savannah or dry grasslands, and the extreme south is thick bush. In the rainy season the watercourses, or *bahrs*, flood the plains. The greater part of the population is concentrated in the south.

The plains are crossed by large sand dunes, resulting from the action of the wind on the sand. As one writer remarks, 'The whole Chad is divided by the dunes of Kanem, which dam Lake Chad and also Lake Fittri to the east.'

Bordering on Niger and Nigeria is the immense Lake Chad, the size of which varies as part dries up because of intensive evaporation, but which is up to 10,000 square miles in extent. The lake is 922 feet above sea level. The rivers Shari and Logone, which flow into it, deposit vast quantities of silt, to add to the sand carried there by the wind. Primarily for this reason, the shores of the lake are flat and swampy. The lake is divided into two basins by the Great Barrier, through which there is only one channel. The waters are rich in fish and the islands are inhabited more or less exclusively by fishermen.

The area seems to have been populated over a thousand years ago at least, but there is very little information regarding its early

Across the river Logone   (W. T. Stunt)

history. Lake Chad was known to Ptolemy, but he provided no information about the inhabitants of the country. Herodotus referred to Negroid cave dwellers as inhabiting the north of the country which lay to the south of Libya (i.e. Chad). Tradition claims that the area around Lake Chad was originally occupied by the Negroie Sao (probably the ancestors of the present Kotoko), remains of whose medieval culture and bronze artifacts were discovered in 1955 not far from the lake.

The Sao culture and political power continued for some centuries, the most important of the Sao kingdoms being the Kanem-Bornou, Baguirmi and Ouaddai. At their peak, these kingdoms controlled practically the whole of present-day Chad and parts of Niger and Sudan. Some historians maintain that the Kanem-Bornou kingdom of the sixteenth century, arising out of the great Sudanese kingdom of the Saharan Berbers, long controlled the trans-Saharan trade route, but that it was finally eclipsed by the Islāmicized kingdoms of Baguirmi and Ouaddai in the following century. It is certainly clear that, in the eighteenth century, the Ouaddai kingdom threw off the suzerainty of Darfur and extended its territories by the conquest of eastern Kanem.

All of these Muslim states enriched themselves by raiding the southern tribes for slaves; but continual conflict and internecine strife rapidly weakened them and, during the period 1883–93, they all fell a prey to the Sudanese adventurer and slave trader, Rabah Zubahr. In 1900, however, he was overthrown by the French, who had already penetrated Chad in 1891 and had established their authority by military expeditions, primarily against the Muslim kingdoms. The defeat of the Sultan of Abéché in 1911 was the final step to the complete subjugation of the country. Initially, the traditional Kanembu dynasty was restored under French protection.

In 1910 the French formed a federation of French Equatorial Africa, composed of what are now the states of Chad, Gabon, the Central African Empire and Congo (Brazzaville), of which Chad was the largest country. After the Second World War, in conformity with the new French colonial policy, the federation was dissolved in 1959 and the four states became autonomous members of the French Community, but in the following year Chad achieved complete independence. It has not been an easy path since. A *coup d'état* in 1975 resulted in the assassination of the President and the assumption of power by a Supreme Military Council with a new President. In 1979 civil war broke out between the army of the north and the national army, i.e. basically between the nomadic Muslim tribes of the north and the ruling Negro river people of the south. In 1981 Col. Qadhafi of Libya added to the tension and political unrest by sending Libyan forces into Chad in an attempt to secure control of the whole country by the Muslims. Five thousand troops, 60 Soviet-made tanks and a number of aircraft were sent into Chad and stationed in and around N'Djamena, within easy striking distance of Chad's neighbours, and Qadhafi announced the political union of the two countries. Nigeria was naturally concerned at the possible threat to cut off her exports of oil to the west and to other parts of Africa.

The capital is N'Djamena (formerly Fort Lamy), which has a population of about 300,000, and other towns are Moundou, Sarh (formerly Fort Archambault) and Abéché, each of which has a population of just over 50,000. Cattle, camels, ostriches, goats and sheep are reared in the north, but cotton, rice, sugar, millet and fruits are produced in the fertile south – which also has a rich variety of trees, including mahogany and kapok. There is a great deal of fishing in the lake, 100,000 tons annually being caught. Natural resources include petroleum, uranium, natron and kaolin, but these still await full exploitation.

N'Djamena   (W. T. Stunt)

The total population is about 4,600,000, and ethnic groups include Sudanic, Nilotic, Arabic and Saharan. Near Lake Chad are tribes of mixed Negroid and Semitic strains, and some Hausa and Fula immigrants from West Africa, in addition to a certain number of Arabs. The great majority of the people are Negroes. The pastoral nomads are represented primarily by the Toda and Daza tribes. These have intermingled very little with the other races. The Arabs, who are engaged mainly in raising cattle, camels, goats and sheep, migrate from north to south with the rains. The Fulani, who are also cattle-raisers, are more static and are mostly located in the vicinity of Baguirmi. The people of Kanem live by cultivating millet, but the Kotoko and Boukouma depend largely on fishing. Fitri, Ouaddai, Sara and other tribes grow cotton, rice, peanuts and maize.

French is still spoken in the cities but to a somewhat diminishing extent. The principal language of the north is Arabic, and that of the south is Ngambai. But Chad Arabic is gradually being adopted throughout the country, although the Muslim is critical of anything resembling a mutilation of the true Arabic of which he is so proud. With over a hundred languages and dialects in use, the language problem is quite a serious one.

People of Sao's Lost Kingdoms

Forty-five per cent of the people are Muslims; in fact, in the north, it is nearer to 100 per cent. In the south, however, the majority of the people are animists. The number of Roman Catholics and Protestants in the country is probably not greatly in excess of 200,000, almost evenly divided between the two. These are found principally in the south.

Islām was introduced from North Africa by the Hausas in the sixteenth and seventeenth centuries. The whole of the northern section of Chad has been virtually conquered by Islām. In the south, in every town of any reasonable size, there are communities of Muslims.

There is complete religious liberty, although the Muslims are seeking increasingly to influence political and religious life and to develop closer ties with less tolerant Islāmic states. The government is composed of Muslims and non-Muslims and, at one time, included three Ministers who were evangelical Christians, while the Prime Minister also stated publicly that he was a believer in the Lord Jesus Christ. Twenty years ago, several M.P.s, two government ministers and a number of administrators were to be found attending the assembly meetings in the capital. But Islām is now gaining ground more rapidly than the gospel. Each year 300 trained teachers of Islām leave Cairo to spread the Islāmic faith throughout Africa. A pagan chief may be surrounded by such teachers and be subjected to their pressure until he finally yields and goes over to Islām with his whole tribe.

Most of the traders come from the Fezzan and are rich and influential and are propagators of Islām. The nomads who wander from place to place with their flocks and herds are all Muslims. The pilgrim road to Mecca runs through the capital, and every year tens of thousands of Muslims from the west coast of Africa pass through the country. These men are intent on winning others to their faith. Arabic must be taught in all schools and often the only textbook is the Qu'rān.

There are other pressures, however. President Tombalbaye, who was assassinated in 1975, was formerly a member of an assembly Bible class. A few weeks before his death, he stated publicly that missionaries must engage in social work and not in spiritual activities. In a reversion to paganism, the government attempted to compel initiation for nationals, involving practices of a nature (including sacrifices to ancestral spirits and an animistic 'rebirth') which many Christians found themselves unable to accept. Consequently some were imprisoned and others put to death. The *New Zealand Treasury* of January 1975 quoted a number of cases of persecution.

'They tried to make X eat food offered to idols, but he refused and they put him in stocks, beat him, broke his fingers, dug a hole before his eyes, and buried him alive.' 'The whole assembly at — has been murdered, except the women.' 'There are numerous cases of the initiation priests coming and taking leading Bible teachers away to enforce initiation – otherwise children will be killed. They shave the Christian men's heads with a broken bottle, force their hair into their mouth and beat them. The village of — is said to have had 131 Christians slaughtered.' Such cases are rare today, but these occurred only a few years ago. The greatest danger today is from Islām subtlety and pressure.

Assembly work began in Chad in 1926 with the coming of Dr. John R. Olley. The Sudan United Mission entered later the same year. Other societies have since opened up stations in various areas and one of the most recent forms of evangelistic activity is a youth movement called Flambeau, i.e. 'little flames', which has a membership of several thousand young people, led by a large number of African leaders.

John Remeses Olley has been described as 'seaman, school teacher and able linguist in Greek, Hebrew and French'. He had a consuming desire to present the claims of Christ to the millions of followers of Muḥammad. He was commended from New Zealand

Preaching at a baptism

(N. J. Taylor)

John Remeses Olley   *(F.O.L., 1958)*

in 1919 and went first to Tunisia to study Arabic and to preach in the port and in markets. In Tripoli he learned of Henry J. Pomeroy's move to enter the Sahara via Nigeria. As he had always wanted to reach the people of the interior, he learned Hausa, the trade language of the Sudan, and went to Italy to obtain medical supplies. In Florence he heard of Henry Pomeroy's death. After visiting Palestine, Turkey and Syria, he took ship for Nigeria and, from the coast, travelled 700 miles inland to Kano (Nigeria). Here he helped to consolidate Mr. Pomeroy's work and saw the little assembly grow to over 70.

The arrival from Abéché of Dugald Campbell, the veteran traveller in Africa, encouraged John in his intentions and in February 1926 he set out from Kano on an 80-day camel journey to Abéché. He learned Sara and prepared a hymnbook and a translation of Luke's Gospel in that language for the growing assembly there. For many years he and his faithful co-workers preached, taught and baptised in Abéché in the east and in Fort Archambault (Sahr), Moïssala and Doba in the south. Despite the slave trade, famine and disease, believers were established and grew in the faith.

In 1928 he felt impelled to take the gospel to the virgin fields lying to the east and prepared for the long journey to Abéché, passing through Fort-Lamy, the administrative capital of the country. When he reached the capital, the Governor of the Chad informed him that missionary work was not permitted in the Chad or Wadai. It seemed extraordinary that, after years of prayer, preparation and patient waiting, when he had arrived at the very place where he had longed to be, in a land virtually without God's good news, with French, Arabic and Hausa at his command, he should be forbidden to open the door to the gospel. Nevertheless, believing that God still rules in the affairs of men and would fulfil His own purpose in His own good time, he left Fort-Lamy and journeyed eastward.

J. W. Clapham paints the picture vividly in *John Olley*, pp. 60, 61, 'Ostriches in groups of six to eight loped away from the passing camels, their males standing out on account of their dark plumage and white tail feathers. Great bustards, at first mistaken for young ostriches, rose awkwardly into the air at the approach of the travellers, returning to their continual search for locusts and grasshoppers as soon as they had passed. Guinea fowl in flocks of fifty to a hundred showed very little fear, sometimes succumbing to the deft swiftness of the throwing-knife carried by some of the party. Grey and red monkeys peered cheekily through the stunted thorn bushes and an odd dogheaded baboon barked his disapproval. Travelling by night was cooler and often preferred by the herdsmen leading their long-horned cattle to watering-places. Great spotted hyenas and their smaller striped cousins lurked a few hundred yards behind the herds, emitting their lugubrious cry, starting on a deep base note and rising to a sharp high yelp. Their massive forequarters and repulsiveness appeared even more unpleasant in the pale light of the moon. The sameness of the terrain was broken about 250 miles east by the unexpected suddenness with which the Hadjarai mountains spring out of the plains, the Pic du Guéra, abode of the pagan priest of the sky-god, the Margai, reigning as monarch of the peaks. Up in the rocky clefts the leopard has his lair and, farther down, its rival, the serval cat with its long, ringed tail, long legs and spotted tawny body, hunts the smaller game. An odd cheetah, champion sprinter of the cat family, summons its strength for great bursts of speed to overtake the black-striped Rufifrons gazelle, prima ballerina of the savannahs which, feeding on the sparse vegetation of the foothills, keeps one ear cocked and trusts one female sentinel in the herd to

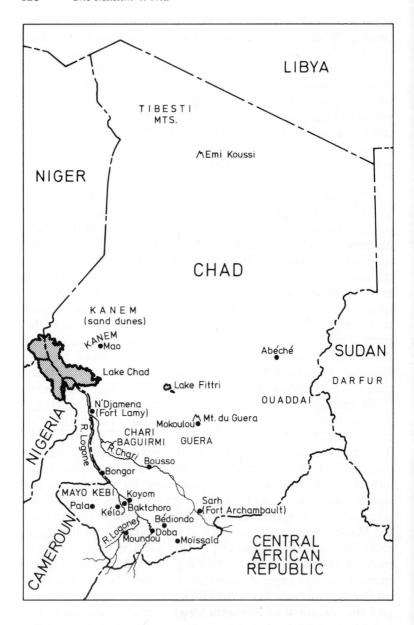

Marrakesh (A. White)

In the land of Two Faces – a Berber tent (H. Ratcliffe)

Tanger market	(H. Ratcliffe)

A Kasbah	(H. Ratcliffe)

warn at the approach of an enemy. The nimble-footed koudore, noblest of all the antelope, lifting his proud spiralling horns, surveys the plains beneath from some rocky promontory. Up in these mountains live the Hadjarai tribes, or people of the rocks,' about whom John Olley was particularly concerned.

Since he could not preach, John opened his house at Abéché to any of the young men from the south who cared to visit him, never failing to tell them of God's way of salvation. They came chiefly from outside the borders of the Wadai. A Greek trader leased a house to him and showed great kindness in many ways. In 1929 there was a change in the administration and he was told that he was 'free to preach in the Chad for all eternity'.

In 1931 he produced Sara–English and Sara–French dictionaries, a hymnbook, Bible primer and Scripture translations, to which he added in following years. At the same time he was preaching the gospel twice daily and four times on Sundays, and he was speaking to French, pagans and Muslims in French, Hausa, Sango, Sara and Arabic. In giving the Mbai New Testament to the Saras, he worked out of love for the people of whom he wrote as a result of his travels:

'The beerpot and the drum are in evidence throughout the land. The history of the Saras is sad indeed. For centuries they have suffered under the old Turkish régime, being constantly raided and taken as slaves to the Sudan and North Africa. With white explorers and Europeanization the situation is worse. The world's "open sore" of French Equatorial Africa has become a gangrene eating out the heart and vitality of central Africa. The Saras are a superior and prolific race with noble traits and are the backbone of the colonial army and labour force. Cruelly exploited and ravaged by sleeping sickness, fevers and imported diseases . . . the Sara has become the vagabond of the Sudan, poor, despised and afflicted. Of no status except the perpetual slave, he bears with calm fortitude the vicissitudes and trials of his lot. From amongst this people is springing up a militant church, a light to an awful, dark place and a bulwark of Christianity against Islām.'

Weariness and fever racked his body, but he laboured on, his ministry attracting an honorary medical degree. But converted Mbais were leading their own people to Christ and themselves establishing assemblies. When the Mbai New Testament was completed, he translated the N.T. into the Kim language.

N'Djamena – assembly hall   (W. T. Stunt)

A new hall was built in 1938 for the assembly in N'Djamena and soon afterwards John Olley began what became annual pastoral journeys to towns and villages throughout the southern area of Chad. He visited Doba, Moissala, Fort Archambault, the Kim villages and the Mayo-Kebbi, and often included Abéché where an assembly had been started in 1926. With his faithful helpers, he continued the translation work during his travels. A Doctorate of Botanical Medicines was conferred upon him in 1944 and a Doctorate of Medicine in 1947. Often laid low by fever and illness, he collapsed in 1952 during a visit to Nigeria to obtain medical and other supplies, and was in hospital in Jos for over three years. On the way to visit his homeland, however, he died in Australia in 1956.

The capital city of N'Djamena, or Fort Lamy, has attracted a number of workers over the years. Jean and Huguette Metz, commended from France in 1952, worked for some years in the area of Baguirmi, east of N'Djamena. To this area also came Mlle. Christiane Bouttet, Mlle. Danielle Gounon, commended from France in 1958, and Marius and Liliane Baar, commended from France in 1952. (Marius has become known in more recent days for his books on prophecy, *The Unholy War*, etc., with which I find it difficult to agree.) The Baars worked mainly in Korbo. Danielle and Christiane were busily occupied in school and dispensary work in Moukoulou. Claude Harel and Georges Ertz, also from assemblies in France, also gave help in school teaching. Unfortunately, political troubles involved the removal of all missionaries from these particular areas. There are over 200 assemblies in this part of south Chad and many Christians, who are in government employ, travel widely in north Chad, where they are in constant contact with Muslims, but very few Arabs are to be found in the assemblies.

Walter Ganz commenced work in Nigeria in 1925 and eight years later married Mrs. Axtell, who had been labouring in that country since 1926. When they moved from Kano to Doba in 1936, some of the believers who had been converted in Kano felt such a strong sense of attachment to them that they moved with them. These proved a great help in the local testimony. For a brief period the Ganz were also joined by Dr. Olley. After a long period of fruitful service, they retired to the U.S.A. in 1952.

Miss Janet MacDougall, commended from Canada in 1956, has the responsibility for the medical work at Doba. The dispensary provides a large captive audience for the preaching of the gospel each day, as some 200 cases are dealt with daily. In the maternity ward some 700 babies are delivered each year. There are also seven other dispensaries in the area, run by national Christians. At a mission school, 125 students are taught by Christians.

Miss Marjorie Winifred Shaw was commended from Canada in 1949. After language study in Paris, she took up children's and

Doba – Miss Janet MacDougall   (W. T. Stunt)

women's work and assisted in the dispensary. Stricken with polio, she returned home for treatment, but in 1960 decided to return to Chad. She got only as far as Paris, where ill-health compelled her to remain. She has remained there until today, but is usefully occupied in guiding and teaching young students and others. (I will never forget Marjorie's most recent return from Toronto, with about thirty bags and pieces of luggage! The airport receptionist, faced with the avalanche – and the airline's restriction to two bags – attempted no argument about numbers or additional payment, but accepted the lot without a murmur. She would have been very ill-advised to argue with Marjorie, who knows what the Lord wants, in any case!)

Miss Margaret King, commended from Australia in 1958, went first to Koyom, where she established a dispensary. She moved later to Doba and directed the Emmaus Bible course work in French, while also assisting in the dispensary there. Miss Ruth Scott, commended from U.K. in 1972, took over the Bible correspondence course work and also engaged in village evangelism, children's meetings, camps and Sunday school as, of course, did most of the workers at Doba, returning home in 1979.

Danielle Gounon, who was a trained nurse, served for many years at N'Djamena, helping in medical work and in the evangelization of women and girls.

Richard and Betty Sanders were commended from U.S.A. in 1965. Betty was the daughter of Mr. and Mrs. Francis W. Rogers, who served for so many years in Chad. Dick took over the responsibility for a small Bible school at Doba, to train young men in the Scriptures and in methods of evangelism, and also engaged in village evangelism and camp work with up to 200 young people in the camps. There are 250 assemblies in this area alone with over 5,000 in fellowship and the missionaries found a great need for Bible teaching in building up the local assemblies. Dick and Betty moved to Moïssala, where they engaged in similar work, Betty selling Christian books from their home. They returned home in view of the political unrest.

Neil R. and Neralie Clark were commended from New Zealand in 1973 and spent two years in Switzerland and France in language study. For some time they helped David and Jean Goold in the Marseille area. Reaching Doba in 1975, they spent two years there, helping the Sanders and learning Mbai. Neil was

Richard Sanders preparing for a journey   (W. T. Stunt)

involved in young men's Bible classes and young people's work, while Neralie helped in the work amongst women and girls. In 1978 they moved to Pala, where there were no missionaries after the Saxbys and Hewletts had left. Here they learned Ngambai and Ka'do, but when the Muslim forces moved south, Neralie and the children evacuated to New Zealand. Eventually Neil also had to leave the station. The New Testament had been translated into Ka'do and in 1981 the Clarks were able to return with printed copies. For a time they were able to work among the Kado without hindrance, Neralie being the first lady missionary to do so. But political unrest is affecting the immediate area.

Alan R. Wheeler, commended from New Zealand in 1969, went to Chad to help in the building programme for the assembly work. He spent three years building schools, houses and halls in the southern area, in Doba, Pala and Bousso. In 1971 he married Miss Lorraine Pegler, who had been commended from Australia in 1969 and had been engaged in medical work. He was, at the same time, commended to full-time missionary work in Chad and gave help in preaching and teaching.

John V. and Dawn Elliott had accommodated John Olley when

he visited Sydney and it was in their home that, at the age of 69, he suddenly departed to be with the Lord. He had spent 30 years in Central Africa without a furlough and had translated the New Testament into two local languages, and only that morning had spent some hours sunbathing on the back lawn, while four-year-old Annette Elliott brushed the grass from his back. In *John Olley*, p. 123, J. W. Clapham tells the consequence. 'John and Dawn Elliott were well aware that there was still very much to be done. They could not help asking themselves why God in His providence had brought him into their home, shown them so clearly the needs of the Chad and then abruptly taken His servant so unexpectedly from their midst. They turned to the passage of the Bible which came in family worship at that time, "My servant is dead . . . arise . . . go" (Joshua 1:3). For a considerable time they had felt that the Lord had some full-time service for them and had been making it a matter of earnest prayer. Strangely enough, they had never considered the Chad, in spite of their vital interest in it and weekly correspondence with John's sister, Ruth Price! Now it became clear to them that the Lord would have them fill the gap in the ranks in distant Chad and they prepared to obey.' After a short period in France for language study, commended from Australia in 1958, they took up service in Doba until 1967, assisting in dispensary work, village evangelization and teaching in outlying assemblies.

In 1975, Mr. and Mrs. Gordon J. Stewart, commended from New Zealand, came to Doba to fill the gap left by the Elliotts.

'In the early days at Doba', writes M. H. Saxby in *Sounding Out*, p. 67, 'the activities of the lion-men were a great hindrance to the progress of the gospel. To their hands and feet they bound pads designed to leave an impression in the soil similar to the pug marks of a lion. They have always been enemies of defenceless folk, and particularly of the Christians. However, despite hardships and opposition, the gospel was proclaimed and many were saved. Here and there a sorcerer or witchdoctor publicly burned the miserable tools of his fraudulent trade and openly confessed Jesus Christ as his Saviour and Lord.'

Francis W. Rogers, having been commended in 1934, became interested in Chad while taking a missionary course at Moody Bible Institute in Chicago. He married Miss Margaret Wagener in 1935. They returned to Australia and in 1938 went as the first

Doba – sewing class run by Betty Sanders   (W. T. Stunt)

Australian missionaries to Chad. After a brief period at Bédiondo, they took up residence at Moïssala, which was then primarily a farming community, growing cotton, peanuts, maize, sweet potatoes, etc. Much of his time was spent in trekking from village to village with the gospel, but his special gift was as a Bible teacher. For many years he conducted a Bible school. Bill's later years were spent in translation of the Scriptures. He died in Moïssala in 1967. Margaret was commended from U.S.A. in 1933. She returned to the field after his death, to help in Doba until she retired to the U.S.A. in 1970.

Neville J. Taylor, commended from New Zealand in 1946, first took a course at the Missionary School of Medicine in London and then spent some time in language study in Paris, actually arriving at Fort Lamy in 1948. After a short stay with Dr. Olley, he travelled south into the Mbai area to make his home at Moïssala. The following year he married Miss Evelyn Rout, the daughter of Mr. and Mrs. Ernest D. Rout, missionaries in Congo. Commended from New Zealand in 1948, she joined Miss Anita M. Lewis (U.S.A. 1946) at Moïssala.

In 1949 the Taylors travelled to Bousso, where they learned Chad Arabic in order to reach 22 tribes with different dialects. At the same time, they ministered to the small assemblies of the area as they moved in long treks around the villages. In 1951 a hall was built at Bousso and they spent two years building up the work there. Evelyn taught the women, and Neville gave systematic teaching to the men to train local believers in evangelism and church building. Travelling was difficult and communications were erratic. Roads were shocking and breakdowns frequent, and many miles had to be undertaken by foot. Nevertheless, many were converted and baptised in the different centres and gradually local elders and evangelists were left in charge.

When Dr. Olley left, the Taylors moved to Doba for Bible teaching and to supervise the work at Bousso, while the Rogers concentrated on Moïssala and Bédiondo and both couples gave help at N'Djamena. Much travelling was involved because so many national evangelists needed help, particularly when it came to interviewing hundreds of people for baptism.

A new hall was opened at Doba in 1956 and 27 were baptised at the official opening, while 930 attended the gospel meeting. The following year 400 evangelists attended a conference there. At the conference at Moïssala in 1956, some 1,200 broke bread, where 30 years before there had not been one believer.

In 1960 the Taylors moved to N'Djamena, and Neville gave his time to translating the Old Testament into Mbai, Bill Rogers undertaking the Pentateuch. At the same time, they paid regular visits for pastoral and teaching ministry to many parts of the country. In 1965 they moved to Moïssala to cooperate more closely with the Rogers in translating. In 1972 they retired to New Zealand to take up work in Auckland Bible School, and the writer can testify to the excellent work they are doing there.

Many missionaries have laboured at Moïssala and the conditions have changed considerably. In the early days, John Olley wrote of the conditions there prior to the rainy season, 'There is a great dearth of food of any kind here. The natives are famished. The workmen climbed trees for seed pods, which can only be regarded as pigs' food. At present there are no schools, no Christian mission.' What has been accomplished, even materially, is a cause for thanksgiving.

Dr. Olley described the magnificent physique of some of the tribespeople, despite some of the ritual disfigurements they were subjected to. The women of some tribes, for example, endured life distortion by metal or ivory discs being inserted in large holes made in their lips when young girls. Some tribes, like the Bananas, were almost entirely naked. Nowadays, at a service in the chapel at Doba, crowds of women gather in brightly coloured dresses and pretty head scarves, and babies strapped on their

Moïssala – Neville J. Taylor and elder.
(W. T. Stunt)

Neville J. Taylor and translation committee   (W. T. Stunt)

Near Koyom – village of the Banana tribe   (W. T. Stunt)

backs. In past days these women would have attended services wearing practically no clothing: they were raw heathen. The problem of a head covering was an acute one, for the scarf worn around their waist was the only available covering. When it was removed to furnish a head covering, further embarrassment was created and the missionaries decided that some other solution must be found. A large number of calabashes of various dimensions was purchased, and each woman was asked to fit a calabash to her head when she entered the chapel. But when heads were bowed in prayer, the calabashes came off and fell to the ground with a clatter and had to be replaced to the accompaniment of many a female giggle. (The apostle Paul had no problems of that kind in Corinth!)

'Travel was arduous and dangerous,' writes M. H. Saxby, op. cit., p. 67. 'When travelling by canoe, they were attacked by angry hippos. Snakes were common, and the spitting cobra was treated with great respect.'

Mr. and Mrs. Colin H. Price were commended from Australia in 1950 and they also commenced at Moïssala, where they spent four years before moving to Koyom and Baktchoro. There they engaged in an evangelistic and teaching ministry, and also translated part of the New Testament into Azumeina. They left in 1966 to work for a time with S.G.M. in England.

Peter A. and Neridah Robinson, commended from Australia in 1957, worked from Koyom in village evangelism and ministry among small assemblies and isolated groups of Christians. Peter undertook translation and Neridah conducted dispensary and midwifery work. They returned to Australia in 1967 for health and family reasons.

Richard J. and Mavis Saxby had long been concerned about the needs of Chad and, in preparation, took a course with Wycliffe in the Summer Institute of Linguistics, and engaged in the study of French and tropical medicine. They were commended from Australia in 1959 and, after a course in Paris, flew to Chad in 1960. Their first two years were spent with Bill and Margaret Rogers at Moïssala to learn the Mbai language. During a journey with Colin Price in the Mayo Kebi area, the few Christians in the Toubouris and Kados tribes implored them to go and teach them the Word of God. Colin Price had built a mud house with grass roof at Pala, intending to use this whenever he could visit there from Baktchoro, where he lived. The Saxbys moved here instead.

The first month was spent in a house lent by Jacob Balardi in the middle of a large Toubouri village. Jacob was a good French speaker and helped in translation and in interpretation. At Pala they began the systematic teaching of the Word – Mavis among the women and Richard in all the little groups of believers in the Kado tribe, as well as in the big town church where eight languages were spoken. In all the three towns in which they lived, Richard taught the Scriptures in French in chapels and schools of higher education. (At that time only French was used in schools.) Many of those to whom he spoke became key men in the government service, the police, military and civil administration.

He put the Kado language in writing for the first time and produced a hymnbook. Then Mavis and Margaret Mansfield (commended from Australia in 1969) produced five reading primers and other literacy materials. Then they taught some to teach others and the literacy programme was successful with the tribe. A Bible school was started and the New Testament translated into Kado. The work done will last for eternity. The Saxbys returned home in 1974.

Laurie and Margaret Cowell were commended from Australia in 1964. Laurie had been invaluable as a builder and Margaret as a nurse in the medical work. They served first in Koyom and later

Pala – translating the Kado New Testament   (R. J. Saxby)

Baktchoro – the dispensary

at Bongor in Bible school, translation and village visiting, returning to Australia in 1975.

Robert and Judy Price were commended from Australia also in 1963 and started at Kélo. Here Robert engaged in visiting the villages, conducting Bible schools and doing translation work. Judy, as a nurse with secretarial experience, conducted the dispensary, took women's classes and typed translation manuscripts.

Miss Margaret Mansfield is a qualified school teacher and went to Chad to establish and teach in a school at Pala for missionaries' children. She also assisted in local work amongst women and girls. Miss Marguerite Byard, commended from Australia in 1971, went to France for language study before taking up medical missionary work in Chad until 1977.

Ivan and Alison Hewlett, commended from New Zealand in 1962, spent two years studying French in France and Switzerland and linguistics in England before arriving at N'Djamena in 1964. Their first years were spent helping in the building programme, assisting in meetings, and studying the Mbai language. In 1967 they took up residence in Pala and there helped Alan Wheeler. Ivan undertook a heavy schedule of teaching, while learning Chad

Pala – Alison Hewlett   (W. T. Stunt)

Arabic. He taught Scripture in the high school and also conducted a Bible class for government employees who spoke French. He visited many villages and cotton plantations to sell Bibles. Much time was spent in distributing literature in eleven languages.

The gospel has affected the south. A missionary describes the scene today. 'Hanging on a sapling slung between two forks outside the meeting-place in every village where God's people gather, can be seen a piece of iron on a rusty wheel. At certain times this is struck repeatedly, thus ringing out a call to come. The work probably began through the arrival of the evangelist from a neighbouring group of Christians, preaching and teaching the Word day by day. The meeting may be for prayer or a word of exhortation. Hymns are always sung, all teaching some aspect of Christian doctrine. Everybody sings lustily. It may be a class for teaching new readers, and the literary material used will most likely be the work of a missionary. In any case, whatever the meeting, there will always be an exhortation and the Word of God read. It may be a Bible study for the believers from many villages. It may be for 300 men and women lasting four days, or for 25 men and last three weeks to three months, depending on the time of the year, planting, harvesting, etc.'

There are over 500 assemblies in Chad, and twelve Bible schools. In the assemblies there are many evangelists, pastors and teachers. These are supported only partially by the assemblies, but they have their farms and grow crops. Gifts enable them to work a little less than normal on the land, and do a little more of the work of God. A few men, engaged in a special teaching ministry or translation of Scripture, are fully supported.

Assembly missionaries have, from the beginning, sought to form autonomous churches so that, whatever changes may come in government, these testimonies will remain to continue the evangelization of their own areas.

Nevertheless, it cannot be ignored that the work has been almost entirely among the tribespeople, and practically nothing among the Muslim population. There is a truly indigenous work at Mao on the southern border of the Sahara. This is a Muslim stronghold, delightfully situated on a hill with several oases near by. Thomas Ulater, a carpenter in government service, who had been converted in N'Djamena, was sent to Mao and found himself an isolated Christian in a Muslim community, surrounded by sin,

Pala – a Christian tailor   (W. T. Stunt)

with no assembly and no fellowship. After a few weeks he met a Christian school teacher and they met each Sunday at his house to pray and study the Word. Sinners were saved, backsliders were restored and believers were attracted to them. Eventually, over 40 met three times a week, and ten of these were baptised believers.

This, of course, is encouraging, but can we sit back comfortably and forget the two or three million Muslims in Chad who have never heard the gospel and apparently will have little or no opportunity of doing so?

8

Volcanoes Dead and Alive

To the north-west of Madagascar (Malagasy) and between it and the mainland of Africa lies the small group of the Comoro Islands. Of volcanic origin, these four islands cover an area of only 863 square miles and the total population is around 300,000.

The largest of the group is Grande Comore, 443 square miles in extent, which still has the active volcano of Mount Kantala. Moroni, the capital of the republic, is located on this island, and there is also the smaller town of Mitsamiouli. The island of Mayotte, which is partly encircled by a coral reef, rises from the coastal plain to a plateau 2,165 feet above sea level. Anjouan, the principal town of which is Mutsamudu, is a triangular-shaped island, which rises to a central volcanic massif 5,177 feet above sea level. Moheli, the smallest of the group, again rises to a plateau, but one only 1,000 feet high. Fomboni and Niamouchoua form its chief towns.

The islands naturally enjoy a tropical climate. From November to April it is hot and humid, but for the rest of the year it is fresh and dry. Rainfall is heavy and at least part of the water supply is derived from reservoirs filled in the rainy season. Except in the case of Grande Comore, the rains give rise to streams and a considerable amount of water is held in the ground, so that wells may be sunk to trap this bountiful supply. In Grande Comore, however, the rain sinks deeply through the lava and porous rock, and wells can be sunk only in the coastal lowlands and, even then, the water is quite brackish and can be drunk only after boiling.

Selling cloth in the Pure Land (Tear Fund)

Pakistan – Homework (Tear Fund)

148

Peshawar

(Tear Fund)

Primitive forest covers sixteen per cent of the land, but in the coastal zones above the mangroves, it is possible to grow coconut palms, mangoes, bananas, coffee, sisal and cocoa. Vanilla and perfume plants are grown for the export of their products. At the highest levels, only broom, heather and lichens flourish. Turtles abound along the coasts, however, and form one of the islands' most important exports. Cattle and goats are raised, and the islanders grow cassava, sweet potatoes and rice for domestic

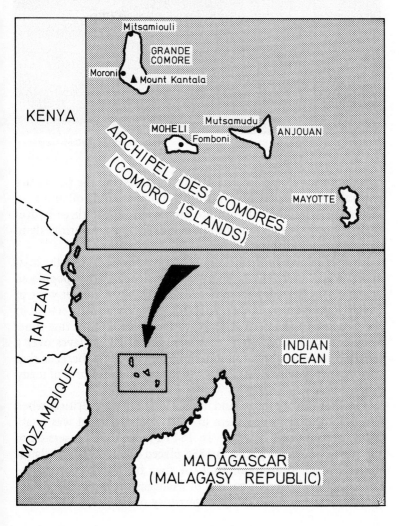

Moroni   (R. Stanford, Wycliffe Bible Translators)

consumption. There are no natural resources and the people are generally poor. Apart from sawmills, there are only oil and soap factories. A number of men are employed by the three hydro-electric power plants, but the remainder are engaged primarily in agriculture and fishing.

Little is known of the history of the islands. It is thought that, apart from early Malaysian seamen, they were populated originally by Sakalava and other Malagasy tribes. A later wave of Malay immigrants and then Arab traders subsequently settled in the Comoros and intermarried with the inhabitants of that time. People of various African races were imported as slaves over a long period, and a small number of French settled there, so that the product is a mixed strain in which are found features of many races.

The first Europeans to land in the Comoros were British, when James Lancaster visited them in 1591. No settlement was established at that time, however. In 1843 France took possession of the island of Mayotte, and in 1886 placed the other three islands under French protection. In 1914 they became subject to the control of the governor general of Madagascar, but in 1947 were given the status of an overseas territory of France, and in 1960

On Anjouan　　　　　　　　　　　(R. Stanford, Wycliffe Bible Translators)

they were accorded internal autonomy. In 1975 Grande Comore, Anjouan and Moheli declared their unilateral independence, and France immediately withdrew all technical and professional workers and assistance from them. At that time, Mayotte retained its links with France, and in 1976 voted to become an overseas department of France. The other three islands remain the federal and Islāmic Republic of the Comoros.

The majority of the population speak Kiswahili but a small proportion speak French or Arabic. Between 90 and 94 per cent of the people are Muslim and the remainder are Roman Catholic, Protestant and others. The Arab traders and settlers naturally brought the teachings of Islām and 99 per cent of the population accepted the new faith. There is, however, complete religious liberty. There is also full opportunity afforded for radio broadcasting.

The Islands Mission commenced work in the islands some ten years ago and, at their invitation, were joined by the Africa Inland Mission in 1974. A number of Malagasians, Creoles and Comorians have been converted and several congregations established, particularly on Mayotte. There is no note of any assembly activity in the islands, but the doors are still wide open.

9

Republic Without Resources

The Republic of Djibouti is located in north-east Africa and is bounded by the Gulf of Aden, Somalia and Ethiopia. Prior to its acquisition of independence in 1977, it was the French territory of the Afars and Issas. It has three geographical regions. The coastal plain rises to 650 feet above sea level; the mountains of 1,000 feet rise to peaks of 5,000 feet; and the plateau behind the mountains is from 1,000 to 5,000 feet high. The land is bare, dry and desolate, and is marked by sharp cliffs, deep ravines, burning sands and thorny shrubs. The rainfall is sparse and the climate torrid.

The country is only 9,000 square miles in extent and its population is about 350,000, composed primarily of Somalis (Issas and Ishaaks) and Afars (or Danakils), 90 per cent of whom are Muslims. French, Somali, Afar and Arabic are spoken, but literacy is only ten per cent.

French interest in the African shores of the Red Sea dates back to Rochet d'Hericourt's exploration into Shoa (1839–42). Further observations by Henri Lambert and Captain Fleuriot de Langle led to the signing of a treaty of friendship and assistance between France and the sultans of Raheita, Tadjoura and Gobaad. In 1884–85 France expanded its protectorate to include the shores of the Gulf of Tadjoura and the hinterland and called the area French Somaliland. The administrative capital was moved from Obock to Djibouti in 1896, because the latter had a good natural harbour and ready access to the Ethiopian highlands and attracted trade caravans crossing East Africa, as well as Somali settlers from

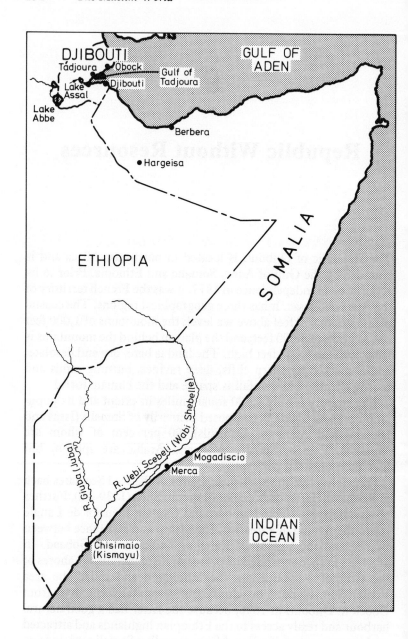

the south. (*See Djibouti and the Horn of Africa,* by V. Thompson and R. Adloff.)

When President Charles de Gaulle visited Djibouti in 1966, he was faced by demands for independence, but a referendum at the time made it clear that the majority of the people wished to retain the association with France. In 1977, however, the electorate voted for independence and the Republic was inaugurated in June of that year.

Djibouti has no natural resources and no productive industry. Eighty-nine per cent of the land is desert wasteland; ten per cent is pasture land and one per cent is forested. It is a port of call on the shipping lanes of the Red Sea and the Suez Canal, and functions as a bunkering port and a small French naval facility. Exports and imports from and to Ethiopia pass through Djibouti, which is now Ethiopia's only effective link with the world. The Republic has no exports of its own and is dependent upon the port revenues.

Its economy has, however, been shattered by the Somali–Ethiopian war and is largely dependent on Saudi Arabian aid. There remains the very real possibility that a communist Ethiopia may at some time dominate and even absorb its tiny neighbour. A glance at the map will show the strategic position of Djibouti if a strong power decided to invade the Horn of Africa in order to close all entry to the Red Sea and to the Suez Canal.

A small Christian bookshop was opened here in 1975 by the Red Sea Mission Team and there is considerable interest in Bibles and Christian literature. Muslims frequently purchase copies, but there is no sign of response to the Christian message. The first Afar was baptised in 1979. No assembly worker has engaged in service in this country.

10

The River State

(Map page 244)

The Republic of the Gambia is a narrow strip of land in West Africa, seven to twenty miles wide along the lower reaches of the River Gambia. It extends 200 miles inland from the Atlantic Ocean and, except for the sea-coast, is completely surrounded by the Republic of Senegal. It is only 4,003 square miles in size and the total population is about 600,000. Banjul (formerly Bathurst), the capital, has only 40,000 population.

The country was originally part of the Empire of Ghana and the Kingdom of the Songhais. When Portuguese navigators discovered it in the fifteenth century, it was part of the Kingdom of Mali. By the sixteenth century, Portuguese slave traders and gold seekers had settled in the lower river area, but in 1588 Antonio of Crato, who was a claimant to the Portuguese throne, sold exclusive trade rights on the Gambia River to English merchants. In 1618 James I of England granted a charter to a British company for trade with The Gambia and the Gold Coast (now Ghana). During the seventeenth and eighteenth centuries, Britain and France struggled for supremacy in Senegal and Gambia. Eventually the Treaty of Versailles in 1788 gave Britain possession of the latter. As a result of the activities of her merchants, Britain had, in 1664, taken control of a number of ports on the river, and in 1843 established a crown colony at the mouth of the river. At the beginning of the twentieth century, this was extended 250 miles up the river.

The Gambia achieved independence in 1965 as a constitutional monarchy within the British Commonwealth, but five years later it was converted into a republic with an elected President. The smallest of the former British colonies, the Gambia also proved to be the most stable.

The people are comprised of a number of ethnic groups. Twenty-eight per cent are Mandinka, sixteen per cent Fula, fourteen per cent Wolof, eight per cent Jola, eight per cent Serahuli, all of whom are negroid, and the remainder are non-Gambians. Apart from the official language of English, Mandinka, Wolof and other indigenous languages are used. Nearly 58 per cent of the people are Muslims, the remainder being Christians and animists. About 85 per cent of the people live in rural areas, and literacy is only twelve per cent.

The Gambia is low-lying, the maximum altitude being 120 feet above sea level. Thick mangrove swamps border the lower half of the river and behind these are river 'flats' which are submerged completely during the wet season, in some cases with salt water. It is perhaps not surprising that the life expectancy is only 32 years.

Agriculture and fishing are the principal occupations. Peanuts, rice, millet, sorghum and palm kernels are produced. Cattle, sheep, goats and pigs are raised. There are small woodworking and metal-working shops and also agricultural machinery assembly facilities, but there is not much scope for industry. Fishing and tourism have developed rapidly during the last decade. Deposits of ilmenite and other minerals have been discovered but have not yet been exploited.

Despite the dominance of Islām, there is freedom for religious worship in the country. Islām is gaining ground in the uncommitted areas, whereas the lack of missionaries and national Christian workers means that little evangelization is going on except near the coast. The Wesleyan Methodists commenced operating in the country in 1821 primarily among Africans repatriated from America to Banjul and they maintained three primary schools and two clinics. They still have seven churches and a total membership of 1,500, but work is difficult. Many of the missionaries in the past died after a very brief period of service. Moreover, in 1945, the government took over all primary schools run by Methodists, Anglicans and Roman Catholics. There are a few expatriate Christian teachers in the country, who are exerting some influence through schools, but the principal evangelical mission in the country since 1957 is the Worldwide Evangelization Crusade, who are operating mainly through medical, agricultural and literacy outreach. Parts of the Scriptures have been translated but supplies are inadequate to meet demands, particularly among the Mandinka people. According to *Operation World*, p. 178, there are one-quarter of a million Mandinkas in Gambia.

No assembly work has ever been attempted in this country.

11

The Nonconformists

(Map page 244)

When General de Gaulle planned the granting of independence to the French colonies, it was his confident expectation that they would respond unanimously by voting to join the French Community. Of the twelve colonies in Africa to gain independence in 1958, Guinea was the only one to vote against joining the Community. This was too much for de Gaulle to stomach and he punished the nonconformists by withdrawing all French administrators and removing all government records from the country. The action was extremely unwise as well as unjustifiable in view of the practical difficulties consequently created, but Guinea managed to survive, even although records had to be built up all over again. She did, however, break off diplomatic relations with France in 1965 and also expelled the Peace Corps in the following year, although they were invited back in 1969.

The Republic of Guinea is bounded on the south by Liberia and Sierra Leone, on the east by the Ivory Coast, and on the north by Mali and Senegal. It has an area of 94,925 square miles and is drained by a number of rivers. The Guinea Highlands are the source of the River Niger, the longest and most important river of West Africa, and the mountains divide the streams that flow north as tributaries to the Niger and those that flow to the Atlantic.

J. C. Thiessen says that the alluvial soil deposited by Guinea's vast river system is fertile and yields rich vegetation. East of the mountains, however, stretch sandy and infertile plateaux. Rice, millet, peanuts, coffee, maize, cassava and bananas are grown, and coffee is one of the exports. Cattle and sheep are also raised. Apart from agriculture, employment is provided by forestry and fishing. The country is potentially a very rich one for it has large deposits of bauxite chiefly at Boké and Fria, and iron ore in the Nimba mountains which are now in the process of exploitation. Gold is also mined. Diamonds have also been found in the Macenta region.

The capital is Conakry, which grew up on a small island near the end of the Kaloum peninsula, to which it is attached by a causeway. John Gunther, op. cit., p. 858, says that 'a literally phenomenal industrial expansion is proceeding, caused by the development of iron and bauxite mines, hydro-electric power, and enlargement of the port. The reserves of iron ore in Guinea are estimated at two billion tons. A few years ago, Conakry was one of the few Gulf cities where young women stark naked still walked without shame down the chief streets. . . . Wherever the white man comes in force, African picturesqueness goes.' Other chief towns include Kankan, Labé and Kindia.

The country has a long history. Over a millennium ago, it was apparently part of the ancient kingdom of Mali. In *The Africans*, p. 48, Naomi Mitchison maintains that centuries ago 'there was a forest culture or civilization along the Guinea coast; there were holy places or shrines around them; ordered groupings of houses on the courtyard principle of several single storey, lightly built houses, round a square, inside one wall, the outer shell, so to speak, of a complex family relationship in which obligations and duties were well known'. In due course, however, the Arab hordes swept right across North Africa to the coast and, like most of the countries in the region, Guinea responded to the teachings of Islām. There is not much trace of the Arab invasion in the present inhabitants of the country, however.

French military penetration began about the middle of the nineteenth century and a treaty was signed in 1880. Following an attempt to expel the French from the Sudan, however, France occupied Guinea in 1898 and it became part of French West Africa in 1904. Colonial reforms after World War II gradually reduced French administration and transferred more power to the Africans, and in 1958 Guinea became an independent republic.

The population is over five million and is composed of some

eighteen tribes, including the Fula, Malinke, Soussou, Kissi, Loma, Konyanke, Bassari, Obago, Lele, Koranko, Yalunka, etc. Although the official language is French, many of the tribes have their own languages. Guinea is a secular state, but the Islāmic faith is dominant. Eighty-five per cent of the population are Muslim and, whilst there are some Christians, the majority of the rest of the people are animists. In the forest areas, they are certainly under the power of the sorcerers and the fetishes of their religious leaders.

Complete liberty was allowed for the practice of other faiths, and the Christian and Missionary Alliance started a work in 1918 and considerable blessing was seen. Unfortunately, in 1967 President Sékou Touré decided that there must be a complete 'Africanization' of all churches, and ordered the expulsion of all foreign missionaries within 60 days. A small number were, however, allowed to remain, but the scope of their activities was restricted.

There is a Bible School at Telekoro, which is run by nationals, and there is one religious bookshop in the whole country, but stocks are limited because of difficulties of importation. Some of the Scriptures have been translated into certain of the languages, but there is a great deficiency. Radio ELWA beams messages into the country, but the greater part of Guinea is completely unevangelized. Conakry has a population of 600,000, but is a staunch – and hard – Muslim city.

No assembly witness has apparently ever been attempted in this country and it may well be that the opportunity has now been permanently lost. Patently, it would be difficult to secure an entry. On the other hand, with the increasing industrial activity, and the educational, medical and social developments which will doubtless follow, there may be opportunities for Christians to take up secular work and to engage in spiritual activities in their spare time. In any case, there is obviously need for prayer that the few national believers may be kept faithful to the Lord and that their witness to others may be blessed.

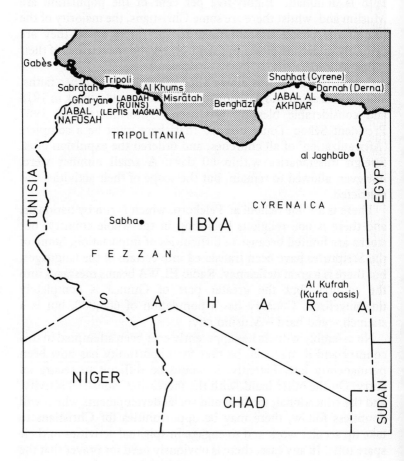

12

World of Oases

The Greeks described the whole of North Africa except Egypt as Libya and the territory is referred to in the Bible under that name (Ezekiel 30:5; Acts 2:10). The name is used today for the Socialist People's Libyan Arab al-Jurnhūrīyah, a large country of 679,536 square miles, which lies to the west of Egypt and borders the Mediterranean. It has been described as the land of oases. 'Even the seaports of Tripoli and Benghāzī,' says J. C. Thiessen in *A Survey of World Missions*, p. 175, 'are but magnificent oases.' He goes on to say, 'Topographically it consists of a maritime plain, then plateaux and the system of oases formed in the depression of the Sahara Desert. There is also an immense sandy coast running the entire length of Libya, characterized by shifting dunes which attain a height of from thirty to a hundred feet, and from three hundred to seven hundred yards in width. These are interspersed with salt swamps or lagoons, some of them very large.' The coastline is 1,100 miles in length and the country is bordered by Egypt, Sudan, Tunisia, Niger and Chad.

Roughly 92 per cent of the terrain is desert or semi-desert, consisting of barren, rock-strewn plains and a sand sea with two small areas of hills and mountains rising to a maximum of 3,000 feet above sea level – Jabal Nafūsah in the north-west and Jabal al Akhdar in the north-east. The Saharan mountains in the south rise to 10,335 feet. Except for scattered oases, only the narrow coastal plain and the slopes of the two northern hill areas are suitable for cultivation. Only seven per cent of the total land area is devoted to agriculture and nomadic herding. Tripolitania in the north-west produces dates in abundance, and Cyrenaica in the north-east produces grain and raises domestic animals. Fezzan in the south-west is extremely barren, but there are some large oases where crops can be grown. Soda and potash are also obtained from the salt lakes, particularly in Tripolitania. The large Kufra oasis in the south-east is also a fruitful area for grain and other crops. Libya is blessed in having large reserves of petroleum and natural gas and the former is its principal export.

The population of over three million is composed mainly of Arabs and Berbers, but there are also some Negroes, Greeks, Maltese, Italians and Egyptians. Ninety-seven per cent of the population are Muslims. The language used is Arabic and the literacy rate is 35 per cent. Conditions are hard, however, and the life expectancy is only 37 years. Nearly half the population is under fifteen. The principal cities are Tripoli, the capital, with a population of 735,000, Benghāzī, the capital of Cyrenaica, with 337,000, Misrātah, Gharyān, Al Khums and Sabha, the capital of the Fezzan, with 113,000.

Libya is the home of the Senūssī Brotherhood, which was originally a religious movement opposed to the corruptions of Islām, but which subsequently developed partly as a political movement. Its founder, Sīdī Muḥammad ben 'Alī es Senūssī, was born in Algeria in 1796. He moved to Mecca and in 1835 founded a religious settlement in Arabia, but later settled in Cyrenaica in the mountains of Derna. He founded another settlement at al Jaghbūb with some 7,000 members. His son, Sīdī Muḥammad al-Mahdī, who succeeded him, removed to Kufra in 1895 and this is now the chief centre of Senūssīsm, and its population of 5,000 includes some of Islām's outstanding professors. Al Jaghbūb is, however, still the leading seat of strictly orthodox Muslim learning in North Africa. The Senūssī aim is the establishment of a purer form of Islām. Some of the members are extremely wealthy and influential.

Senūssī settlements spread right across the country and are found, not only in Libya, but in Egypt, Algeria and Morocco as well. They cling largely to the oases. As one writer remarks, 'The desert is the natural home for the contemplative religious life, and in these oases will be found masses of men, adepts in Ṣūfī mysticism, intensely studious and ready to pay a remarkable

Camp 1973 (Mrs. R. Solly)

Thadia – Miss Barbara H. Prentice and Dr. Jean Orr

(Mrs. R. Solly)

homage to able teachers of divine truth.' Here are men to whom
the gospel might well come in a new freshness.

In the southern desert of Libya there are also settlements of
Touaregs, although not in the numbers found in Algeria. More
interesting possibly are the Troglodytes, who are cave dwellers
and who live most of their lives underground and are rarely seen
by strangers. The Khologhli are also peculiar to Libya; these are
descendants of Libyan women who, long ago, interbred with
Turkish Janissaries and who do not normally mix with other races
in the country.

The history of Libya goes back many centuries. It was certainly
colonized by the Sidonian Phoenicians sixteen centuries B.C. and
the aboriginal Berbers were then pushed back into the interior.
Later it experienced the domination of the Carthaginians, Greeks,
Romans, Vandals and Byzantines. The remains of the cities of
Sabrātah and Leptis Magna, built by the Romans, are said to be
the most incomparably noble and beautiful Roman ruins in the
world.

In his book, *North Africa*, Fletcher Allen gives a concise history
of Libya. He says, p. 280 *et seq.*, 'The Libyans, a Berber race, are
at first encountered in history as warring with their neighbours,
the Negroes of the Sudan. They were reduced to paying tribute to
Egypt under the eleventh dynasty, but under later dynasties they
succeeded in establishing in the Nile Delta a flourishing colony,
which reached its apogée on the accession of the Libyan King of
Egypt, Sheshork in 945 B.C. In 631 B.C. the Greeks founded a
settlement at Cyrene, which became a centre of Greek influence
and the metropolis of the five cities known as the Pentapolis. The
trade at Cyrenaica, as the region was called, attracted large
numbers of Jews.'

Later, the Phoenicians established a number of colonies, but
these were taken over by Rome after the conquest of Carthage in
140 B.C. They were followed by the Vandals and then the
Byzantines, and later by the Arabs. With the weakening of
Muslim power, Spain, Turkey and Italy successively took possession of the area.

When the hordes of Islām invaded in the seventh century A.D.
under Abdullah in 647 and 'Ukbah ibn Nāfi in 648, the Berbers
fought back and regained part of their country. In the eleventh
century, however, the Banū Hilāl and the Banū Suleim tribes

from Egypt settled in the country and strengthened the Arab stock, and in the following centuries, the Arabic language, culture, practices and religion were adopted by the majority of the population. In 1510 it was conquered by Spain, but in 1551 it was conquered by the Ottoman Turks and remained part of their empire for over three centuries. For centuries it was the home of the Barbary pirates, but ultimately it was invaded by the Italians in 1911 and became an Italian colony.

King Idris I, then Emir of Cyrenaica, led Libyan resistance to Italian occupation and after the Second World War the country achieved independence in 1951. Idris ruled the kingdom until the government was overthrown by a military revolution in 1969. The monarchy was then abolished and a new régime introduced, headed by a Revolutionary Command Council and Col. Mu' ammar al-Qadhafi became Chief of State. The Council was later succeeded by the Secretariat of the General People's Congress, but Qadhafi has continued to rule.

The country is financed by its sale of petroleum. The economy has rapidly expanded, but industrialization has been slow. With higher incomes and a growing population, the demand for consumer goods, and particularly for food, constantly increases.

Col. Qadhafi's military excursions and constant sabre-rattling over the last few years have caused some concern in the political realm, and this has not been relieved by the steady build-up in military strength. To take merely one example, Libya has 2,700 tanks and nearly 600 tank crews (she would, therefore, be dependent on Russia for tank crews if trouble broke out); her army, of course, is now 40,000. Her neighbour, Egypt, has fewer tanks for an army of 400,000 – ten times the size of Libya's.

Many Bible students have concluded from Ezekiel 38:5 that Libya will be associated with Russia in a future day in a military attack upon Israel. It is probable, however, that the prophet's use of the name, 'Libya', was in a wider sense and not restricted merely to the present country of that name. It would, nevertheless, include present-day Libya.

There is little doubt that the gospel reached Libya in the first century. Cooksey, op. cit., pp. 16, 17, claims that the origin of the North African Church 'must probably be sought for at Cyrene – the modern Tripoli – in the person of Simon, who bore the cross for the Redeemer, and walked by His side to Calvary. His two

Tripoli gateway   (North Africa Mission)

sons, Rufus and Alexander, early became eminent in the early church (Mark 15:21), and the early believers of Cyrene were foremost in evangelizing the Greeks at Antioch, where Lucius, their compatriot, was a leading figure (Acts 13:1). From that Cyrenian source probably flowed also the stream of truth which fertilized in its western flow the Phoenician colonies dotted along the littoral unto Carthage. This was followed by another of greater volume when the Phoenician trading galleys bore to the African shore a remnant of the church at Jerusalem, fleeing from the destruction of the Jewish people by Titus, A.D. 70.'

When, in 533, the armies of Justinian re-established Roman rule after the Vandals' conquest, the emperor was anxious to establish the Christian faith in the regained areas, and some Berbers definitely became members of the Catholic Church. According to K. S. Latourette, after the Muslim conquest, the Roman Catholic counter-advance of the thirteenth century gained a few thousand converts in Libya. Conrad of Ascoli, a Franciscan monk, is reported to have won 6,400 Muslims to Christianity at that time, but there is no evidence that they remained faithful or did anything to propagate the faith.

Protestant work began in 1829, when the Christian Missions to the Jews commenced distributing Bibles in Tripoli, repeating the efforts in 1870 and 1890. In the latter year, the North Africa Mission opened a centre in Tripoli for the spreading of the gospel message, and have continued operating in various centres ever since. Italian Baptists also started a ministry among Italians in Tripoli in 1913. When Italy took over Libya in the 1930's, all Protestant missionaries were expelled in 1936. They were, however, allowed to return in 1946 and the North Africa Mission engaged in medical and evangelistic work. Conversions have been few among Muslims and Jews and direct missionary work is, in fact, forbidden. The churches which exist are for the benefit of expatriates.

Literature enters the country in various ways and some, at least, of the people listen to Christian radio broadcasts.

Apart from assembly workers who have been associated with the North Africa Mission, only one assembly missionary has engaged in any activities in Libya – and then only for a brief time. Dr. John R. Olley of New Zealand, an able linguist in Greek, Hebrew and French, went to Tunisia in 1919 to witness to Muslims. After learning Arabic, he attempted evangelization in various centres in that country. He had to leave Gabès because of the water pollution and the fever sweeping through the area, and apparently moved to Tripoli in 1923. While there, he found a few openings among Jews, chiefly fanatical Talmudists, who seemed remarkably ignorant of their own Scriptures. Then he learned that Mr. Henry J. Pomeroy was planning to enter the Sahara via Nigeria. Since his desire had always been to reach the people of the interior, he learned Hausa, the trade language of the Sudan and in 1924 travelled to Italy to obtain medical supplies in preparation for his new sphere. His time in Libya was, therefore, quite brief, and the country does not seem to have attracted any other assembly missionary. It is a long time since the poet wrote of Job's words (Job 31:17), but maybe his words are still pertinent:

'If I have eaten my morsel alone,'
    The patriarch spoke with scorn,
What would he think of the church were he shown
    Heathendom – huge, forlorn,
    Godless, Christless, with soul unfed?
While the church's ailment is fulness of bread
    Eating her morsel alone.

'I am debtor alike to the Jew and the Greek,'
    The mighty apostle cried,
Traversing continents, souls to reach
    For the love of the Crucified.
Centuries, centuries since have sped,
Millions are famishing; we have bread,
    But we eat our morsel alone.

Ever of them who have largest dower
    Shall heaven require the more.
Ours are affluence, knowledge, power,
    Ocean from shore to shore.
And East and West in our ears have said,
'Give us, give us, your living bread?
    Yet we eat our morsel alone.

'Freely as ye have received, so give,'
    He bade, Who has given all.
How shall the soul in us longer live,
    Deaf to their starving call,
For whom the blood of the Lord was shed,
And His body broken to give them bread,
    If we eat our morsel alone?

13

The Coral Islands

Four hundred miles south-west of Sri Lanka is a chain of some 2,000 low-lying coral islands, grouped into clusters of nineteen atolls. Few of them rise to a height above five feet and none is larger than five square miles, their total area being only 115 square miles. The majority of the islands have few, if any, sources of potable water and they also lack arable land. The 220 which are inhabited have a tropical vegetation ranging from grass and scrub to dense groves of coconut palms and fruit trees. The climate is hot (27 degrees C.) and humid (80 per cent humidity) and there is little variation, but since the islands lie on the route of the monsoons, they receive an annual rainfall of 100 to 150 inches. This archipelago is the Republic of Maldives.

The islands are said to have been inhabited for 3,000 years, but there is no real confirmation of that. The original inhabitants were apparently Aryan and Dravidian, but Sinhalese and Arab strains have been added since.

According to Maldivian legend, a Sinhalese prince named Koimale was becalmed with his royal bride in a Maldivian lagoon. They were so entranced by the islands that they made their home there and Koimale became the first sultan. The Maldives were subsequently governed as a sultanate by members of the Didi clan from 1100 to 1968, the only exception being a brief period of republican government in 1953. (See *The Two Thousand Isles* by T. W. Hockley.)

Arab traders visited the islands in 1153 and, through their

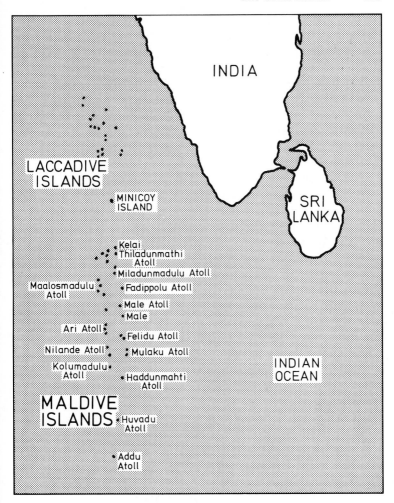

influence, the inhabitants accepted the Islāmic faith. Mopla pirates from the Malabar Coast (i.e. from the Indian Kerala of the present day) long harassed the islands. In the sixteenth century, they were plagued by Portuguese raiders, but these were eventually driven out by the warrior leader, Muḥammad Thakurufar Al-Azām. For a brief period the Maldives came under the rule of Portugal, but from 1887 to 1965 they were under British protection. They achieved independence in 1965, but three years later the sultanate was abolished and the country became a republic with a president elected by the legislature and confirmed by popular referendum. The legal system derives from traditional Islāmic law.

The total population is under 150,000, of whom nearly 30,000 live in Male, the capital, in the centre of the archipelago. The principal ethnic groups are Dravidian, Sinhalese and Arab. Although English is spoken by government officials, the common language is Divehi, derived concurrently with Sinhalese from the common root language of Elu.

The islands' economy is based almost entirely on fishing and tourism. The Maldivians are developing their own fish-processing industry and have been aided in this by the Japanese. The tourist industry is growing and since there is no taxation in the islands, the republic may well become a tax haven for the wealthy in a future day. Apart from fishing, there are really no natural resources. Coconuts, millet, corn and sweet potatoes are grown, but the entire grain requirement (including rice, the staple diet) must be imported, as well as sugar, drugs and textiles.

In view of the Maldivians' origin, it is not surprising that, at one time, they were practically all Buddhists. But they were converted by Arabs to Sunnī Islām in the twelfth century, and virtually the entire population is now Muslim. There is a strict adherence to Islāmic religious precepts and crime is consequently punished severely.

Christian propaganda is not permitted. So far as can be ascertained, little attempt has ever been made to introduce the Christian faith to the islands and no portion of the Scriptures is available in the Divehi language. This should surely be a matter for prayer and heart exercise.

14

Country of the Lion Prince

A completely landlocked country, the Republic of Mali (which was previously known as French Sudan) is situated in the interior of West Africa, and is bordered by Algeria, Mauritania, Senegal, Guinea, Ivory Coast, Upper Volta and Niger. Most of the country lies in the West African savannah region, between the coastal rain forest and the desert. It is drained by the Niger River (known locally as the Djoliba) and its tributaries, which is navigable from June to December. The country is 478,832 square miles in size. Its principal cities are the capital, Bamako (population 404,000), Ségou (65,000), Mopti (54,000), Sikasso (47,000) and Kayes (45,000).

The total population is roughly seven million. Mande (Bambara, Malinke, Sarakole) make up 50 per cent of these, Peul (or Fularic) seventeen per cent, Voltaic twelve per cent, Songhai six per cent, and Touareg and Moor five per cent. About 65 per cent are Muslim and one per cent Christian. French and Bambara are the chief languages used.

The Malinke kingdom of Mali had its origin in the Upper Niger River area. The earliest kings of Mali were members of the Keita race and they ruled for some centuries as subjects of the emperor of Ghana. In 1230 there came to power in Mali an outstanding ruler named Surchata or Mari-Djata (literally the Lion Prince, from which his empire became known as the Land of the Lion Prince), who immediately started to expand his small kingdom by the absorption of the fragments of the old empire of Ghana and

the countries of western Sudan. In *Discovering Africa's Past*, p. 71, Basil Davidson says, 'The rise of Mali, and its rule over wide West African lands, was largely the work of the Mandinka people of Wangara, the ancient land of gold production, and of neighbouring areas. After about 1250 Mali steadily expanded to become one of the largest states of any part of their world, whether in Africa or not. Mali became famous for the wealth of its rulers, for the peace which prevailed in its territories, and for the influence of its learned men.' A German map of 1375 showed something of the extent of the Mali empire. It included a large number of the cities of North Africa and reached as far as the Atlas Mountains.

The ancient Mali empire was an extremely powerful and wealthy state. As Colin Nicolson says in *The Making of Africa*, p. 13, 'Under a succession of strong rulers, Mali enjoyed a period of great prosperity. The wealth of the trans-Sahara trade gave rise to rich towns; Djenne, Kumli and, above all, Timbuktu, became renowned as centres of learning and scholarship.' The archaeologist has revealed something of the wonder of Timbuktu. In *The History and Description of Africa*, John Pory quotes Leo Africanus as saying of Timbuktu in the sixteenth century, 'Here are shops of artificers and merchants, and expecially of such as weave linen and cotton cloth. And hither do the Barbary merchants bring cloth of Europe. . . . Here are great store of doctors, judges, priests and other learned men, that are so bountifully maintained at the king's cost and charges, and hither are brought divers manuscripts and written books out of Barbary, which are sold for more money than other merchandise.'

Mali reached its peak in 1325 and thereafter began to decline. A century later it had shrunk to a fraction of its former size. It came under the domination of the Songhai empire for a period, until the latter was destroyed by the Moroccans in 1600. French military penetration began about 1880 and, in due course, Mali became part of the Federation of French West Africa. In 1959 Sudan and Senegal joined to form the Mali Federation, which became independent in 1960. Almost immediately Senegal seceded from the Federation, and Sudan thereupon proclaimed itself the Republic of Mali, thereby perpetuating the ancient name. A bloodless coup in 1968 led to a new constitution and an elected president and a single political party.

Fishing and agriculture are the principal occupations. Rice, cotton and millet are grown and cattle and sheep are also raised. Deposits of bauxite, uranium, iron, copper, manganese, gold and phosphate exist, but very little mining has taken place, primarily because of the inadequate transport and power facilities.

Despite the Muslim majority, there is almost complete freedom for the propagation of the gospel. The Gospel Missionary Union opened the first station in the country in 1919 at Bamako and has since engaged in educational, medical and evangelistic work. A complete Bible in the Bambara language appeared in 1962. Other societies have since entered the country and a considerable amount of work is going on. The bitter opposition evidenced in so many Muslim countries has not been seen in Mali and, at present, there is far greater liberty than in most of the neighbouring countries.

There is no assembly in the country and no assembly missionary has laboured there, but there seems no obstacle at the moment to evangelistic work and there is a need for prayer that workers may be raised up to work in this country.

15

A Desert Land

The Islāmic Republic of Mauritania is situated in north-west Africa with a coastline on the Atlantic, and is bounded by Algeria, Mali, Senegal and Western Sahara. It is 419,229 square miles in size, and it has three geographic regions. A large northern area, representing two-thirds of the country, is arid, barren desert, characterized by shifting sand dunes, rock outcroppings, and rugged mountainous plateaux with elevations of more than 1,500 feet. A narrow belt along the valley of the River Senegal in the south possesses the soil and climatic conditions for agriculture to be carried on. A broad central plain, nearly a third of the whole country, runs from east to west, and is characterized by vast sand plains and fixed dunes held in place by sparse grass and scrub trees.

The population is 1,680,000 and is composed of Moors and Berbers and also includes some negro people of the Wolof, Toucouleur and Sarakoles tribes. The languages used are French, Arabic and native dialects, and the predominant religion is Islām. Apart from the agriculture in the region of the Senegal River, the people engage in fishing and in the raising of livestock. Ninety-nine per cent of the people are Muslim.

Thousands of years ago the Saharan regions were verdant and filled with game. The original inhabitants were apparently Berbers, of whom there were repeated migrations. Tribes of negroes evidently followed them and the two peoples lived together harmoniously. The precise origin of the Berbers is not

known. They were a great white nation which spread all over North Africa. Cooksey, op. cit., p. 100, says that there are five main groups, viz.

'(1) The *Zenatia* group in the Djebel Nefousa in Tripoli, the Chawias and Beni M'Zab in the south of Algeria and the Riffs of Spanish Morocco.

(2) The *Zouaoua* group, represented by the Kabyles of northern Algeria.

(3) The *Taberberiat* group of Berbers found in the Middle and High Atlas of Morocco.

(4) The *Tashelhait* group found in the Sous country, and the Anti-Atlas of Morocco.

(5) The *Tamashek* group of Touaregs in the Algerian Sahara and the Sudan Sahara.

Other groups are found in the Niger and Senegal. . . . though fifty Berber dialects are spoken, the grammatical basis is broadly the same. Their numbers are known only approximately, but they certainly cannot be less than several millions.'

Gunther says that the Mauritanian women are quite distinctive. They 'wear purple-blue gowns, and have sumptuous head-dresses, with bows sticking out like artificial ears.'

Archaeological evidence suggests that Berber and Negroid Mauritanians lived beside one another before the spread of the desert drove them southward. Migration increased in the third and fourth centuries A.D. when Berber groups arrived, seeking pastures for their herds and safety from political unrest and war in the north. The Berbers' use of the camel allowed them to range widely over the expanding desert regions and also supported the development of a caravan trade system throughout the region. This trade in turn promoted the Berbers' loose Ṣanḥājah confederation. Trade involved gold, slaves, and ivory going north in exchange for salt, copper and cloth going south to Timbuktu and beyond. Important trading towns were established, and the Islāmic faith spread along the trade routes. A copper mine near Akjoujt was still being worked in the fifth century.

The antiquity of some of the country's ancient cities is considerable. The ruins at Koumbi Saleh, the ancient capital of the empire of Ghana, according to J. D. Fage, in *A History of Africa*, p. 67, 'have produced a carbon 14 date around A.D. 1200. Their extent – there is about a square mile of stone ruins and a further two square miles of cemeteries – together with the considerable number of comparable sites known but as yet hardly investigated in the surrounding country, suggests that the beginnings of urbanization here must at least go well back into the first millennium A.D.'

In the tenth century the Ṣanḥājah Confederation was broken up by Ghanaian warriors and the Ghanaians became the dominant force in the eastern and southern regions. In the following century, however, a tribe of Berbers conquered the western Sahara regions, destroyed the Ghanaian kingdom and firmly established Islām throughout Mauritania. These Berbers were, in turn, defeated, in the sixteenth century, by Arab invaders led by the Benī Hassan.

Portugal made conquests in certain parts of north-west Africa in

Nouakchott   (North Africa Mission)

the fifteenth century, and these included Mauritania, but in 1903 the French extended a protectorate over it and in 1920 designated it a French colony. In 1958, however, it became a separate republic within the French Community, but two years later became completely independent.

The capital, Nouakchott, has a population of 135,000. Other cities, such as Nouadhibou, Kaédi, Atar Zouerate, Kiffa and Rosso have populations ranging from 10,000 to 22,000. The country is poor and undeveloped, but there is little prospect of any considerable development. The Moors of earlier days were extremely successful slave dealers. Although it is over twenty years since independence was achieved, the *Daily Telegraph* of

Baltistan – a typical rural scene   (Dr. A. G. Stewart)

The Saltoro Spires   (Dr. A. G. Stewart)

Setting out to reach the Balti (Dr. A. G. Stewart)

Balti townsmen (Dr. A. G. Stewart)

12th August, 1981, stated that the United Nations was informed the previous day that there were still 100,000 slaves in Mauritania. A decree in 1980 to abolish slavery had had little effect and was intended to restore the government's image and to calm the slaves while a way of coping with the country's anti-slavery movement was found.

Under a papal bull of 1534, the king of Portugal was made responsible to provide and support Catholic missionaries in Mauritania to meet the spiritual needs of the conquered peoples, but the R.C. priests had little influence.

No Protestant work has been undertaken in modern times, although the Gospels are available in Moroccan Arabic, which can be understood by the people. No attempt has apparently been made to circulate the Scriptures in the country, despite the relative freedom to do so, and no assembly work has ever been undertaken, although no difficulty would evidently be experienced in entering this Muslim country. As Islām tightens its hold, access may, in due course, become impracticable. If the evangelization of the Mauritanians is ever to be engaged upon, it is obviously imperative that it should start at the earliest possible date. The challenge is clearly one that ought not to be ignored.

16

Two Faces

Facing the Mediterranean Sea on the north and the Atlantic Ocean on the west (and, therefore, described as the land with two faces), Morocco has a coastline of 1,250 miles. It is separated from Europe only by the Straits of Gibraltar, and the Jebel Mousa in Morocco and the Jebel Tarik in Gibraltar are described as the Pillars of Hercules: they are not only the gateway to the Mediterranean, but centuries ago represented the end of the known world so far as seafarers were concerned. The country is bounded on the east by Algeria and on the south by Western (Spanish) Sahara and Mauritania, and occupies the north-west corner of Africa.

It has open, agriculturally rich plains in the north-west, but economically poor mountains and plateaux in the east and south. The coastal plains and plateaux on the Atlantic are cut off from the interior by the High Atlas and Middle Atlas mountains, the peaks of which rise to 13,000 feet. The Rif Massif sweeps sharply upward from the coast to heights of 7,000 feet. The coastal plains are densely populated and nearly all the major cities like Oujda, Kenitra, Rabat and Safi are in this area. The eastern region of the country is a series of arid rolling plateaux that form a continuation of the Algerian High Plateaux.

Morocco is 171,953 square miles in size, and its principal industry is agriculture, a very large percentage of the population being engaged in the production of barley, wheat, citrus, sugar beet, etc. There is also a reasonable fishing industry. Reserves of

Quarzazate – High Atlas mountains   (North Africa Mission)

iron, manganese, lead and phosphates exist, but comparatively little mining is carried on. Tourism provides a not inconsiderable proportion of the national revenue, but despite the appearance of prosperity in some of the cities, there is a great deal of poverty as well.

The population of nearly twenty million is usually described as mainly Arab, including Berbers who have become 'Arabized'. It would perhaps be more accurate to describe the population as Arab, Rîfis, Susîs, Drawis, Kublawîs and Shluh. The Berbers were the original inhabitants and they dominated the country for centuries, their principal tribes then being the Almoravides, the Almohades and the Zenetes. With the expulsion of the Jews from Spain in the fifteenth century, a large number settled in Morocco and, at one time, there were over 20,000 in the country. They exercised a considerable influence in the commercial sphere and also in the administration, but a general hostility developed, particularly with the Arab–Israeli conflicts, and the majority of the Jews have now left the country. Negroes, whose ancestors were brought from the Sudan as slaves, and a small number of Europeans – primarily French and Spanish – make up the remainder of the people. The life expectancy of 54 years is higher than that in most North African countries.

Marrakesh – High Atlas mountains   (North Africa Mission)

The Berbers (of whom incidentally Augustine was one) seem, as already mentioned, to have been the original inhabitants of the country. It is commonly thought that they originated in the Iberian peninsula and travelled across the Straits of Gibraltar some thousands of years ago. They are obviously a distinct race from the Arabs and are much fairer in countenance. Unlike the Arabs they are generally monogamous, also they do not adopt the Arab practice of homosexuality, and often their women are unveiled. A. H. Brodrick, in *North Africa*, p. 20, describes them as 'settled mountain agriculturalists', and certainly larger numbers are to be found in the mountain areas. The Shluh, in the south of the country, have a definitely European appearance. Their ancestors were Christians, who were forced to accept Islām, but they follow their own customary laws, the Kanouns, rather than the Qur'ān.

Harry Ratcliffe classifies the Berbers under three main headings, viz. the Masmouda, the Senhaja and the Zenata tribes. He says that the Masmouda were the most numerous of the Berber tribes and that the majority of the Moroccan population belonged to that race 'when the Muslims swept through North Africa. They controlled all the plains along the Atlantic coast as

well as the Grand Atlas and the Anti Atlas. The Sousi Berbers,'
among whom he worked, 'are direct descendants of this tribe.'

The language in general use is Arabic, but several Berber
dialects are used and French is also spoken. Islām is the state
religion and 98 per cent of the people are Muslims.

The Phoenicians from Canaan – and particularly from Sidon
and Tyre – colonized a great deal of North Africa and they
invaded Morocco as long ago as 1300 B.C. and established a large
number of settlements in the country. They were followed in 550
B.C. by the Carthaginians, but in 146 B.C. Carthage gave way to
Rome, and from the first century B.C. until the sixth century
A.D. Morocco was part of a Roman province. During that time,
the Romans built roads and cities and brought a new civilization
to the country. The Vandals, Visigoths and Byzantines followed
in quick succession, however, and then there came the Arab
conquest in 682. A native sultan did seize power in 788 and laid
the foundation of a Moroccan kingdom, but he was eliminated by
a present of poison (masquerading as perfume) sent to him by
Hanen el Rashīd, of *Arabian Nights* fame.

French interest in the country dates from 1830, and the
Algeciras Conference of 1906 formalized France's 'special
position', while the Treaty of Fès in 1916 made Morocco a French
protectorate. Spain retained control over the small enclaves of
Ceuta and Melilla in the north and the enclave of Sidi Hri in the
south, however. The latter became part of Morocco only in 1969.

Boumalne   (H. Ratcliffe)

The Roman city of Volubilis had been the first capital, but it was succeeded by Fès in 808. The French, however, built a new capital, Rabat, by the side of an old Arab settlement, dating back to the twelfth century. Eventually the country recovered its political independence in 1956, and was governed by a king and an elected parliament. In 1965, however, parliament was suspended and the king ruled the country by decree.

Harry Ratcliffe says that 'Volubilis has been excavated and partly rebuilt, and it reveals something of the beauty and grandeur of the early Roman cities in Morocco. Some of the mosaics, which have been exposed to the elements for many years, are still beautifully preserved, and they are a permanent reminder of the artistic perfection of the Roman artisan. The records available indicate that the Berbers were on good terms with the Roman rulers, and that for many years the land enjoyed prosperity and peace.'

Christianity evidently reached Morocco at a fairly early date. It is known, for example, that two martyrs were put to death at Tanger towards the end of the third century. Christian lamps and tombs have been excavated at Volubilis. There also have been discovered epitaphs, dated A.D. 599, 605, 653 and 655, a confirmation of the survival of the Christian faith up to the date reasonably close to the Muslim invasion. Arabian historians mention the existence of a Christian church at N'fiss in the foothills of the Atlas mountains, and reference is also made to Christian tribes being found in the plains towards the end of the eighth century. In *Decline and Fall*, Gibbon says of this area, 'The northern coast of Africa is the only land in which the light of the gospel, after a long and perfect establishment, has been totally extinguished.' The major reason has obviously been that the people did not have the Scriptures in their own tongue and had no defence against the attacks and seductions of Islām.

Missionary work has never been easy in Morocco. Even under the French Protectorate, it was merely tolerated. The French did not desire any difficulties for their administration, and if missionaries were too aggressive in their presentation of the message, it provoked the Muslims and caused trouble for the government. Under a treaty between the French and the Sultan of Morocco in 1926, it was expressly provided that Islām should be protected. Consequently the activities of missionaries were

restricted to their own homes or premises. It was not possible, for
example, to hold even an informal meeting in a café or in any place
where the public would congregate. The missionary had to
inform the local authority if he intended to be away from home for
more than four nights and had to report to the police on arrival at
his destination.

An edict of 1963 made it a punishable offence to attempt to
convert a Muslim to another religion, or to use educational or

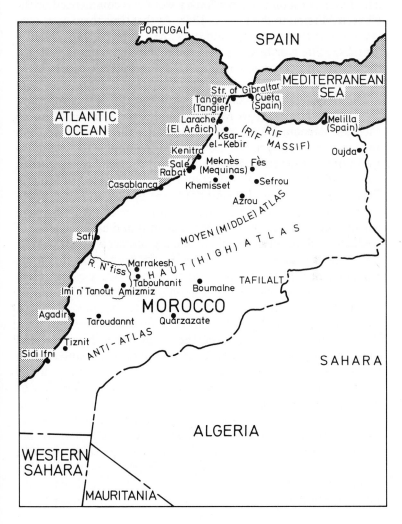

medical help or orphanages to this end, and also provided for the closing of the establishment where such an offence had been committed. Open-air meetings and evangelistic campaigns were impossible, so that work could be carried on only on a personal one-to-one basis.

Followers of Francis of Assisi started preaching the gospel in the country in the thirteenth century, but little impact seems to have been made, and no permanent impression was apparently left. The earliest modern missionary work was commenced by the Church Mission to the Jews in 1875. At that time there were over 20,000 Jews in the country and the C.M.J. interest was primarily for these. The North Africa Mission followed, however, in 1881, the Southern Morocco Mission in 1888, and the Gospel Union (U.S.A.) in 1895.

The first missionary connected with assemblies was Matthew C. Taylor, who went to Morocco under the Central Morocco Medical Mission. He left the Mission after three years and from 1901 began to look to the Lord alone to supply his needs. He spoke Arabic fluently and worked first in the area of Meknès (then known as Mequinas), but itinerated widely. He was particularly interested in the large Jewish population in that area.

The Jewish population numbered well over 10,000, who were not allowed to live in the city. Mr. Taylor found his knowledge of medicine and surgery valuable in making contact with the people.

In 1903 he removed to Larache on the coast, and this town remained his base for the duration of his missionary career. Here Mr. Taylor witnessed to the Jews, some of whom readily assented to all he said but were afraid openly to become disciples. Sometimes Mr. Taylor had as many as 80 Jews at his meetings. He gave much time to visiting the shops of the Muslims, and gained a ready hearing for the gospel. Often he had to stop reading and remind the shopkeeper that people were waiting to be attended to. As soon as customers had been served, Mr. Taylor continued the witness.

From Larache he itinerated widely, visiting the Rhurb and Khuboot tribes, in addition to villages and weekly markets. He also spent some time at Ksar-el-Kebir, on three sides of which were refuse dumps 30 to 40 feet high, draining into the bed of a small river flowing through the town. As the river dried in the summer, the stench was awful. During the rainy season the banks of the same river would overflow and carry great quantities of refuse into the town. Despite the dreadful conditions, Mr. Taylor found good opportunities here for preaching the gospel and many of the Jews accepted a New Testament. During the First World War, he went to the U.S.A. and apparently never returned to the field.

John Crane served in Venezuela and then in Spain, before his marriage to Miss G. May Willie while on furlough in Wales in 1923. Soon after their marriage they set out for Melilla, deeply exercised to spread the gospel there. Although they had made a good start, within five months Mr. Crane died of typhoid fever. Mrs. Crane left for Spain and although she intended to return to Melilla she married missionary statesman, Ernest H. Trenchard, and remained in Spain.

In 1915 Albert and Daisy Fallaize went to Morocco under the auspices of the North Africa Mission. They both learnt Arabic and Albert served on the translation committee from 1920 and worked on the translation of the New Testament in Mogrebi Arabic, which was printed by the British and Foreign Bible Society in 1932.

In 1918 Daisy was having their first baby. One evening near the time the child was due Daisy became ill. No hospital was available, and no doctor. Both Daisy and the baby died.

In 1922 Albert remarried. Lucy Yarde was a Nurse with the N.A.M. In 1925 they returned to England on furlough, and after exercise of heart they were commended by the Assembly at South Park, Seven Kings, Essex. They returned to Morocco looking to the Lord for guidance and support for their future service.

Salé – a walled city with 20,000 Muslims and 2,000 Jews was opened for Europeans to reside there in 1922, and as it was a strategic centre and unoccupied by missionaries Mr. and Mrs. Fallaize went to live there and continued until 1947. From 1946 to 1950 Mr. and Mrs. John Sietman also worked here, and witnessed steadily amongst the Europeans. Lucy Fallaize opened a dispensary for midwifery and dentistry, and trained an Arab woman to help her. She was beloved of the Arab women for her loving care and had wonderful opportunities to speak of Christ's love to them. She was called home in 1970.

Classes and meetings were conducted in the house and a bookshop was also opened. Albert and Lucy also visited the Jews'

John Crane
(*Echoes*, 1923)

Fès – a sculptor

little shops and held encouraging weekly meetings amongst them. They were cheered by the numbers who attended. Mr. and Mrs. Charles Gabriel joined them from time to time and Charles and Albert for many years travelled to the tribal markets with Christian literature and sold thousands of copies of the Scriptures. At first they travelled by mule and cycle, frequently sleeping in Bedouin tents but eventually purchased a second-hand Ford truck, putting on it a body suitable for sleeping purposes. They were able to travel on the military roads laid down by the French Foreign Legion. One notable convert was a sheikh, who was brought to the Lord through the preaching in the markets where he did business.

These tribal markets provided immense opportunities to proclaim the gospel. There were more than 600 such markets in south and central Morocco, from the sea to the Sahara Desert, some were held in almost uninhabited country. Before 1933 many of the markets could not be visited because in endeavouring to establish the Protectorate the French Foreign Legion prevented access. After 1933 Messrs. Gabriel and Fallaize were able to evangelize not less than half the markets. On one tour in 1926 they travelled 1,125 miles, preached to several thousand Muslims and sold nearly 1,000 Scriptures. On some occasions as many as 800 tribespeople would listen to the preaching. Their meetings were frequently opposed by those who sought to draw off their hearers by shouting or singing, and by using horrible insults and blasphemies. Surprisingly, at times, there was no antagonism and many in the crowds agreed with the missionaries regarding their sin and the ineffectiveness of their endless prayers and fastings.

There were so many believers and others interested that the missionaries began to hold Bible teaching conferences in various centres. People came from all parts to meet for several days and to hear the exposition of the Scriptures in Arabic. Numbers grew to about 120. It proved a great encouragement to isolated believers, living under severe pressure in their villages, thus to meet other believers who were living in similar circumstances of persecution and hostility. On such occasions, as many as 40 or 50 national believers would partake of the Lord's Supper with the missionaries.

Albert Fallaize (who, incidentally, is still preaching in England at 93) paid a number of visits to his old field to visit scattered

Fès – nature market

Fès – narrow corridors

believers from Islām. At 88 he paid his last visit, travelling with Harry and Chris Ratcliffe over 2,000 miles into the desert. They called on believers and had meetings in their homes. He quotes a typical case of God's saving power. Si Edrees was a native of the great oasis of Tafilalt, with its thousands of date palms of the quality favoured by Arabs and rarely exported. Because of a family feud, he fled the district and joined the Arab Legion of the French Army. One night a stranger appeared in the Arab café, selling Scriptures. He was quickly hustled out and a tumult ensued. Struck by his attitude, Si Edrees and another soldier escorted him to safety.

In course of time, Si Edrees tired of the military discipline and deserted. Following routes he knew, he eventually arrived at a cosmopolitan coast town and was soon swallowed up in the general population. One night, not having money to pay for a bed in an inn, he drifted into a room where tribesmen could spend the night. This place had been hired by Albert Fallaize for this purpose, so that he could preach the gospel each night to the men who gathered there. Night after night Si Edrees listened to the preaching. One Saturday evening, when the room was packed, the missionary read Romans 1. One of the tribesmen asked what book made statements so descriptive of the way they lived, and was told that the words were written 1,900 years ago. When the appeal was made after the preaching, Si Edrees was one of those who accepted Christ. He was later baptised and years later met the preacher again – and was still reading the Scriptures and bearing witness.

Mr. and Mrs. Charles Gabriel, who had been with the North Africa Mission until 1933, resided at Casablanca, the second largest city. Built on the Atlantic coast, to the south of the capital, Rabat, this is the financial and commercial centre of the country. It is an extremely modern city, with a 'facade of white buildings, most of them bright with glass and hung with balconies'. Despite its magnificent hotels and attractive restaurants, the Arab slums on the outskirts are constructed of flattened petrol cans and the conditions are deplorably wretched. The Boushir at Casablanca is the largest and most spectacular brothel area in the world and contains over 11,000 registered prostitutes. Mrs. Gabriel had regular classes for women and girls and Charles itinerated extensively in the area. Regular gatherings for the Lord's supper were held at Salé, Casablanca and Tabouhanit. This was the most prosperous and encouraging period for the Lord's work. Conditions were not nearly as favourable after the Second World War.

The former capital of Fès is located in a secluded valley far from the coast and is still described as the country's intellectual, spiritual and artistic centre. It has one of the best-known universities in the Islāmic world. In some parts there is a pronounced Andalusian atmosphere, due to the descendants of Spaniards who fled from the Córdoba caliphate centuries ago. Its streets are narrow corridors of dirt and cobbles and it has unattractive physical features in addition to its more interesting ones. It is a very poor city and at night many sleep on the ground in the railway station and elsewhere. Despite the spiritual need, there has never been any attempt by assembly missionaries to evangelize this city. However, workers of the North Africa Mission have served in Fès since 1888, mainly women. In early years a young N.A.M. missionary was stabbed to death here by a fanatical Muslim. The opposition to any further attempt to evangelize Fès would be considerable and there may have been justification for turning to more responsive areas, especially in view of the small number of workers available.

Marrakesh also lies some distance inland and closer to the mountainous area. The original city was founded by the Romans, but the present city originated with the Almoravides in 1062. It is an important market town for the desert tribes. Gunther, op. cit., p. 52, says that this city, 'under the creamy white canopy of the Atlas, is a proliferating mass of blossom. Here are orange trees and cypresses slim as pencils, bougainvillaea and hibiscus, gardens boiling with roses, date palms etched like saws against the sky, and jacaranda the colour of candied violets.'

The busy streets present people of every colour too. Here are the light-skinned, fair-haired and blue-eyed Berber, the 'sienna-coloured Touareg in indigo veils and Sengalese black as blindness. Skins are mahogany, bronze, chocolate, beige, russet, tar-paper. Tribesmen bring in wool and goats, and go out with sugar, spices and brilliantly dyed cloth. . . . In the dye market are lambent pools of ultramarine and scarlet.' In *Mauretania*, Sacheverell Sitwell describes the fascinating public square of Djemma el Fna, which is packed with stalls and places of

Marrakesh – the busy streets

entertainment. Snake charmers, fire eaters, magicians, water carriers, blind beggars and children with faces half destroyed by sores. The city is known too for its celebrated red tower, the Koutoubia, resembling the Giraldo in Sevilla (Seville), and for the rambling ochre palace of El Glaoui.

It was near here that Eric G. Fisk and his wife Dorothy (née Smith) commenced work in 1928. In the previous year, they had taken up responsibilities at Casablanca with the North Africa Mission.

Charles F. Frazer-Smith had gone to Morocco in 1926. At first he considered joining the N.A.M. but finding his ambition to earn his living by farming to support himself, as Paul had tent-making, did not fit into the Missionary Society set-up, he set out on his own. Cuthbert Nairn was, however, his Arabic tutor for two or three months until a farm was purchased between Marrakesh and the Atlas mountains.

Besides his own farm in Morocco, he managed farmlands for both the Moroccan Royal family and the chief religious judge of Morocco. 'I had thirty Berbers, the original people of Morocco, working my land in partnership with me. Their civilisation went back three or four thousands years to Abraham's time and through them I had wonderful understanding of the people of the Bible', *Challenge November 1981.*

Charles Frazer-Smith invited the Frears to evangelize in that area and, with the approval of home assemblies, the Fisks moved to Tabouhanit, fifteen miles south of Marrakesh and built a house there, followed by the erection of a hall and buildings to accommodate visitors and helpers.

Dorothy was a qualified nurse and, with the approval of the French authorities, started a dispensary. This medical work proved of great blessing to many and it helped considerably in removing prejudice. Hardly a week passed but the Fisks were asked to go to someone sick in one of the scores of surrounding villages. On such occasions they were often asked to explain God's Word, and almost everywhere they went they found an interest which was not merely curiosity. This led Eric and Dorothy to hold weekly Bible-classes in various villages. On one occasion, in 1933, they were even invited to go to a group of villages for no other purpose than to preach. Many of these villages were frequently revisited, involving tortuous journeys. On one occasion, accompanied by Mr. and Mrs. Fallaize, on a road of fifteen miles they traversed 162 hairpin bends in ascending 6,000 feet to reach villagers working in a mountain mine. After two years' famine, children were thrust upon them and the circumstances compelled them to start an orphanage. Thomas W. Frears and Harry Ratcliffe joined them in 1938, but these two young missionaries had hardly settled before the Second World War broke out and Eric and Mrs. Fisk had to return to England for a time. The younger men remained, however, learning Arabic, French and Shilha (a Berber language).

When Eric and Dorothy returned, there was still a reasonable degree of liberty, primarily because most of the missionaries' activities were carried on within the limits of their own compound and the authorities did not wish to interfere with what were regarded as private meetings. Good numbers attended the hall and many also came for medical treatment. As recorded in Eric's book, *The Prickly Pear*, there were many conversions during the years.

Thomas Frears, as a boy was always interested in missionary work, and his first interest in the Muslim world was created by a visit to his assembly by Henry Mitchell of Egypt. This was

Dakar – street traders   (S. F. Warren)

Dakar – craft village   (S. F. Warren)

Life in the Horn (Tear Fund)

Málaga – about to visit
Morocco
(T. Frears)

Tom Frears

followed by correspondence with the Fellowship of Faith for the Muslims. Finally a visit from Mr. E. G. Fisk of Morocco, led Tom to feel the call of God to help there. So, as already mentioned, he went in 1938, along with Harry Ratcliffe.

Dorothy (née Ashbridge) was also interested in missionary work from her mid-teens, chiefly through missionaries who visited the assembly, and through Missionary Study Classes held in the Lake District. The Lord brought Tom into her life, and through this, an interest in Muslims. She eventually went to Morocco in 1948.

After helping Mr. and Mrs. Fisk in their orphanage work, Tom moved up into the hills to learn the Berber language. After their marriage in 1946, Dorothy stayed at home to do her midwifery training while Tom went back to build a house and prepare a language course.

Work in Amizmiz was entirely in Berber, in which language there was neither Bible, nor hymnbook, though they did have John's Gospel. Tom had daily classes for boys and some accepted the Lord, whom they still visit. Dorothy had classes for girls. Her qualifications as a nurse and midwife were a great help in work among the Berbers, and her early experience in typing in an office, has stood her in good stead in the production of literature in Arabic which has occupied both her and Tom in recent years.

They later moved to Casablanca (170 miles away) and Tom was busy with Mr. Fisk on the translation of the North African Bible into Arabic. The Lord blessed and a little assembly was established, with some very capable brethren both Arabs and Berbers.

After independence, a new law was passed forbidding the preaching of the gospel to Muslims, and some missionaries were expelled. The Frears returned home and for five years engaged in secular work. On visiting some former missionaries to Morocco, who live in Málaga, Spain, Dorothy was asked to check some Arabic script for printing and through this the Lord spoke to them. After much prayer, they decided to return to the work as itinerant missionaries. So for the past nine years they have been living in a caravan, and alternating between Spain and Morocco. Their main work apart from visiting has been translation of several books from English into Moroccan Arabic. Recent news from Morocco is not encouraging. Several missionaries and national believers have been interrogated by the police and it is possible that some missionaries may be expelled. The Frears retired from full-time work early 1983.

When Sir John Laing and Alec Pulleng visited Tabouhanit in 1952, they found a thriving work. One hundred and forty attended the annual conference and, beside the five assembly missionaries, twenty other missionaries were present.

Some of the converts from this area removed to Casablanca to find employment, as believers found this difficult in the rural areas because of the antagonism to Christianity. Eric Fisk and Charles Gabriel accordingly endeavoured to shepherd them, and the former made a round journey of 300 miles alternate weekends for the purpose. Today there are many committed Christians living in remote villages and townships and witnessing for Christ in their own circles. They found the Saviour at Tabouhanit and the majority were taught to read the Bible and possess their own copies. It is sometimes said that very few Muslims turn to Christ but Eric Fisk's book, *The Cross Versus the Crescent*, provides a complete refutation of this. Some, like Jean Padilla, now labouring in Marseille, France, carry the gospel even farther afield.

In 1954, when Morocco achieved independence, the medical and orphanage work at Tabouhanit had to cease. Conditions became more restrictive and Albert Fallaize says, 'No public halls are allowed, no public preaching, no circulation of Christian literature, no visiting of tribal markets with Scriptures, and no missionary schools for children, on penalty of expulsion or

Casablanca
(T. Frears)

imprisonment. No medical missionary work is permitted, but the spiritual work goes on.'

Miss Jean Orr joined the work at Tabouhanit in 1948 and lived in a native house just outside the compound. She held meetings for women in a nearby village. When Mr. and Mrs. Fisk removed from the area, she moved to a large village immediately outside Marrakesh. In 1954 she acquired a small native house and commenced a work amongst girls. At that time there were not sufficient schools to provide education for all the children who needed to go to school, and the courtyard was, therefore, always well filled with girls. One day, when Jean was reading Patricia St. John's book, *News of Heaven*, an official walked in and enquired what she was doing. She explained that she was conducting a school at the request of the parents of the children. As a result, a decree was issued, directing that all private schools should be registered and that no religious instruction was to be given.

Jean managed to rent a large house with a more secluded courtyard, and began a new work with classes for girls and women. No religious instruction was given at these classes, but the women and girls were invited to attend informal meetings on Sundays. In addition, there was a gospel meeting for women on Wednesdays and a Bible reading for believers on Fridays. Unhappily all this work was brought to an end by the instructions of the authorities.

Tanger (Tangier), almost opposite Gibraltar, is a picturesque town on a beautiful bay, surrounded by wooded hills. Its present population is 188,000. A large number of Jews formerly lived here – Sephardic Jews, who were descendants of those who came from Spain in the fifteenth century, most of them extremely wealthy. By contrast, there were also large numbers of Jews living in miserable ghettos in the Atlas villages. But the Jewish population has almost completely disappeared with the national revival of Israel.

Probably a Berber settlement prior to the advent of the Carthaginians, who made it a trading post, Tanger was under the Romans, at first a free though tribute-paying city, but it was created a colony by Claudius, becoming the capital of Mauretania Tingitana. Thereafter it shared the common history of the country. In 429 the Vandals entered; in 524 came a feeble echo of Rome in the Byzantines. In 621 the Visigoths landed, and the

Arab invasion of the same century brought the Muslim general Okba Ben Neb to the town in 682. In 1471 the Portuguese captured the city, but in 1662 it was given by Portugal to Britain as part of the dowry of Princess Catherine of Braganza on her marriage to Charles II. In 1684, however, the British abandoned it on the ground that it had become 'a nest of papacy where Irish troops and Romish bastards could disport themselves unchecked.'

Mr. Maynard Beattie (U.K. 1946) spent some time in the work at Tanger before moving to Kasbah, Taroudannt, for a brief spell.

Mr. Joseph J. Grossholtz, who was born in Switzerland but who spent his boyhood in America, worked for a number of years in Tanger amongst Spanish-speaking people before returning to the U.S.A. in 1940. He and his English wife, Catherine, who had formerly laboured in South Spain, were commended by U.S.A. to the work in Morocco in 1946, and they accordingly returned to Tanger. Here they concentrated on the Jews, who after some time became increasingly open to the claims of the gospel. Joseph also distributed literature to Arabs. After some months' illness Catherine died in 1952. Mr. Grossholtz later married Bessie Gould of Ascot, Berks. Bessie went to Morocco with a faith mission but after her marriage resigned from the mission. Together Mr. and Mrs. Grossholtz worked in Tanger until his death in 1959. After a furlough in the U.S.A. Bessie returned to Morocco.

In Socco, Tanger, there was a house large enough for public meetings and a residence for missionaries and Bessie carried on a work here. Part of the house was rented to a missionary couple in 1961. Bessie's work consisted principally in personal witnessing and the distribution of literature. In 1968 she fell asleep.

The North Africa Mission carried on a medical work for many years and, apart from the dispensary work, this included the Tulloch Memorial Hospital. Two aunts of Charles Frazer-Smith nursed in Tulloch Memorial Hospital, Tanger and died there aged 26 and 27 respectively from typhoid.

The assembly at Tanger had a number of converted Moroccans, as well as Dr. Farnham St. John, his wife Dr. Janet St. John, Dr. W. Campbell, Mr. T. R. Wilson, Mrs. Harold St. John, Miss Patricia St. John and some of the hospital staff. Much fruit had been seen from the labours of the missionaries over many years.

Desert-dwellers
interested in the gospel
(H. Ratcliffe)

First recording of Berber
broadcast
(H. Ratcliffe)

When all the medical work was nationalized, Dr. Farnham St. John, Dr. Janet St. John and others left the country in 1975, after 30 years of sacrificial service, which had opened many doors to the gospel.

In 1946 Tom Frears and Mr. and Mrs. Harry Ratcliffe removed to Amizmiz, some forty miles from Marrakesh in the foothills of the High Atlas Mountains. They built a house and a meeting room and classes were held daily and some conversions were seen. At the same time, Miss Alice L. K. Bates, who had served for some years in French Guiana, was living in a native house in the town itself and visiting the women. Mrs. Frears engaged in medical work, which provided an access to homes. In 1956 the Frears moved to Casablanca to care for the growing number of believers there, including some who had removed from Amizmiz. A house was obtained on the outskirts of this large modern city and the garage was converted into a meeting room. Miss Rona M. Carroll (U.K. 1958) lived close by and gospel work was attended with blessing. Mrs. Frears conducted a small dispensary but, after a time, this had to be closed because of the attitude of the authorities, although she continued to give help in maternity cases. In 1964 Miss Carroll had to give up her work amongst girls because of a complaint lodged with the authorities. This was regrettable because her house was ideally suited to the work.

Harry and Chris Ratcliffe left Amizmiz in 1949 to open up a new work at Tiznit in the far south of the country. It was a walled town where no gospel work had previously been done. He managed to secure and reconstruct a native house. The Muslims here were very fanatical and at least one attempt was made to poison him. He won the favour of many of the boys, who delighted to come into the courtyard of the house and to see pictures of Biblical stories and scenes thrown by the projector on to the whitewashed wall of the courtyard. There were 37 who regularly attended, but one was beaten unconscious by his uncle for attending. The Imām's son, who lived opposite, played truant from school on one occasion. A blacksmith was summoned to hammer leg irons on the young truant, which were left in place for three months. They prevented his leaving the street but, as soon as his father went to work, he hopped the ten feet across the road into the Ratcliffes' home and, before the leg irons were removed, the truth of the gospel had set him free from the bondage of Islām.

On occasions, people attacked their car and tried to overturn it and to drag Harry out. Their ultimate escape from Tiznit was a miracle. With their station waggon loaded with bedding, clothes and crockery, they drove quietly towards the main gate very early one morning. As they approached the gate, a lorry rushed out from a side street and drove ahead, churning up a great cloud of dust. Having heard of the packing-up, at least 50 men were waiting for the Ratcliffes at the roundabout. But following the lorry and shielded by a cloud of dust, the missionaries could not be seen until they turned north for Agadir. Then, raising their heavy clubs, the men gave pursuit, but it was too late to accomplish their designs.

They moved to Tanger in 1956 and attempted to reach the derelict young men on the streets. Their first contact was a murderer, who had seen an Arabic New Testament and wanted a copy for himself, and who eventually accepted the Saviour. Another became a missionary. Some fifteen attended Bible readings. They had no home and were sleeping in a disused graveyard. After nine years of comparative freedom, the work was greatly restricted by a government decree of 1963. They still visit Morocco, and broadcast the message regularly on Trans World Radio and E.L.W.A. and by correspondence and visits still keep in touch with isolated believers.

At Taroudannt, a much larger walled town than Tiznit, Mr. and Mrs. R. Lightbody (U.K.) commenced their service for the Lord in 1948, but their period was brief. They incurred the suspicion of the French authorities because of their contacts with the Arabs and they were expelled in 1953.

Carlton L. Whitaker was stationed in Morocco during his military service and realized the spiritual need of the country. After his marriage to Doreen M. Weismiller, they were commended by U.S.A. assemblies in 1961. They rented a house at Imi n'Tanout, 60 miles south-west of Marrakesh, where there were 13,000 Berbers, but unfortunately had to leave the country.

For some years a conference was held at Khemisset, but when the missionaries were obliged to leave here, it was held at Meknès and was attended by Christians from Fès, Sefrou, Rabat, Casablanca and Azrou. This city owes much to the abominable Moulay Ismail (1642–1727), who surrounded the city with a wall and built palaces and mosques there. A. Pulleng, who was at the

Tiznit – before the
cinema show
(H. Ratcliffe)

Listening to a cassette
(T. Frears)

conference there, comments that the work was done by Christian slaves, 60,000 of whom at any one time were incarcerated in vast underground prisons. The notorious pirates of Salé, Algiers and other cities captured many European ships and the unfortunate prisoners were thrown into Moulay Ismail's prison. Busnot says, 'For the slightest faults they were impaled, burned alive, or hung by the feet over the mouth of a lime-kiln. The king often had them strangled; he passed loaded waggons over the bodies of others; and others still he had tossed into the air by four negroes, beside unnameable mutilations.' Those who were too weak to work were crucified.

Many of these prisoners were offered manumission if they became Moors. A large number did so and were transported to various parts of the country. A Moorish name was bestowed upon them, together with a wife – invariably a negress – and they were given some employment. It was a desperately unhappy lot, with no hope of being redeemed by money provided in some European lands, as was done for some of the other prisoners.

In 1967 the attitude of the authorities became harsher and most missionaries have either been expelled or have withdrawn. There are now no assembly missionaries openly in the country.

17

Slave Trade Centre

Completely landlocked, the Republic of Niger is surrounded by Algeria and Libya on the north, Chad on the east, Nigeria, Benin and Upper Volta on the south, and Mali on the west. It shares with Chad a small section of the northern shores of Lake Chad and is 458,000 square miles in extent. N. C. Pollock says in *Africa*, p. 227, 'most of the country is Saharan in climate and vegetation, and only a narrow belt in the south comes within the Sahel zone with about twenty inches of highly variable rainfall along the Nigerian border. Nearly half the country has less than four inches of rainfall a year.'

The northern section of the country is virtually part of the Sahara Desert, the monotony relieved occasionally by mountain massifs and by oases. During the brief rainy season, as one writer says, 'a green film springs from the sandy soil as if by magic', and then 'camels, cattle and goats have room to wander endlessly, licking up the sparse grass and thorns. There are as many cattle as people and twice as many sheep.' The central zone provides more pasturage than the north. But it is in the south that agriculture occupies the people, especially in the Chad basin in the south-east and along the tributaries of the river Niger in the south-west. Here are cultivated rice, millet, cotton, cassava and groundnuts. At Gouré gum arabic is also produced for export to Nigeria. The Niger and its tributaries are really the salvation of the country. It has been appropriately described as a country which is partly jungle, partly savanna and partly desert.

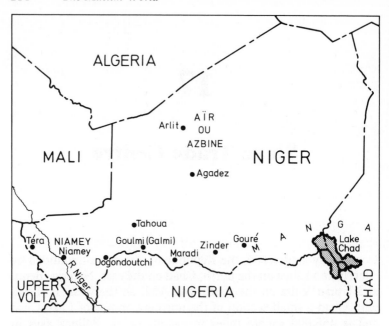

Niger has attracted attention in recent days because of her large uranium deposits at Arlit, which have not yet been exploited. She has also supplies of salt and natron at Agadez and in the Manga and tin, which should prove a source of revenue in the future, is found in the mountainous Aïr region. The country was once the centre of the inhuman slave trade which proved so profitable a few centuries ago. Zinder, which was formerly the hub of this traffic, is still the starting point of many of the camel caravans of the desert today, but little revenue is derived from this source.

The capital, Niamey, is a small town with a population of about 226,000, but other towns, like Maradi, Zinder, Agadez and Tahoua, are even smaller. The population is over five and a half million and is composed mainly of fourteen African tribes, the largest being the Hausa. The Fulani, Songhai, Djerma, Beriberi-Manga, Touareg, etc. comprise the remainder. The blue-veiled Touaregs and the Tibbus are nomadic shepherds, whom it is difficult to contact.

When the ancient African empires suffered the inroads of the Muslim hordes, Niger – like so many North African countries – accepted the new faith and 86 per cent of the population is

Muslim today. There are about 20,000 Christians (including Roman Catholics), but most of the remaining inhabitants are animists. The country became a French colony in 1922 and was one of the three states forming French West Africa, but in 1958 it became a republic, associated with the French Community. In 1960 it achieved complete independence, but there was a military coup in 1974 and the constitution was suspended. The country's official religion is Islām and is actively encouraged and there is a School of Islāmic Studies at Niamey. Nevertheless, there is complete liberty for religious worship and the preaching of the gospel.

Evangelization of the country in modern times did not commence until the Sudan Interior Mission opened a station in 1923 at Zinder, later extending the work to Tsibiri in 1928 and then to Maradi and Dogondoutchi. Dispensaries were opened at each station and schools were also established at a number of centres. The S.I.M. hospital at Galmi was at one time the only one in Niger and the leprosarium close by was the only hospital for lepers.

The Evangelical Baptist Missions, who work primarily among the Djerma tribe, established a centre at Niamey in 1929, and opened several branch stations along the River Niger. Medical and education work was carried on at each station. A Bible School was also opened at Téra for converts from Islām.

Despite the freedom for Christian work, except Mlle. Mari-Jeanne Berney who was commended from Switzerland in 1968, and is serving in Galme par Madous, no assembly missionary has apparently been attracted to Niger, and the country is virtually held by the prophet of Mecca.

18

The Pure Land

The Islāmic Republic of Pakistan extends from the Arabian Sea across the Thar Desert and eastern plains to the Hindu Kush and the foothills of the Himalayan mountains. It is bounded by Iran, Afghanistan and India, and is drained by the Indus river and its tributaries. It has four provinces – Punjab, Sind, North-west Frontier and Baluchistan. It has an area of 310,527 square miles. The name 'Pakistan' means 'pure land' or 'holy land'.

Although its present status as a separate country dates only from 1947, Pakistan has a long history. It certainly goes back some five thousand years to the ancient civilizations of Harappa and Mohenjo Daro. Muslims reached the coast of Sind early in the seventh century A.D. and made a temporary conquest of Sind in the following century. Subsequently Afghan and Turkish invaders gradually spread across northern India, and Islāmic influence increased.

By the eighteenth century Britain had begun to assume political responsibilities in the Indian sub-continent, and from 1857 onwards it exercised some control over the whole of what was then India. It was not long before agitation came for a national voice in the country's affairs, and from 1885 the Indian National Congress took an active part in representations. Muslim leaders felt that they needed some means of presenting their views more effectively and the All-India Muslim league was accordingly formed in 1906. It proved impossible, however, to agree on a formula for the protection of Muslim religious and economic

A vale of the Pure Land   (Mrs. J. Solly)

rights and representation in an independent India Government. Mounting tension over the question of Hindu–Muslim relationships, coupled with widespread disappointment at the limited extent of British reforms, led to a series of bitter communal disturbances at intervals from 1920 until the outbreak of the Second World War. The idea of a separate Muslim nation was adopted in 1940 by the All-India Muslim League, led by Muḥammad Ali Jinnah.

After long negotiations, it was decided in 1947 that full dominion status should be given to two states – India and Pakistan. The latter was to be a bifurcated country, separated by

Peshawar – a tonga   (S. F. Warren)

the thousand miles' breadth of India. Pakistan became a self-governing dominion within the Commonwealth on August 14th, 1947. The death of Jinnah in 1948 and Liaqat Ali Khan's assassination in 1951 dealt severe blows to the new nation, and the situation was aggravated by gradual economic deterioration. In 1956 Pakistan ceased to be a dominion and became a sovereign Islāmic Republic within the Commonwealth. Following a military coup in 1958 the Army Commander in Chief, General Ayub Khan, became President, but retired in 1969. After a bitter civil war, East Pakistan became independent as the People's Republic of Bangladesh in 1971.

Zulfiqar Ali Bhutto succeeded to the presidency in 1970 and strove in every way possible to restore the national confidence which had been so badly shaken by the events of the preceding years. By 1977, however, the people and the army had become increasingly restive and ultimately General Muhammad Zia-ul-Haq seized power and in 1979 Bhutto was executed.

Pakistan has a large and growing population, but the literacy rate is only 24 per cent, and there is a shortage of needed skills. She has adequate resources to develop a vigorous economy. With the Indus and its tributaries and the canals and dams which have been constructed, she has the largest irrigation system in the world, and the river system also powers a number of large hydro-electric stations. Natural gas, oil and chromium ores are also

Gossiping the Gospel in Somalia   (Tear Fund)

Somali woman and child
(Tear Fund)

The Kushite Kingdom – Shilluk tribe, Melut (J. Paul, M.E.Ph.A.)

Multan – little mother   (S. F. Warren)

being exploited. Eighty per cent of the work force is engaged in agriculture and there is a very large production of rice and cotton. Industry was virtually non-existent at the date of independence. The textile industry, based on the fact that she is a major cotton grower, has developed rapidly, but food processing, cement, fertilizers and light metal fabrication are growing in importance. There is a wide range of minerals available and some of these, like coal, limestone, graphite and copper, have been exploited.

The population is 84 million and the ethnic groups are Punjabi, Sindhi, Pushtan (or Pathan) and Baluchi. Over 40 languages are spoken, but the principal are Urdu (the language employed officially), English, Punjabi, Sindhi, Pushtu, Baluchi and Kashmiri.

Pakistan is an Islāmic country and over 97 per cent of the population is Muslim, but there are small minorities of Christians and Hindus. During 1979, actions to implement an 'Islāmic economy' were announced. The first move in this direction was the imposition of Zakāt, a wealth tax to support charity to the poor. It is likely that further moves will be made cautiously. At present, freedom of religion is maintained, but it is not known how long this will continue. The few Christians in Pakistan come largely from the depressed classes of Hindu society, and they find it difficult to witness to the Muslim community.

According to tradition, the apostle Thomas preached in Taxila in the north-east of Pakistan during the reign of Vindafama (A.D. 20–48). Taxila was then the leading seat of Hindu scholarship and was famous for its medical school. Today it is famous as one of the major archaeological sites of the Indus Valley civilization. Being only 40 minutes away from the capital, Islamabad, it is a favourite stop for foreign travellers. It has an active church based on the American mission hospital.

It is known that there were groups of believers in various centres in the third century. Then Nestorian Christians came as traders from the Persian Sāsānian empire. They were zealous and active in testimony, but saw few results from their witness, and no enduring indigenous church was established. One major difficulty was that Syriac and Pahlavi (Farsi) were the ecclesiastical languages, and scarcely anyone understood them. Christianity was regarded as a foreign religion and there was little response to it. By the fourteenth century there was little, if any, active witness in Pakistan.

In 664 and in the following three centuries, raiders from Afghanistan had repeatedly swept over the mountains of the Hindu Kush and crossed the Indus to raid the town of Multan. They eventually established some form of Muslim sovereignty over the area. By the sixteenth century the Mogul empire, which was Muslim, held sway over Pakistan and northern India. Armenian Christians entered the country at this time, however, and brought the message of the gospel.

Then, in 1576, the reigning emperor, Akbar (1556–1605), who had found no satisfaction in Islām, heard of Christian missionaries at Goa and invited them to his court. They were Jesuit priests, but knew the truths of the gospel. At his request, three more arrived in 1594, led by Jerome Xavier, a nephew of Francis Xavier, who had such an influence on India. The visit resulted in the establishing of a church in 1601 in Lahore, then the capital of the empire. A Farsi translation of the New Testament was produced, and a proclamation allowed citizens to convert to Christianity if they wished to do so. Almost inevitably, the work died out. Only a few low-caste servants remained

Multan   (S. F. Warren)

nominally Christian and the number of Armenian believers
dwindled. Today there are 20,000 Roman Catholics in Karachi.

The first Protestant work was opened in the Punjab by the
American Presbyterian Mission in 1849, when educational work
was started in Lahore. The Church Missionary Society commenced in Karachi in the following year. Various other bodies
followed, but one report says that 'All of the missions concentrated their efforts at first upon the educated, higher classes of
Hindus and Muslims, with few results. Later, large numbers of a
depressed caste, the Chuhras, began to ask for instruction and
baptism. Between 1880 and 1935 the movement accelerated until
nearly the whole caste had been won to Christ. Over 90 per cent of
the Christians in Pakistan today trace their ancestry to this
Chuhṛa caste.'

More recently, however, there have been other encouraging
developments. After a visit to Pakistan in 1969 David Bentley-
Taylor of the International Fellowship of Evangelical Students
said that he 'was amazed at the progress made by the previously
rather nominal evangelical student movement. With David
Penman as its executive secretary, it has leapt into life among
graduates and faces now the problems of rapid growth.' In the
same year a four-man team of Indonesian Christian leaders paid a
two-week visit to the country, when hundreds were led to Christ.
In *World News*, January–March, p. 4, David Bakhsh wrote, 'In

one meeting, so many stood up, indicating their desire for
salvation, that the speakers had to warn them that those who did
not mean business with God should sit down. Instead, even more
stood up. In these meetings a large number of non-Christians
were present. In the Lahore meeting, so many came forward for
salvation that the counselling team was completely overwhelmed.'

The religious liberty enshrined in the national constitution is
not a dead letter and it has afforded excellent opportunities for
Christian work in Pakistan.

No account of the Lord's work in Pakistan could omit mention
of the name of Bakht Singh. An engineer from Sargodha, he was
converted in Canada. He returned to North India and with
Ghulam Masih and others, he toured the country, mainly in the
Sindh and Punjab areas, during the 1930's preaching the gospel.
Those inter-war years were, however, largely barren and
unproductive. Nevertheless, Bakht Singh and Ghulam Masih
were greatly used of God and they saw many individuals born
again. Unfortunately, on returning to them after a period, Bakht
Singh found that the apathy and nominality of the existing
churches had done nothing to encourage or develop their growth,
so that little remained of the work which he had initiated.

Against this background and, through his study of Scriptures, a
pattern of church planting emerged which, in most respects, was
similar to that regarded as characteristic of assemblies. During
succeeding years, particularly in the early days after the birth of
Pakistan in 1947, there was a rapid growth of newly-formed
assemblies. This was, of course, due not only to the activities of
Bakht Singh, but also to those of assembly missionaries, together
with a considerable number of Pakistani Christians engaged in
full-time service, and local believers who were active in their own
towns and villages. New assemblies are still springing up. It is
perhaps significant that the report, *Status of Christianity Country
Profile*, said of Pakistan, 'The Brethren Church is quite
indigenous in its leadership and methods, though a number of
missionaries are affiliated with it. Most of the pastors support
themselves at secular jobs and do church work in their spare time,
relying on offerings from their people to support the work. Their
local assemblies meet in homes, are unstructured and only loosely
connected with other brethren groups. Although a small

movement, it has had a strong ministry of revival among nominal Christians.'

The 1940's and particularly the period immediately prior to partition in 1947, saw the first activities of assembly missionaries in what was then north-west India. Local churches were established in Lahore and Peshawar. Those primarily involved at that

Peshawar – Dennis E. C. Clark   (S. F. Warren)

time were Dennis E. C. and Gladys M. Clark, the daughter of
Charles and Martha Wright of Tibet and India. Associated with
them in Lahore were such men as Jordan Channan Khan. In
Peshawar, Sohan Lal Isaac was the national Christian whom God
used to continue the work of the assembly after the Clarks had
returned to Lahore, and his influence as a wise and moderate
leader has continued. Over the years both of these local assemblies
have faced not only external opposition but, unfortunately,
internal division. Nevertheless they have continued to exist as
centres of truth and life in a hostile environment.

Wilfred and Christina Durham had founded the Gospel
Literature Service in Bombay, which had proved a great blessing
in India. In 1945 Dennis Clark and Wilf Durham met in Karachi
to consider expanding literature work in India, and a tentative
agreement was reached to divide the country into broad spheres of

interest on a language basis. It was envisioned that there would be two centres, from which evangelistic literature would be distributed throughout the country. It was anticipated that, in both areas, printing presses and publishing wings would be established.

With the coming of partition in 1947, it became apparent that the original intentions needed revision. The initial vision of literature in Urdu for North India as a whole was necessarily aborted, and the Clarks, in consultation with others, took the initiative in founding the Masihi Sahitya Sanstha (i.e. The Gospel Literature Institute) at New Delhi. Robert Duff agreed to become a co-founder in the early years, until he became involved in the development of Delhi Bible Institute.

At Lahore was started the Masihi Isha'at Khana (i.e. The Christian Publishing House) in 1947–48, the M.S.S. developing subsequently in New Delhi. M.S.S. majored in Hindi publications, while M.I.K. majored in Urdu and literature for the Muslim World. Mr. John A. Renvoize, who, along with his wife Ethel, served at Lahore (1949–53), recorded that during the first three months of 1952 M.I.K. printed 1,000 books of 200 pages on Bible Doctrine, 3,000 copies of Genesis, 15,000 copies of St. John's Gospel, 15,000 copies of Luke, 5,000 S.G.M. portions, and other material.

During this period, Dennis arranged for the import of book-binding equipment. Working with Bishop Chanda Ray, then the secretary of the Bible Society at Lahore, the Tibetan Bible was rapidly bound and taken through to the border between Pakistan and India before it was closed.

From the inception of the publishing work, Christians in the United Kingdom saw the strategic importance of its ministry. The Clarks were joined over the next few years by other missionaries from Britain, and also had the cooperation and help of national Christians. From 1952 to 1966, for example, Paul W. Marsh had a major share of responsibility for this work. Subsequently, Heinrich Becht became general manager.

Ingrid Hauer went to Lahore in 1968, and Peter and Barbel Seewald at the same time, although the Seewalds later transferred to Rawalpindi. The literature work has steadily grown, and the number of books published and sold constantly increases. The property was purchased with financial help from U.K. and

Germany. The distinguished Pakistani scholar Prof. Khair Ullah has now completed a very comprehensive Bible dictionary in Urdu.

Among the objectives of the M.I.K. was the production of evangelistic literature for Muslims and also for nominal Christians. Further, the publishing house was committed to the production of conservative evangelical literature to build up the churches. The majority of the staff are now Pakistani Christians. After ten years of operation it became apparent that the printing press had fulfilled its function, and the machinery was sold and the proceeds ploughed into the publishing house work. The M.I.K. is the only evangelical publishing house in Pakistan.

Despite much poverty, ignorance and disease, there are still reminders in Lahore of the long history and past civilization. There was, in fact, a highly developed culture and civilization in the Indus valley as long ago as the time of Abraham, and the Khyber Pass on the Afghanistan boundary is a reminder of the invasion of Alexander the Great in 326 B.C. The magnificent buildings in Lahore include the Badshahi mosque, probably the largest mosque in the world, Shalimar Garden, Jehangir's tomb, and others calling up memories of the renowned Mogul era. In a visit to the German missionaries there, Ernst Schrupp saw something also of the work in the villages around the city. With no previous announcement of the missionaries' coming, within a few minutes of their entry into a village, over a hundred people would gather to hear the message.

Mr. and Mrs. William S. Penfold took out a truck in 1951 and converted it into a 'book bus', carrying literature to cities and villages from the centre of Lahore. The bus also carried a team of workers for campaigns in various centres and to assist in the distribution of literature in bazaars, markets and homes. W. T. Stunt wrote that, in two years, half a million people were reached with literature over a very wide area, and that as many as 1,500 Muslims have gathered at an evening meeting to hear the gospel preached through amplifiers and with the help of transparencies. Gospel songs recorded on tape were frequently used.

Robert W. Orr and his wife, Dr. Jean M. Orr, were exercised about missionary work for some years before they sailed for Pakistan in 1951, just two months after Jean had graduated at Edinburgh. They took up residence at Lahore for two years,

Jean Orr's women's class   (S. F. Warren)

Robert W. Orr   (S. F. Warren)

during which she served at the Christian Hospital, while Robbie engaged in preaching and visiting. In 1953 they moved to Multan with all their worldly goods (including their bicycles) in a truck given them by Dennis Clark. They rented a house in Multan and used one of the rooms as a clinic.

Colin F. Blair was commended from New Zealand in 1953 and spent the first two years learning Urdu with Robert Orr in Multan. He went on to work at Lahore, Landour and Murree,

Karachi   (S. F. Warren)

Heinrich Becht
(Mrs. J. Solly)

using literature to reach both Muslims and Hindus. While in Lahore he was also involved in the production of literature. He married Miss Gladys Fehr in 1956 and they continued in Lahore, producing literature for Muslims. Following their furlough in New Zealand in 1958, they engaged in a wider sphere of ministry.

Mr. and Mrs. Ronald Beckett (U.K. 1950) were also based for some years at Lahore and then at Murree. In the former they found open doors all around for the gospel and daily meetings were held in three locations within twelve miles of Lahore. At Murree Mrs. Beckett gained free entrance into many Muslim homes and during the summer Ronald visited villages outside the town and distributed thousands of tracts. They worked in the villages of the Multan district too, and while Mrs. Beckett engaged in medical work, Ronald, with the aid of a gramophone and loudspeakers, would preach the gospel to as many as 1,000 people. The Becketts left Pakistan in 1965.

Mr. and Mrs. Ian H. Douglas (U.K. 1949) also served for a few years in Lahore.

Based at Karachi were Mr. and Mrs. Edward G. Williamson, who had served in India since 1949 and 1936 respectively. Their ministries included weekly jail visits, bazaar evangelism, Sunday-school work, and ship visitation. There was fanatical opposition. Two young students who were converted and baptised were cut off by their parents and were compelled to give up their studies and search for employment which was difficult in view of the discrimination against Christians.

Heimann Janzen, who had formerly worked in Turkestan, and Ernst Max Hoppe repeatedly tried to emphasize to German assemblies their responsibility to the Islāmic world. In consequence, Daniel Herm and his brother Bruno responded to the call in 1955, the former to go to Pakistan and the latter to Arabia. Daniel worked in association with the Afghan Border Crusade on the Pakistan–Afghanistan frontier.

Some time earlier a work had been founded by Bakht Singh, which was being carried on by Heinrich and Renate Becht (commended in 1957) and Hans Peter Züblin. Through these two brethren a number of assemblies came into being and had fellowship with the missionaries working among the Pathans in the north-west border region adjoining Afghanistan. Other missionaries left for the field in 1960, commended from German assemblies, including Martha Brauner, Ruth Späte and Irene Wrona. As a result of a visit by Ernst Schrupp, the work was co-ordinated as the Brethren Christian Fellowship.

In 1962 Gustel Fuchs was commended to Multan and was joined there in 1966 by Wolf and Inge Munzinger. An evening Bible school was started at Multan, which has met a real need over the years.

Howard F. Harper was commended from New Zealand and left for Pakistan with Colin Blair in 1954. He commenced language study in Urdu at Multan and Murree and later visited Quetta in Baluchistan amongst the nomadic tribes people. He went to Edinburgh to undertake a full course of medical training. He graduated in 1962 and returned to New Zealand with his wife Monika, who was born in East Germany and trained as a nurse in West Germany and in England. Commended from New Zealand they returned to Pakistan in 1963. In Taxila, Howard worked with Dr. Christie in a hospital with 500 patients. While learning Urdu, they were able to help in other ways. Later they moved to Lahore and helped in the Christian Hospital.

In fellowship with German brethren Dr. Howard and Monika Harper moved to Kohat near the Afghanistan border in 1965 and were able to enter that land once a month for medical work. The following year they were able to spend some time at Kabul, before returning to Pakistan. As already mentioned in an earlier chapter, they went back to Afghanistan in 1971 until they were required to leave in 1973. Later they went to Iran.

At the end of 1973 the outpatients' department at Kohat had to be closed because there was no lady doctor available, but Dr. Hansmartin Killguss and his wife Thekla took up the work at the Bach Hospital in Qalandarabad in the north of the country. Eva Maria Munzinger was also commended to the work in 1977, and Ruth Späte had been there for some years. With other doctors and nurses, Dr. Killguss was able to undertake medical work in the mountains of Chitral several times a year.

When Alex Moore (U.K.) was commended to Pakistan in 1958 as a young man of 24, no one foresaw that the Lord would call him home the following year. But his death constituted a challenge to his sister, Elsie S. Moore. She found it hard to accept the principle of a 'faith missionary', but in 1965 heard of a new hospital at Lahore, at which all her expenses would be paid. She applied and was accepted – but told that she must pay her own fare and partially support herself. She went committing herself to the Lord. Due to fighting in Lahore, she was diverted to Multan and spent three weeks with the Orrs at Aman Clinic. When she went to Lahore she knew no Urdu and was the only foreign nurse, but she proved that God was sufficient. After a period at home, she returned in 1968 to Multan to learn the language and to help in the Clinic. At the request of Heinrich Becht she spent some months in 1971 at M.I.K. at Lahore. Subsequently she joined the German friends at the clinic at Kohat, where there was a small assembly, but due to the absence of a doctor, the clinic was closed in 1973 and she returned to Multan to serve at the Mission Hospital there, as Nursing Superintendent.

In 1954 the Orrs were joined at Multan by Barbara H. Prentice and Agnes C. Hislop and the clinic was expanded to occupy another house. Barbara and Agnes became friends during their nursing training in Britain and were both commended to work in Pakistan by their assemblies. They were able to help in the spiritual work amongst women and children as well as in the Aman Clinic. After returning home in 1973, Agnes went back in 1982 to act as Nursing Superintendent at the mission hospital whilst Elsie Moore was on furlough.

Elizabeth M. Greig undertook nursing training in Glasgow and Aberdeen. She had been exercised about Christian service for many years, but her interest in the mission field was deepened as a result of serving with G.L.O. teams in Italy and Germany. Commended from U.K. to Pakistan in 1981 she went to Multan to help in the medical work while learning the language. Other sisters joined later from Scotland, Germany and the U.S.A., and helped with the medical work and in the evangelistic work amongst the women and children. The contribution to the work made by German sisters was notable. They came from various assemblies in Germany but through the Wiedenest Bible School.

Sylvia R. Tarring took courses at Moorlands Bible College, Capernwray Bible School, the Missionary School of Medicine, and Wycliffe School of Linguistics to fit her for the Lord's work. She and M. Ann Hughes (whom she met at M.S.M.) were exercised regarding the Lord's will for their lives. After a week with the Orrs at Edinburgh, they had no doubt and both were commended (U.K.) to the work in Multan in 1969. After initial

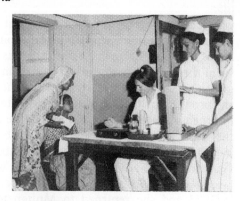

Elsie S. Moore

Multan – Sylvia R.
Tarring's class
(S. F. Warren)

language study, they helped in the Urdu Sunday School at Murree, where there are now 100 girls. During their first ten years their ministry was mainly among nominal Christian communities around Multan which were numerous at that time, but they also share in the presentation of the gospel to Muslim patients in the hospital and help in children's meetings and Bible study groups and in visiting Muslim villages. Some blessing has been seen. Since 1979 Sylvia has been encouraging small assembly groups in villages within a 50-mile radius of Multan. A girls' group of 30 has been established at Shantinagar. In Chak twelve children have trusted the Lord.

Rose Brooks (daughter of Cyril and Anna Brooks of the Philippines) trained as a nurse and served in Pakistan, at first with a missionary society. In 1970 she was commended by a U.S.A. assembly and joined the Orrs in Multan to help in the medical work. Ruth Cushing (U.K. 1970) and Elizabeth Greig are all helpers in the medical clinics and with midwifery cases. Margaret McKenzie (U.K. 1978) also helped until her return to Scotland in 1981.

An excellent building was erected in 1978 in Multan containing a fine school-room, a residence for a Pakistani family, a small courtyard for women, a basement and a baptistry. Youth camps are now held there. Wolf Munzinger (now working with his wife, Inge, in Multan) made a major contribution in building a clinic and a residence for four sisters alongside the assembly premises.

A common language school is conducted in Murree and all evangelical local churches and missionary societies co-operate in this as well as in radio programmes, literature work and the Bible correspondence courses. Missionaries' children are cared for in a mission school and a boarding school. Flora McGill who was commended from Scotland in 1978 was located at Murree, and taught in the Christian School, as well as engaging in visiting and general assembly activities, until she returned home in 1981 and married in the following year.

The building up of the assembly at Multan was a slow and painful business. Robbie Orr was cheered in 1957 by the arrival from Wiedenest Bible School of Heinrich Becht and a Swiss brother, Hans Peter Züblin, who now directs the Christian Publishing House of Brunnen Verlag at Basel. The three brethren preached in many towns and villages. Messages were given to patients at the start of the day, and Gospels and booklets were given to those who sought them. In addition to caring for the assembly, Robert Orr engaged in open-air preaching, visiting villages and literature distribution. Evangelization and church planting are regarded as the major activities, but the principal means to this end are medical mission work for women and children in Multan and Kohat and the literature service in connection with the publishing house M.I.K. at Lahore. There are now probably more than 200 assemblies in Pakistan.

Ruth E. Warren, a highly qualified radiographer first served with Voluntary Service Overseas for a year until she was

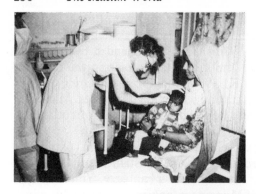

Multan – Rose Brooks
dressing a child's ear
(Mrs. J. Solly, née Warren)

Baltistan – coping with
widespread disease
(Dr. A. G. Stewart)

evacuated at the time of the Indo–Pakistan War. Subsequently assured of the call of God she returned having been commended from Preston (U.K.) in 1973. After completing her language study at Murree and Multan she was not only involved in the clinic at Multan, but in children and young people's work and in following up clinic patients in the homes. She was also in constant demand by mission hospitals because of her radiography qualifications. She returned home in 1977 to marry John Solly.

Ruth Twamley had been exercised about the mission field for a long time and it was through Charles R. Marsh that she saw the possibility of working among Muslim women and children in Pakistan. Commended from Dublin she went to Pakistan in 1976. Ruth had done a full summer at the mission language school before Dr. Alex G. Stewart's arrival from Scotland and at first they were separated by 100 miles. Alex had had contacts with Dr.

Port Sudan
(Red Sea Mission Team)

Sudanese land reclamation (Red Sea Mission Team)

Sudan – their daily bread (Red Sea Mission Team)

Edward S. Short, Dr. James W. McMillan and Miss Elsie Moore, Alex being commended from Glasgow in the same year as Ruth. They returned home in 1977 to be married and then Alex took a locum at a small village hospital at Abbottabad, the most northerly mission hospital in Pakistan. He was also school doctor for Murree Christian School for a time.

Jean Orr became Medical Superintendent of the Mission Hospital in Multan and Robert Orr subsequently became Director. Lal Din and Yunis Lal Din, who were elders in the asssembly and appreciated for their work there, helped in the Multan Hospital as well as in various Christian activities. Yunis had been saved in the Sunday School as a boy. Dr. Shirley Scott (U.K.) also gave help in 1978 and, after further medical study in Britain, returned to Multan in 1982.

By 1979 the Orrs felt it was time to hand over the work to others and Yunis Lal Din succeeded Robbie in his responsibilities as Director at the Hospital.

After 26 years at Multan, Robbie and Jean moved to the Northern hills to be joined by Dr. Alex and Ruth Stewart. Stephanie J. Shaw (U.K. 1982) is presently studying Urdu in Lahore with a view to joining them.

Baltistan is in the extreme north-east of Pakistan and lies between the Himalayan range and the Kunlum mountains of south-west China. The Orrs had paid several visits to this area and were accompanied on occasions by Dr. Alex and Mrs. Ruth Stewart. Their account of the air journey to Baltistan is worth quoting. 'On this bright September morning we are climbing up on track, and before we are half an hour out of Rawalpindi airport, snow-capped mountain walls tower *above* the little plane! It is only in clear weather that the flight can be attempted, and our plan to fly in earlier in the summer had had to be abandoned because of the monsoon clouds. Down on our left is the 50-mile-long reservoir held by the great dam at Tarbela, conserving the waters of the Indus a thousand miles from the sea. One hundred and sixty miles away, above those grey-blue waters, glistens the huge bulk of Tirich Mir, monarch of the Hindu Kush. As our trip ends, we cross a void, making for a rocky shoulder. We glide over it with several hundred feet to spare, and ahead of us, to the right, is the deep and narrow gorge down which the young Indus is rushing towards us. A quarter of an hour later we emerge into a

To Baltistan
(Dr. A. G. Stewart)

broad sandy valley, and soon touch down at the airfield nine miles short of Skardu, the district headquarters town. We step out into the painfully brilliant sunshine and crisp, cool air, and are greeted by airport hands, who are by now old friends.'

Conditions are difficult; water is often contaminated, accommodation is poor, and food is sometimes a problem. But the Lord's servants continue for the sake of the souls for whom Christ died. The Orrs and the Stewarts now work for the summer half of the year in Baltistan and for the winter half in Multan.

Local assemblies in the Punjab have been built up by solid Bible teaching and God has greatly used Robert Orr and Paul Marsh in this respect, both in the assemblies and at the large annual conventions. Pakistani brethren are beginning to fulfil their responsibilities in similar fashion, but there is still a need for teachers. It has also been important to gather together the 30 or so full-time workers from time to time to give them sustained and concentrated Bible teaching for a week or more. These are the future leaders of the assemblies and they need help and guidance that they may be fitted for the work.

19

Spanish Sand

(Map page 180)

The Sahara Desert, which runs across most of North Africa and effectively divides it from the south, has been aptly described as a sea of sand. Yet the description is not entirely accurate for, as one writer justifiably remarks, it is 'an area so vast and so diversified that it is impossible to generalize about it. There are oases in the Sahara with a million palms, moist as wet blotters; there are also areas so blindingly hot and arid that they have never yet been traversed. In Arabic, the word "Sahara" means "emptiness" or "nothing".'

The province of Spanish Sahara is located on the Atlantic coast, bounded by Morocco on the north, and Mauritania on the east and south. It is very largely desert but, while the hinterland is raw emptiness, there are a few unattractive coastal towns and, inland, a number of unkempt settlements. The total area is 102,703 square miles. It comprises two zones: in the north is the region of Saquia el Hamra, and in the south Rio de Oro between Cabo Blanco and Cabo Bojador.

The country was formerly occupied by Sanhajah Berber tribes, but these later came under the domination of Mali-speaking Bedouin. Cabo Bojador was founded by Portuguese sailors in 1434, and two years later, they discovered a bay, which they named Bahia de Rio de Oro (Bay of the River of Gold). The local population brought gold down the Rio de Oro and bartered it for spices. Spanish merchants arrived a decade or so later, but they made little attempt to explore the country, and were content to settle at one or two locations in Morocco.

In 1884, however, Emilis Bonelli of the Spanish Africa Society came to Bahia de Rio de Oro and signed treaties with the coastal tribes on behalf of his country. As a result, Spain shortly afterwards claimed a protectorate over the coastal zones. France had already penetrated northern Africa quite deeply and frustrated any Spanish designs on Mauritania by claiming it herself. A Bedouin sheikh who had founded the town of Smara (now the capital of Saquia el Hamra) at an inland oasis in 1904 also presented resistance to attempts to push farther into Sahara. Eventually the Spaniards occupied Cap Juby in 1916 and proceeded to take possession of Guera and Smara. In 1958 Spanish Sahara became a province of Spain. Cabo Juby was transferred to Morocco in 1958 and this left Sahara without any suitable port, and it is without any proper roads.

There is very little agriculture, but there is a small fishing industry, and dried fish is exported to the Canary Islands. Camels, goats and sheep are raised. Potash and iron ore are available at Agracha and there are vast phosphate deposits existing at Bu Craa, to the south-east of El Aaiún, the provincial capital. Water shortage is a serious problem for the extraction of the phosphate, however. Villa Cisneros, the principal town of Rio el Oro, has to import drinking water. Explorations for oil have not been very promising, but there is still a possibility of reasonable reserves being discovered.

The population is a fluctuating one, ranging from 25,000 to 76,000, because large numbers of nomads migrate for part of the year to Mauritania. There are more than 16,500 Europeans, mainly at the substantial military establishments. The nomads, fishermen and negroid tillers in Saquaia el Hamra speak Hassanizah Arabic. Apart from Smara, with its celebrated Kasbah and mosque, and Villa Cisneros, there is a small fishing harbour at Gillua.

The country is 78 per cent Muslim, but there is no evidence of the fanaticism evidenced in some other countries. The nomadic character of the majority of the population would make it extremely difficult to contact them, and there is no record of any serious attempt to evangelize them. There is a remote possibility of some being brought into contact with the gospel in Morocco or Algeria, but the probability is small. Islām has established itself firmly in Sahara.

20

Blackest Black

John Gunther declares that the Senegalese are the blackest blacks in Africa, and this is generally said. The Senegalese are, of course, excellent soldiers and, during the period of the French régime, the area was an important reservoir of French military manpower. There is a distinct educated class, deriving from the area known as the *Quatre Communes*.

Senegal is the westernmost country of Africa and is situated at the tip of the bulge of West Africa, facing the Atlantic Ocean. It is bounded by Mauritania, Mali, Guinea and Guinea-Bissau, and it completely surrounds the country of Gambia. Most of the country has low, rolling plains with savanna-type vegetation, but in the south-east, plateaux rise to over 1,000 feet to form the foothills of the Fouta-Djalon mountains. Senegal is in the Sahel strip of West Africa. The desert sands of Mauritania lap at its northern border and the south verges into the rain forest of Guinea. Marshy swamps interspersed with tropical rain forest are common in the south-west. It is drained by the rivers Senegal, Saloum, Casamance and Gambia, each of which is navigable for a considerable distance. The country is 76,342 square miles in size.

The climate is hot and humid and at times very oppressive. Malaria is endemic and hepatitis is prevalent. The service of a number of early missionaries was cut short by early death, but conditions are said to be greatly improved today and the general level of health in the capital, Dakar, for example, is reasonably good. The national life expectancy, however, is only 44 years.

The population is 5,660,000 and there are 22 tribes. There are many ethnic groups here: Fulani shepherds, Mandingo griots, Dyola warriors.

Six major languages have been approved for literacy purposes. French, the official language, Wolof, Pulaar, Dyola, Kandigo and Sarakole. Amongst these, Wolof has the leading place.

The Wolof are grouped in the peanut basin of northern Senegambia, almost a million in Dakar, the rest in smaller towns and countless villages from St. Louis in the north to Kaolack in mid-Senegal, spilling over into the north bank area of Gambia and Banjul, and going east 100 miles from the Atlantic. The Wolof cultivate peanuts and millet in the three-month rainy season from

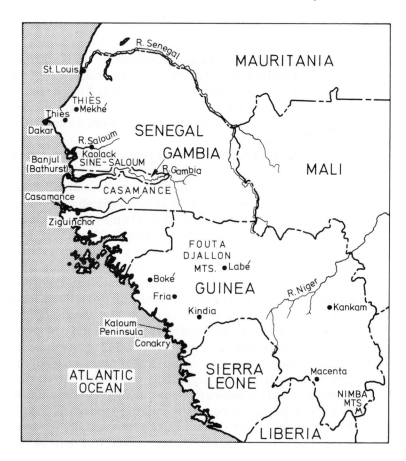

July to September. A veneer of Islām has coated their original animism, so that 99.9 per cent of the Wolof would assent to the belief that 'there is only one God and Muḥammad is his messenger'.

Senegal has rich phosphate deposits and there is a thriving fishing industry and also some light manufacturing, but the main occupation is agriculture. The country is the biggest peanut producer in the world, but millet, sorghum, manioc, rice and cotton are also grown.

Archaeological findings indicate that Senegal was inhabited in prehistoric times. It is said that the country was first settled by the Normans. In the thirteenth century it occupied a position of some importance as the Djoloff Empire of Senegal. French traders, interested in the trans-Saharan traffic, were in evidence in the country from the seventeenth century and, by the nineteenth century, France had gradually established control over the interior.

At one time there was a thriving slave trade based on the island Goree off the port of Dakar. Slaves were sold in the interior to the traders often by their own chiefs. They were taken to Goree in chains, graded and sold there in a market which has been preserved as a testimony to posterity of this evil trade. Having been sold to the merchants, the slaves were shipped to the new world passing through the 'Door of no hope' to waiting ships.

Originally a protectorate and from 1920 a French colony, Senegal became a member of the French Community in 1958

The island of Goree   (S. F. Warren)

with internal autonomy. But, in the following year, Senegal and Sudan merged to form the Mali Federation. In 1960, however, she seceded from the Federation and proclaimed herself completely independent as the Republic of Senegal, Sudan becoming the Republic of Mali.

The predominant religion of the country as a whole is Islām. At least 80 per cent are Muslims, five per cent are Christians and the remainder are animists. Although the country is a Muslim one, there is complete freedom for the propagation of the gospel. Surprisingly also, many of the women do not bother to wear a veil.

The gospel was brought to Senegal in 1862 by the Paris Evangelical Missionary Society, but in the first 60 years most of the men who went out as missionaries either died or were invalided home after a few months. Conversions were disappointingly few and the society's work was accordingly curtailed, although there are still a church, dispensary and bookstore in Dakar. Other societies followed and work was started at Ziguinchor, Thiès and Dakar, but results did not prove very encouraging although there is still a bookshop at Thiès.

Assembly missionary work commenced when Eric D. Church arrived in 1962 followed by Eithne in 1963, both having studied at the Sumner Institute of Linguistics camps, and having the express purpose of translating the Scriptures into Wolof. Eric lived in a village with an African family for much of his first year. It was a time of intensive language work that laid the foundation for their translation ministry. It was a time of getting the vowels straight; *wer* – a worm, *wér* – to be healthy, *weer* – the moon, *weér* – to lean against, and the consonants *bàkk* – to praise, *bax* – to boil, *bàq* – the stomach. Mistakes were easy to make as Eric found when he mispronounced the q of *boqi* – to stare at, and achieved *bukki* – a hyena, while trying to pass the time of day with a lady on the train whose baby was staring at him! The mother angrily retorted that her baby was not a hyena though the missionary resembled one.

After their marriage in 1963 the Churches settled at Mekhé in the heart of Wolof country, the Cayor, where the language is profound, and, like Saxon, 'sweet as a nut'. The last battles against the French colonialists were fought in this area in 1882 and the last Wolof king died on the battlefield. Though tried by much illness and going through much cultural adaptation, they

Dakar – Eric D. and Eithne Church   (S. F. Warren)

enjoyed the four years of learning Wolof there. It was there that they began to translate the Word of God into Wolof.

They subsequently moved to the modern city of Dakar with all its possibilities of evangelism. Ten thousand copies of the Gospel of Matthew in Wolof were distributed by Geneva Bible House workers, and much other literature has since been distributed. The government finalized the alphabet in 1971, which helped in translation.

Eric has been involved with the radio programme for some years and Eithne has had a sewing class of fifteen to twenty girls where the gospel was clearly preached. Eric has also given a lot of time helping the French I.V.F. in the University, with its twenty or so members from the various African countries. Eric writes that there are probably no more than ten baptised Wolof believers.

Graham and Hermina Bode (U.S.A.) went to Dakar in 1976 and are holding meetings in their own home. Hermina also has a women's class. The need is great but it takes time to contact people.

Paul and Carol Bramsen (also from the U.S.A.) also went to Dakar in 1981 and are still busily engaged in acquiring the language.

When so many other doors are closing today, those in Senegal are still wide open and, despite the difficulties, there is an ear for the gospel. The opportunity thus presented must surely constitute a powerful challenge for those seeking the mind of the Lord as to the area of their future service.

21

The Horn of Africa

(Map page 154)

Somalia or, to give it the official name, the Somali Democratic Republic, is situated on the east coast of Africa and, with Ethiopia and Djibouti, is often referred to as the Horn of Africa. It is bounded on the north by Djibouti, on the west by Ethiopia, and on the south by Kenya. It comprises two areas previously under British and Italian control until 1960, when they received their independence and joined to become one sovereign state.

The central and southern regions are flat but, in the north, hills rise to 7,000 feet. The country is drained by the Juba River, into which flows the Wabi-Shebelle. The country is 246,155 square miles in extent. The capital is Mogadiscio, and other towns include Hargeisa, Kismayu, Merca and Berbera.

The population is approaching four million and is composed primarily of Somalis (98.8 per cent), the remainder being Arabs and Asians. The official language is Somali, but Arabic, English and Italian are also spoken. The people are Hamitic and, as early as the seventh century, they began to mingle with Arab and Persian traders along the coast. They became prosperous traders and by A.D. 900 had developed their own Swahili culture and civilization. They built cities of stone at many points along the sea-coast of Somalia and adjoining countries. The majority are nomadic in character and large numbers of Somalis are to be found in the Ogaden province of Ethiopia, in north-east Kenya, and in other East African countries. Sixty per cent of the population is dependent for a livelihood on the raising of camels,

Somali homes
(Tear Fund)

Spreading the gospel
(Tear Fund)

sheep and goats. Only 25 per cent are settled in the fertile zone between the rivers, and they produce bananas, sorghum, maize, beans, peanuts, sugar and cotton. Some textile manufacturing is carried on and there is a small canning industry. Deposits of iron ore, beryl, columbine and gypsum have been discovered, but have not yet been exploited.

An Arab sultanate was founded in the seventh century by immigrants from Yemen. The Portuguese landed in the fifteenth century and ruled some of the towns along the coast. French, Italian and British traders established themselves in the country in the nineteenth century and various treaties were entered into. After a rather muddled history, independence was achieved in 1960. There was a bloodless coup in 1969. Five years later a treaty of friendship and cooperation was entered into with the U.S.S.R. From 1972 tensions began along the frontier with Ethiopia and the Somali army invaded Ogaden to support insurgents in Ethiopia. The U.S.S.R. switched their support to Ethiopia and 15,000 Cuban troops poured into the latter country. Although military activity has ceased, there is still considerable unrest and there are one and a half million refugees in Somalia.

Remains of an early Christian civilization of the fourth century were discovered in 1854, but the country is now almost completely Islāmic. Over 99 per cent of the population are Muslims. Initially, religious liberty was guaranteed, but it was illegal to propagate any religion but Islām. Swedish missionaries entered Eritrea in 1866 and Somalia in 1875, when several hundred Muslims were converted. In the early part of the twentieth century the same mission sought an entry into Somalia. Apparently little was achieved, however, and they were expelled when Italy invaded Ethiopia. The Eastern Mennonite Board commenced schools and hospitals from 1952, but in 1962 Merlin Grove, one of their missionaries, was murdered by a Muslim fanatic. The Sudan Interior Mission commenced work in the country in 1954 and operated several schools. Unfortunately, in 1963 the government insisted that religious teaching should be from the Qur'ān and not from the Bible. The S.I.M. accordingly closed the schools, but many of the students came to the homes of the missionaries and there were many conversions. The New Testament was translated into Somali in 1966 and the Old Testament has since been completed.

One major problem is that all the converts have been young men, and there are no Christian young women for them to marry. It seems evident that conditions generally may become more difficult and that, if the gospel is to be spread through the country, opportunity must be taken without delay.

No assembly missionary has apparently been engaged in this country and no assembly work has been established.

22

The Kushite Kingdom

The largest country in Africa and the one with the greatest number of neighbours, the Democratic Republic of the Sudan lies across the middle reaches of the River Nile and is bounded by Egypt, Ethiopia, Kenya, Uganda, Zaire, the Central African Republic, Chad and Libya, and is completely landlocked. From north to south, the country has tropical forests, savanna, immense swamplands and scrublands, while sandy, arid hills lie between the Red Sea and the Libyan and Sahara Deserts. The White Nile flows through the country from south to north for 2,340 miles. Extreme desert conditions in the north-west give way to sandy steppes north of Khartoum. The total area is 967,500 square miles.

The principal occupation of the Sudanese is agriculture. Cotton, peanuts, sesame seeds, gum arabic, sorghum, wheat and sugar-cane are grown. Cotton and cotton-seed account for over half the country's export earnings, but large quantities of gum arabic are exported. Camels and sheep are reared and are sold to Egypt and other Arab countries. Sudan has also modest reserves of iron ore, copper and chrome. Her industries are small and are mainly the manufacture of cement, textiles, pharmaceuticals, shoes, and food processing. There has been extensive petroleum exploration, both off-shore in the Red Sea and also inland in the south-west, but reserves do not seem to be large. Hydro-electric power, generated by the Blue Nile grid, supplies most of the country's needs. Sudan receives considerable financial aid from

In the Gezira District   (S.G.M.)

the OPEC nations and is regarded as an economic link between the Arab and African countries, as is indicated, for example, in the location in Khartoum of the Arab Bank for African Economic Development. She has also received extensive assistance from Russia and China.

The population is over eighteen million, more than two million of whom are concentrated in a relatively small area at the junction of the White Nile and the Blue Nile. The principal cities of Khartoum, Omdurman and Khartoum North form a single metropolitan area. Other cities include Juba, the capital of the southern region, Wad Medani, Kassala and Port Sudan. The population is composed of two distinct cultures, and effective collaboration between them poses one of the principal internal problems.

The twelve northern provinces cover almost two-thirds of Sudan and include most of the urban centres. Two-thirds of the population live in this area and these are Arabic-speaking Muslims, with several distinct tribal groups, viz. the Kababish of northern Kordofan, who are a camel-raising people; the Jaalin and Shaiqiyya groups of settled tribes living along rivers; the semi-nomadic Baqqara of Kordofan and Darfur; the Hamitic Beja in the Red Sea area and the Nubians of the nothern Nile area, some of whom have been resettled on the Atbara River; and the negroid Nuba of southern Kordofan and Darfur in the western reaches of the country.

The three southern provinces have nearly a quarter of the population and a predominantly rural subsistence economy. The people here are mostly animists. The south contains many more tribal groups and languages than the north. The Dinka, numbering a million, is the largest of the many negro tribes. The Azande, Bor and Jo Luo are Sudanic tribes in the west, and the Acholi and Lotuho live in the extreme south and extend into Uganda.

The ethnic groups, therefore, are Arab-African and Nilotic-African. The official language is Arabic, but English and tribal dialects are also spoken. The religion of 70 per cent of the people is Islām; 25 per cent are animists or have their own indigenous beliefs; and only five per cent are Christian (including Roman Catholics). The literacy rate is only 28 per cent, so that it is necessary to teach people to read if a spiritual work is to be firmly established. Life expectancy is only 49, which again necessarily affects the attitude of the misionary.

The history of Sudan goes back nearly four thousand years, and possibly longer. The Kushites of the seventeenth century B.C. developed a remarkable civilization and by 1000 B.C. had established the great kingdom of Meroë. Among the remains of that period, one of the most outstanding is that of the Kushite temple to the sun at Musawarat, which is dated 500 B.C. The inner chambers still retain their fine glazed wall tiles of blue and red and their floor tiling of black and white.

Meroë traded with Rome, India and China, as well as with nearer countries. For some centuries the Kushites, or Nubians as they were then known, were under the domination of Egypt and they adopted the Egyptian gods and goddesses in their worship. When the New Kingdom of Egypt (1580–1050 B.C.) collapsed, the Kushites took possession of the country by the eighth century B.C., but in 650 B.C. they were driven back south by the invading Assyrian army. They retired to their old capital of Napata but, for economic and political reasons, King Aspelta (593–568 B.C.) transferred the capital to Meroë, 250 miles south.

'There now opened the second and greater stage of the Kushite

Kairouan – a saddler
(Tunisian National Tourist Office)

Hammamet – fortress – beach   (Tunisian National Tourist Office)

Kairouan – traditional costume

(Tunisian National Tourist Office)

Tunisia – feast costume

(Tunisian National Tourist Office)

Port Sudan   (Red Sea Mission Team)

kingdom, centred on the city of Meroë', writes Basil Davidson in *Discovering Africa's Past*, p. 21. 'The power and influence of Meroë lasted for about eight centuries.' The Meroë culture and civilization were quite remarkable. The Kushites had their own alphabet of 23 letters, for which there were signs, and their system of writing was superior to that of the Greeks. They built stone cities, where scholars taught and craftsmen produced pottery and metalwork. They mined and smelted iron and were far more advanced practically than their neighbours. Their queen mothers were always described as Candace (cf. Acts 8:27), one of the most famous Candaces being Queen Amani-Shakete, who ruled 41–12 B.C. In the fourth century A.D., the Greek-influenced Semitic kingdom of Axum in Ethiopia had begun to dominate the trade with the interior and in A.D. 350 King Ezana of Axum invaded the country and destroyed Meroë.

Sudan disintegrated into a number of smaller states until its conquest and unification by Egypt (or by Turkey as the dominant power in Egypt) in 1820. During the second half of the nineteenth century, Britain having replaced Turkish influence in Egypt, British governors, such as Sir Samuel Baker and General Charles Gordon, were sent to the Sudan to put a stop to the iniquitous slave trade in negroes, which was causing untold misery. In 1881, however, a religious leader appeared, who proclaimed himself as Mahdi. Taking advantage of conditions resulting from Ottoman-Egyptian exploitation and maladministration, he declared a *jihād*, or holy war, against the corrupt Egyptian administration. His army swept all before it; he wiped out the Egyptian army, led by the British general, Hicks Pasha, captured Khartoum in 1885 and killed General Gordon, one of the great heroes of Victorian Britain. But in 1898 General Kitchener routed the Mahdi and his army at Omdurman.

In his book, *The Boer War*, Sir Winston Churchill, who was at the Omdurman battle as a young man, wrote, 'Suddenly the whole black line, which seemed to be the Zeriba (a defence work of branches and thorns) began to move. It was made of men, not bushes. Behind it other immense masses and lines of men appeared over the crest; and while we watched amazed by the wonder of the sight, the whole face of the slope beneath became black with swarming savages. Four miles from end to end and, as it seemed, in five great divisions, this mighty army advanced swiftly. The whole side of the hill seemed to move. Behind the masses, horsemen galloped continually; before them many patrols dotted the plain; above them waved hundreds of banners, and the sun, glinting on many thousand hostile spear points, spread a sparkling cloud. Despite the terrifying appearance of the Mahdi's army, the spears of his warriors stood no chance against the

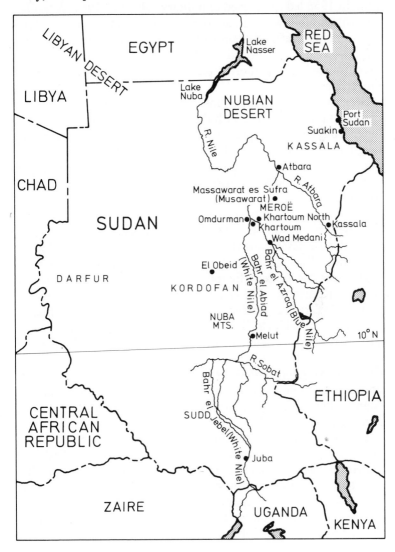

Maxim guns and artillery of the British. In a few hours, 11,000 of the Mahdi's followers lay heaped in the desert.'

Sudan was proclaimed a Condominium in 1899 under joint British and Egyptian administration, but in 1953 an agreement provided for Sudanese self-government and self-determination, and complete independence was achieved in 1956. A bloodless coup in 1958 led to a period of military rule until 1964. A civilian government followed, but another military coup occurred in 1969 and General Gaafar Muhammad Nimeiri became Prime Minister and, two years later, President. Administration has been formally decentralized and authority placed in the hands of Provincial Governors.

Because Sudan occupies most of the Nile basin, it is obviously in a position to interfere with the flow of water to Egypt, and the latter country has repeatedly sought to control its southern neighbour. Additionally, it has not been forgotten that Sudan was once part of Egypt. There is, therefore, always the possibility of some political move to bring the two countries more closely together.

Christianity was introduced to Sudan at an early date. H. S. Darling writes, 'In A.D. 548 Christian missionaries first crossed the Sudanese deserts and the country was quickly converted to the new faith. Two Christian kingdoms arose, one in the extreme north near the present Egyptian frontier, and the other to the south of Khartoum. The ensuing Christian era lasted for nearly a thousand years. Long before the end, however, the power of Islām was making itself felt. The more northern kingdom was under sustained pressure from Muslim Egypt for hundreds of years before it was finally overrun about A.D. 1350. The southern Christian kingdom lasted for perhaps 150 years longer than its northern neighbour, when it too collapsed before the armies of Islām. There is evidence in this case that great spiritual decline preceded the end.'

The Arab invasions not only introduced Semitic blood into a Hamitic race, but also brought, of course, the Muslim faith and the Arabic language and, as H. S. Darling says, These 'together have spread over the northern half of the country, superimposing themselves on tribal tongues and traditions and bringing about a surprising degree of unity. The Muslim influx failed to penetrate the fastnesses of the Nuba Mountains, where the tribes are still largely pagan and where Arabic, though the *lingua franca*, is not the natural tongue of the people. The southward drift of the tide of Islām was halted by the forbidding swamps and *Sudd* land of the White Nile and its tributaries. Crossing latitude 10° N the traveller moves south from the Muslim Middle East into pagan Central Africa. The transition is the more abrupt because the tribes that inhabit the *Sudd* area are resolute, almost arrogant, in their indifference to both Islām and Christianity. They are conservative pagans, adhering firmly to their traditional customs. Their lives are centred on their cattle, which they love above all else.'

Although Islām is the official religion of the country, considerable religious liberty was originally allowed. Indeed, a writer in 1952, referring primarily to the south, said, 'Every encouragement is being given to Christian missions to replace the negative and apathetic pagan beliefs with a dynamic Christian faith, which it is hoped will lead to the growth of moral stamina and of a sense of responsibility.' In the north, Christian missions were permitted to run schools and hospitals and some converts were won. Evangelistic work, specifically directed at Muslims was, however, forbidden. A government decree of 1933 stated, 'No mission station may be formed north of the 10th parallel of north latitude in any part of the Sudan which is recognised by the government as Muslim.' It is further laid down that no Muslim may change his or her faith without permission from the civil authorities.

Modern Christian activities commenced with the Church Missionary Society who, in 1899, opened a station at Omdurman. They were followed in 1900 by the American United Presbyterian Mission. A great deal of blessing was seen for many years. One report, for example, said that after 1916 the number of Christians increased by tens of thousands.

Assembly missionaries were in the country at a fairly early date. Mr. Alfred A. Hewstone, a widower from Canada who later went to Nigeria, spent 1913 to 1916 in Sudan, and Mr. and Mrs. Francis Parks, also from Canada, served there during 1913. Originally they had purposed to travel inland 300 miles by foot, to the north-east of Lake Chad and to settle at Kordofan in the hilly country of Darfur where several tribes numbering four million lived. But with many difficulties in the way of beginning this

Suakin – in the Muslim north   (Sudanese Embassy)

Shilluk tribesmen   (Sudanese Embassy)

work, Francis Parks began working at a trade on a mission station, while Alfred Hewstone made his headquarters at the city of El Obeid and began a work amongst the Copts. Soon after Alfred transferred to Melut, where he built his own bungalow. From there he travelled up the Sobat River, using medicine to open doors for the gospel amongst the Arabic-speaking members of the Shillucks, Nuers, Aswaks and Dinkas. Dinkas from Melut also exhibited an interest in the gospel. Mr. Hewstone also visited the Nuba Hills in order to reach the primitive Nubas, but because of war conditions the government prevented him from commencing work there in earnest. Within three years of coming to Sudan, Alfred Hewstone went to the U.S.A. where he married Annie D. Gillett and did not return to Sudan. There are no 'open' assembly missionaries in Sudan now, although there was for many years a small assembly in Khartoum.

Following the setting up of the Condominium in 1899, 'large numbers of foreigners and Egyptians entered the country to take up posts in the new administration. Among these were brethren belonging to "exclusive" assemblies, of which many were found in Egypt. These Christians found an active leader in Louis Schlauhort, an exclusive brother of German nationality. Halls were built and assemblies formed in Khartoum North, Omdurman, Atbata, Wad Medani and El Obeid. These assemblies were almost entirely made up of non-Sudanese, and evangelistic work does not seem to have been one of their main activities. Few, if any, Sudanese were converted through them. About 1925, political repercussions following the murder of Sir Lee Stack in Cairo resulted in a great reduction in the number of Egyptians working in the Sudan. Many officials seconded from Egypt were recalled to their home country, including the majority of those supporting the assemblies, which declined rapidly. The gatherings at Atbara, Wad Medani and El Obeid collapsed. Those in Khartoum North and Omdurman shrank to a shadow of their former size, and their weakness was accentuated by bitter internal strife. In 1948 assembly testimony ceased altogether in the Sudan.'

Nevertheless, God was still working out His purposes. In 1938 an old brother named Yassa Effendi, who was a member of the Khartoum North assembly, a B.F.B.S. colporteur, sold a Bible to a man named Enfedgian, an Armenian who owned a tailoring

Khartoum   (Tear Fund)

business in Khartoum. This led to the latter's conversion. 'The new convert grew spiritually and, after experiencing the fellowship of various Christian bodies in Khartoum, he became convinced of the truth of assembly teaching on baptism, worship and fellowship. He was greatly helped by Dr. John R. Olley and was led to reject the "exclusive" principle of the "closed" table. With the final collapse of the exclusive assemblies in 1948, he, in common with others, was exercised as to what path should be followed by the few scattered believers who remained.'

In 1949, Mr. and Mrs. H. S. Darling, from assemblies in Northern Ireland, went to live near Khartoum. They did not know of the existence of any assembly in Sudan and, therefore, broke bread in their own home. In 1950 they came into contact with Mr. Enfedgian and, through him, with the small circle of believers in Khartoum. In early 1951 an assembly testimony was re-established, the believers meeting each Sunday to break bread together in the house of one or another. This aroused some local interest and others were added to the company. At that time the B.F.B.S. representative in Khartoum reported that he had never known such a demand for the Bible as then existed.

In 1962, however, The Missionary Societies Act was passed,

which made missionary work almost impossible. This was designed, *inter alia*, at replacing missionaries, as far as practicable, with national workers. Every missionary society was compelled to apply for a licence to operate in the Sudan. The licence, if granted, was to be for one year only (renewable on application) and could be revoked at any time. Phil Landrum, writing in 1963, said, 'Missionary societies may not witness to persons professing any religion other than their own. Each missionary society will be assigned a limited area in which it may work. No missionary may talk of his Christian beliefs to any national under 18 without the written consent of his parent, which a government official may declare invalid.' Charitable work, famine and flood relief, the care of orphans, medical and educational work were severely restricted.

But, as J. H. Kane says in *A Global View of Christian Missions*, pp. 372–3, 'the final blow came on the 17th February, 1964, when the Minister of the Interior announced the "repatriation of foreign missionaries from the three southern provinces."' The missionaries 'were given seven days to settle their affairs, including the closing of hospitals, schools and dispensaries, and leave the country. The reason given by the government was that the missionaries were interfering in the internal affairs of the country, which was just a euphemistic way of accusing them of aiding and abetting the cause of the African insurgents who were fighting for their civil rights in the three southern provinces.

'The real reason for the expulsion was that the government was about to commit genocide in an attempt to force Arab culture on the south, and it did not wish to have any foreigners on hand to witness the slaughter. So the missionaries had to leave. Those in the north were permitted to stay on for the time being. In 1970 the government ordered the expulsion of all American missionaries who were registered with the Ministry of Education and some who were registered with other Ministries.'

In the subsequent movement against the south, thousands of innocent people were killed, and 250,000 fled as refugees to neighbouring countries. Kane says that the 'destruction has taken place in the smaller towns and villages in the high country; and the Christians, because they are the educated élite, have been singled out for special attack. Pastors and other church leaders have been killed, and churches and schools have been burned; but still the

Khartoum – a mosque
(Tear Fund)

C.M.S. Hospital,
Omdurman – leprosy
patients hear good news
(S.G.M.)

church not only survives but continues to grow. Revival has broken out in some places and thousands of new converts have registered their decision to follow Christ.' National believers have taken up the work laid down by the foreign missionaries – and the work goes on! Men cannot withstand God.

Many years ago Karl Kumm wrote in his book, *The Sudan*, 'Travellers have crossed the Sudan in all directions. They have gone at the risk of their lives. Many of them, like Mungo Park, have died in exploring it. They have left their tracks and traces all over it, but the missionary of the Cross has never entered most of its kingdoms. The Arab has gone there. He has conquered and killed and boasted of Allāh and Muḥammad, and multiplied houses and wives and slaves. But the messengers of the Cross have shunned the region. Only a handful have dared to enter it. Merchants have gone there; gold seekers have gone; hundreds of each are getting the riches of the land. . . . There is just a handful of missionaries on the Lower Niger, but in Central Sudan along the Upper Benue; around the vast overflowing waters of Lake Chad, in the mountains of Adamwa, in the plains of Wadai, in the rugged ranges of Darfur, in the deserts of Kordofan, among the teeming millions of the Sudan proper no missionaries are found, no voice is lifted up to cry "Behold the Lamb of God, which taketh away the sin of the world." '

The words are not completely accurate today. Some progress has been made since Dr. Kumm's day. But the greater part of the country remains untouched, and the Crescent has taken the place of the Cross.

Yet, what a pity that there was no one to take up the work when the opportunity was there in the last half century!

23

Home of the Pirates

During the decline of the Ottoman Empire, Tunisia became known as the shelter of the many 'Barbary' pirates who flourished along her coast. At a much earlier date, when the Roman Empire was the dominant universal power, she was described as the granary of Rome. Prior even to that she had been the centre of the mighty Carthaginian empire, but modern minds will probably associate her with the desert warfare of Rommel and Montgomery.

The smallest country in North Africa, with an area of only 63,378 square miles, Tunisia is located on the Mediterranean and lies between Algeria and Libya. The eastern end of the Atlas Mountains, with an average elevation of 4,000 feet, protrudes into Tunisia from Algeria. The central steppes, which represent a third of the total area, merge into the Sahara and are largely arid desert. The central coastal plains are devoted mainly to cattle grazing, although olive groves are also cultivated. The northern area is well-watered and fertile, and yields good crops of grain, citrus fruit, dates, figs, olives and almonds; it is this region that produced the large quantities of grain that satisfied the Roman needs. The country's resources also include petroleum, phosphates, iron ore, lead and zinc.

According to F. Allen, in *North Africa*, p. 221, 'Native industries are few. Tanning, leather-dyeing, mat-weaving, basket-making, the manufacture of carpets and clothing, leather-working, and the distillation of perfumes, and sponge and general fishing are the chief occupations.'

Tunis – native industry   (Tunisian National Tourist Office)

The total population is under seven million and is composed almost entirely of Arabs, although there are a few Europeans. Most of the people live along the coast or in the major cities, and almost half of them are under 21 years of age. The official language is Arabic, but French is also spoken. Ninety-nine per cent of the people are Muslims, but there are a few Christians (mostly Roman Catholics) and a small number of Jews.

Tunisia, Algeria and Morocco were described by the Arabs as Jāzirat al-Maghrib, or 'Island of the West'. Tunisia itself was formerly known as Numidia, but its people became known not only as Numidians, but also as Berbers (from the Roman *barbari*, referring to those who did not belong to the Roman civilization). John Gunther rather cynically remarks that 'Arab civilization is no more than a thin, brittle veneer on a hard Berber underlay. . . . Berbers are fairer than Arabs,' he says, and 'some have blue eyes.' Although Muslim, they are not as orthodox as most Arabs. 'An old apophthegm is that "a Berber is not a true Muslim, but only thinks he is". A good many Berbers were converted to Christianity before the Arabs came and engulfed them. Berbers have their own language, which is totally unlike Arabic and which does not exist in written form. Berbers have no written records and there is no Berber literature.'

The history of Tunisia may be traced back 3,000 to 4,000 years, although some writers claim that it is very much older. It is certainly over 3,000 years ago that the Phoenicians, who for centuries sailed along the north coast of Africa, founded settlements in what is now Tunisia. There are indications that it was they who introduced the Tyrian and Sidonian worship of Baal and Ashtaroth to the area. Tradition claims that it was a Tyrian princess who built Carthage and laid the foundation of the great Carthaginian empire, and there seems some ground for this.

Because her brother, Pygmalion, had murdered her husband, a priest of Melkarth, in order to confiscate his wealth, Elissa, the daughter of Matton I, King of Tyre, gathered her husband's fortune together and, in 822 B.C., fled with a small fleet to Africa. She landed near Tunis, regarding the nearby mountain Bou Kornine, with its two horns, as a symbol of the Tyrian goddess, Ashtaroth, the queen of the night, who was crowned with the horns of the crescent moon. Here she built Kirjath Hadeshath (i.e. the New City), or Carthage, of which she became queen under the name of Dido ('the fugitive'). Three centuries earlier, Phoenician explorers had founded Utica to the north of modern Tunis, as well as many other trading posts along the coast.

It was Carthage, however, which was to rise to fame and to become the most important Phoenician settlement outside the Levant. It was built on a promontory of red rock in the Bay of Tunis reaching out towards Sicily. It was an excellent location. As N. Nelson says in *Tunisia*, p. 15, 'To the north were impassable sea marshes, while to the south the large lagoon of Tunis formed a splendid natural harbour. Landward an isthmus, only three miles wide, could be defended easily. By the almost landlocked lake harbour the newcomers built on a low hill and, from the start, established friendly and commercial relations with the Berber

Near Tamerza – an oasis in arid desert (Tunisian National Tourist Office)

Carthage (Tunisian National Tourist Office)

horsemen of Numidia.' The sea entrance to the harbour was only 70 feet wide and, in emergencies, could be closed quickly by chains.

'The new city became rich, and magnificent palaces and temples arose. The central low-walled hill called Borsa, the fort, grew into a mighty citadel. Down from the citadel, with its arched recesses and parapets, to the market-place ran three streets edged with mansions six storeys high, each impregnable for they overhung steep ravines. Beyond the market-place slaves excavated a great waterway 1,066 feet wide in a cuplike shape which encircled an island. It was called the Cotlon, or drinking cup. From a palace-fortress on the island the leader of the Carthaginian fleet could study the shipping en route to the city. In the harbour were three- and five-tiered rowing galleys with metal beaks for ramming an oncoming enemy.'

Originally, Carthage had been little more than a supply port for the Phoenician ships sailing to and from Spain, but by 500 B.C. (and possibly earlier) the then powerful city had become the centre of an independent kingdom, commanding the trade of the neighbouring countries and becoming a strong commercial centre. Through Berber links, some kind of control was exercised over the trans-Saharan caravans and African gold and other goods were diverted to Carthage rather than other trading centres. They ruled over most of what is now Tunisia, occupied the Balearic Islands, and Sardinia, probed into Sicily, established colonies in Spain and conducted trade with Cornwall. The city itself had a population of 700,000.

The Carthaginians enjoyed their prosperity for some centuries, but were ultimately confronted with the rising power of the Roman republic. In 265 B.C. Carthage plunged into war with Rome for the domination of Europe. At one time during the long period of war, the Carthaginian general Hannibal, with an army including battle elephants, invaded Europe and crossed the snow-covered Alps and swept down into Italy with his elephants. The Carthaginians were eventually defeated at the naval battle of Mylae, and three Punic wars followed and in 146 B.C. Carthage was captured and destroyed. It was nearly a century before the Roman Senate agreed to the rebuilding of the old Punic capital.

The Romans took over the trade as well as the territorial possessions of Carthage. Julius Caesar and Augustus Caesar, in

Sousse   (Tunisian National Tourist Office)

Traditional marriage in the
Home of the Pirates   (Tunisian National Tourist Office)

Village mosque (Tunisian National Tourist Office)

A bedouin
(Tunisian National Tourist Office)

Sfax – Tunisia's modern face   (Tunisian National Tourist Office)

particular, extended the African dominion westward and eastward. But Rome fell and Genseric and the Vandals established control from A.D. 430 until A.D. 533, when they were driven out by the Byzantines. The Byzantine 'reconquest' did not last long. Arab Muslims, moving out of the Arabian Peninsula and across Egypt and Libya, conquered Tunisia and most of North Africa in the seventh century A.D. And, almost completely assimilating the existing population, they made Tunisia a major centre of Islāmic culture and political power.

In 1574 the Turks invaded Tunisia and incorporated it into the Ottoman Empire. As the empire declined in strength, the links with Constantinople began to weaken. In 1881 France occupied the country and converted it into a French protectorate. As in other Arab countries, the first half of the twentieth century witnessed a rise in nationalist movements and in 1934 Habib Bourguiba became the national leader of a movement for Tunisian independence from France. Full independence was finally achieved in 1956 and Bourguiba became Premier and later President. The country is divided into eighteen governates for administrative purposes, the governors being appointed by the President.

Since independence, Tunisia has moved towards a more modern secular society. Tunisian women are among the most emancipated in the Arab world. Polygamy was prohibited in 1957 and Tunisian women enjoy full civil and political rights. Consideration has also been given to the possibility of abolishing the Islāmic month-long fast of Ramaḍān, because of its effect upon industry. In 1974 Habib Bourguiba was appointed President for life and his incumbency has been marked by stability and progress. At the same time, the country is plagued by limited resources, acute problems associated with rapid decolonization, high unemployment and rapid population growth. An attempt in the 1960's to collectivize agriculture led to considerable unrest and farm production fell dramatically. The discovery of oil deposits in 1964, however, has been a great boon; petroleum exports now account for a third of export revenues. Very great financial aid has been given to the country by the U.S.A., but there is need for even greater investment. As a non-aligned country, Tunisia maintains friendly relations with West

Cathage – the cathedral   (Tunisian National Tourist Office)

and East, but emphasis is placed on the former rather than the latter.

The official religion in Tunisia is Islām. J. H. Kane says that 'at one time there were 200,000 Europeans in Tunisia, most of them Roman Catholics; but under an agreement between Tunisia and the Vatican in 1964, all but seven of the 109 Roman Catholic churches were closed. The churches, including the cathedral at Carthage, have been converted into museums, historical monuments, public libraries, or schools. In recent years the government has maintained strict surveillance over missionary activities.'

Christianity spread along the north coast of Africa, including Tunisia, at a very early date in the history of the church. At one point, there were over 500 bishoprics in North Africa – an indication of the extent to which the message had spread. Some of the outstanding church leaders of the past were North Africans, including Tertullian, Origen, Cyprian and Augustine. The Donatist schism and the Vandal invasion seriously weakened the church, and the reconquest by the Byzantines did little to revive it. Then came the Muslim invasion in the seventh century. The dwindling Christian witness finally died out by the twelfth century and Islām became completely dominant.

Yet, at the end of the second century, there was a large Christian community at Carthage, with Agrippinus as bishop, while the catacombs at Hadrumetum, containing the graves of thousands of believers, indicate the size of the church in that city in the south. It was at Carthage that the great Christian apologist Tertullian debated with the heathen Celsus with unsurpassed dialectical skill. His words to the senate at Carthage are still worth recalling. He said, 'We grow up in greater numbers, as often as we are cut down by you. The blood of the martyrs is the seed of the church. We are of yesterday, and yet we have filled every place belonging to you – cities, islands, castles, towns, assemblies; your very camp and companies, palace, senate, forum; we leave you your temples only.'

It was in the amphitheatre of Carthage in A.D. 202 that the noble Perpetua, her maid Felicita and a company of other Christians, were thrown to the wild beasts. When the great church administrator, Cyprian, succeeded Tertullian in the third century, the number of Christians had become so great that their shepherding taxed his abilities (and those of others) to the full. It

Bizerte – one of Tunisia's oldest cities   (Tunisian National Tourist Office)

was at Carthage (following his return from exile to Corbous, the popular thermal station still on the Bay of Tunis) that he was beheaded in 258. The decade of the Diocletian persecution took its toll of the church in Tunisia. It was at Carthage in 411 that Augustine (who was born at Souk Ahras in Algeria in 354) defended the faith against the Donatist teaching.

Yet, by the fifth century, the church was in a state of decline. The basic reason was probably that 'the Scriptures were never translated into the languages of the great Berber nation, which formed the mass of the people outside the coast cities. They were taught by men who were Latin scholars, working through teachers who spoke the native tongues.'

Secondly, there was never an appreciation of the responsibility of missionary enterprise. As one writer points out, 'The desert marches to the Sudan were open, and the Pax Romana was imposed upon all the desert tribes. The material, the open door, the opportunity under Roman security, all concerned to give to the North African church an unsurpassed opportunity to win Africa for Christ, from Carthage to the Cape. . . . A splendid opportunity, and a variety of human material, eminently fitted to use it, was granted by God to the North African Church; but the clash of her internal strife deafened her to the whisper of the still small voice. And with her downfall, and the removal of her candlestick out of its place, was delayed the evangelization of the Dark Continent for twelve long centuries.'

The country was – and still is – almost completely Islāmic. J. D. Fage argues in *A History of Africa*, p. 45, that, because they shared 'a common Afro-Asiatic linguistic and cultural background with the Phoenicians, the Berbers proved particularly receptive to Semitic cultural influences, and Phoenician influence paved the way for their later acceptance of the great monotheistic religions, first Judaism, then Christianity and Islām.' This is rather open to question, however. Although there was at one time a fairly large number of Jews in the country, the number of Berbers who became proselytes was relatively small. Certainly, comparatively few have been converted to Christianity from Islām in more recent days.

Louis IX of France, who led the Eighth Crusade, had determined to recover Tunisia from Islām for the Roman Catholic Church, and he accordingly landed on the ruins of Carthage in 1270. But in five months his army was decimated by the plague and he personally lay dead.

Twenty years later an attempt to present the gospel to the Tunisian people was made by a young Roman Catholic named Raymond Lull, to whom reference has been made earlier. Born in Majorca in 1236, Raymond Lull enjoyed the life of a courtier to the king of the Balearic Islands. One night he saw a vision of the crucified Saviour, which led to his conversion. He turned his back upon his old sinful and immoral life, and determined to give himself to the service of Christ. He was an accomplished scholar and had already published works on theology, philosophy and poetry. As the Saracens were laid upon his heart, he made a study of the Islāmic religion and also wrote a treatise contrasting it with revealed religion.

After studies in Arabic, he went to Genoa in 287 with the object of sailing to Tunis. But he was so overcome with the fear of torture and martyrdom that he did not join the ship. His conscience convicted him of his failure and led to a complete physical breakdown. When a second sailing was announced, he persuaded friends to carry him aboard and to leave him there, but

Sousse – The Great Mosque   (Tunisian National Tourist Office)

as soon as he was at sea his fears left him and he returned to mental and physical health.

On arrival at Tunis in 1292 he assembled the Muslim leaders and sought an opportunity of debating their religion against his, and said that he was open to conversion to Islām if their arguments proved stronger. For 23 years he debated in this way with the Muslim Ulema and won quite a number of converts to Christianity. On two occasions he was expelled from the country but was saved from death by the intervention of a Muslim doctor.

On his return to Italy, he spent several years lecturing and promoting the cause of Christian missions, and his representations to the Council of Venice resulted in the foundation of Chairs of Oriental Studies at Paris, Salamanca and Oxford. After labouring among Saracens and Jews in his native Majorca, he moved all over the Middle East, including Cyprus and Armenia, and Neander says, 'All of this he undertook with only one associate, without being able to gain the assistance of the powerful and opulent.' Returning to North Africa in 1306 he narrowly escaped death by stoning and had to leave in 1307.

In 1314 he returned once more, this time to Algeria, and laboured for some time among believers whom he had won to

Christ. Unable to suppress his longing for men's souls, he commenced preaching publicly, but was attacked by fanatical Muslims and stoned to death on 30th June 1315 on the sea-shore at Bougie.

Tunis, the capital of Tunisia, has a population of over a million. It is situated on the Lake of Tunis and is connected with the sea by a narrow canal. The Kasbah, which formerly contained the Palace of the Beys, barracks, and a prison for Christian slaves, is now merely a fortress. The Great Mosque dates back to the thirteenth century, and the Bardo, formerly a vast palace, and the K'sur Sa'īd nearby which was formerly the Bey's harem, and other buildings give an impression of the earlier splendour of the city.

In the nineteenth century large numbers of Jews lived in Tunis and the earliest missionary work of modern days was conducted here from 1829 by the Church's Ministry among the Jews. The mission had a church, bookstore and two schools. The North Africa Mission commenced work in Tunis in 1882. A Bible correspondence course was initiated and by 1964 over 20,000 Muslims had enrolled for the course. Unfortuantely, the government closed the bookstore which had been the headquarters and the N.A.M. were forced to transfer operations to Marseille. They still maintained work in Tunis and also at Sousse, which was the ancient Christian city of Hadrumetum. The Sousse catacombs, dating from the second century, are among the most authentic and interesting in the world and are the clear indication of the extent to which Christianity flourished there at that time. The Algiers Mission Band also had a station at Tozeur, on the edge of the Sahara Desert.

Assembly activities commenced in 1896, when Mr. S. Wasserzug went to Tunisia. Occupying a hall very near the centre of Tunis, they used those facilities to the full in selling Scriptures and in personal evangelism. His witness there was brief, however. He later served in Israel.

At about this time Miss Alice M. Case and Mr. Arthur V. Liley, assisted for a while by Miss L. Ethel Roberts, began a work in Tunis amongst Italians. After four years of considerable discouragement, they were greatly cheered when names on the Sunday-school register increased tenfold from eight to 80 within a comparatively short time. After twelve years Miss Case was in 1910 enabled, after much prayer, to transfer the meeting (with its

numerous classes) to another building with superior facilities in a different part of the city. Miss Case also engaged in an encouraging work at Bizerte and there, as well as at Tunis, she was signally helped by the young Italian evangelist, Signor Varvelli.

Mr. and Mrs. Ebenezer W. McGavin, who had previously served the Lord in India and Italy from 1893 and 1896 respectively were commended to Tunisia in 1909 by Australian assemblies. They commenced at the port and cosmopolitan city of Sousse and ran a Bible shop in the main street, where Scriptures in English, French, Italian, Arabic and Hebrew were sold. The Italians, of whom about 60,000 lived in Sousse, offered more encouragement in gospel work, and it was amongst them that the McGavins were for a long time engaged. A mission hall was the venue for meetings in various languages, and opportunities were also afforded of witnessing amongst naval personnel on French and British warships visiting the port. Sousse was also a transit centre for Italian troops and the missionaries were able to contact many of these. During the 1914–18 War, Mons Berthier, having been twice severely wounded, took an active interest in the Bible shop and was of great assistance to Mr. McGavin. Having been awarded the Croix de la Guerre, this enhanced his influence as he helped Mr. McGavin witnessing to soldiers and sailors. They lived through difficult days during the war between Italy and Turkey. Many Italians were killed by Arabs and constant police patrols were necessary. The activity of German submarines in the Mediterannean often rendered the McGavins short of personal necessities and material to minister to the poor.

Ebenezer McGavin was responsible for the well-attended meetings at Bizerte, but even with the help of Alice Case and Signor Varvelli, they found the work very exacting. The McGavins also carried on a work amongst Jews, especially Jewish children, but this proved hard and unrewarding. They returned to Australia in 1919 and Ebenezer eventually joined F. Kemp, H. H. Halls and R. Byrne as a Treasurer of *Australian Missionary Tidings* until his death in 1946. Mrs. McGavin predeceased him in 1926.

Dr. John R. Olley, M.D., D.B.M., a school teacher who was an able linguist in Greek, Hebrew and French and who later engaged in medical studies, was commended to Tunisia in 1919 by New Zealand assemblies. He had a consuming desire to present the truth to the then 200 million followers of Muḥammad. He went first to Gabès, where he studied both written and spoken Arabic, while helping in a Christian book depot and visiting British ships which came into the port. In 1921 he moved to the market town of Tozeur, the capital of the Djerid, a district which comprised four oases. There 12,000 people lived on the oasis bordering the great Tunisian Sahara of 2,500,000 square miles of desert – the home of twenty million Moors, Berbers and Arabs. Subsequently he lived at Monastir on the coast and then the oasis of Djara. He had to leave Djara because the people all around were either dead or dying of fever and the streams of the oasis were polluted with washing and sewerage. He accordingly moved to Tripoli (Libya) and later to Chad, eventually dying in Australia in 1956.

In 1922 Mr. and Mrs. J. Robb transferred from Algeria to Tunisia and laboured in the latter country till 1924. They had thought of settling at Monastir originally, but soon felt that the

Oasis de Gabès   (Tunisian National Tourist Office)

Lord was leading them to Sousse. There the Robbs opened a Bible depot in the Arab town, but discovered that the Jews and Europeans were more open to the Scriptures than their Muslim neighbours. From Sousse Mr. Robb toured many of the nearby towns and villages, in which he was nearly always well received.

After three years with the N.A.M., Mr. and Mrs. Peter J. Patching were commended to Tunisia from the U.K. in 1953 and were able to help in the small assembly at Tunis. Writing in 1956

In Tozeur
(Tunisian National Tourist Office)

Peter commented particularly on the churches excavated at Carthage and Dougga and the clear evidence that the baptistries were built for baptism by total immersion. At that time there was a Bible depot at Gabès. Also at Bizerte, then regarded by the French as the most important naval base in the Mediterranean after Toulon, and which was one of Tunisia's oldest cities, a Swiss couple and two Swedish ladies were witnessing to Muslims. Peter and his wife moved to France in 1958, but he died in 1971.

Mr. and Mrs. Paul Ferree commenced labouring at Aïn Draham in 1941 and saw the first fruits of their work nine years later. A small assembly of national believers witnessed fearlessly there in the face of very strong opposition. They opened a primary school for Muslim boys and girls, based on the daily study of the Bible. Academic studies were in the hands of Mlle. Marie Trautmann, commended by Switzerland assemblies, who had been trained under Dr. René Pache. The government social service sent them the neediest and most neglected children in Tunisia, and quite a number were converted. Some years ago Paul Ferree wrote, 'Thirty Mecca-bound pilgrims and two Ministers of State listened to our outdoor Bible class. Chedly, Ayyad and Tahar were teaching the Scriptures in the first years of their Christian lives, yet with a persuasion none of us possesses, and with an ability none of us acquires, teaching indeed the very doctrines we had taught them – sometimes with deeper insight.'

Peter Patching showed them the New Testament principles for the church – baptism, the Lord's Supper, discipleship – and it was not long before an assembly was established.

Mr. and Mrs. Donald R. Rickards went to Tunisia in 1951 and opened a shop in Kairouan, the fourth holy city of the Muslim world. From the day they entered it, the bricks came pounding against the door. Many Arabs came, nevertheless, and listened to an explanation of the gospel. In 1956 they were threatened with death, the shop was ransacked and the shop front smashed. In 1962 their main helper, a convert, was seized in front of the Gospel Hall and carried off to be interrogated by the police and then beaten. The next day the authorities closed the Bible centre in Tunis.

Donald presents some of the problems and the only possible solutions after considered thought. He says, 'Crises are unpleasant in experience. We do not deliberately, consciously provoke them. Our obligation, as Christians, is to live peaceably with all men. The questions might well be asked, "What produces crises?" "Can they be avoided?" "Why do you not carry on quiet ministries, as others are doing?" To answer these is not easy, for what one replies tends to be construed as a moral judgment on the efforts of fellow-workers. We certainly do not want to be guilty of that. However, a few things may be underlined.

'If we are determined to build a church in a Muslim country, and there are genuine results following our ministry, then the conflict or crisis situation will be in proportion to the importance of the results to the society. We simply cannot avoid experiencing this, if we seek to carry out our Lord's command. We can avoid it if we modify our operation. But we lose, at the same time, the effectiveness of our ministry in producing born-again persons. As a consequence, the church is not established.

'The answer is to win from Islām enough persons, in a limited time period, from several family networks, who can be brought to a sufficiently mature position in the Lord to carry on after the missionary has been forced to leave. This plan may call for at least 20 to 30 persons to be so trained. To see that number of Muslims converted, the particular ministry selected is of prime im-

Aïn Draham   (Tunisian National Tourist Office)

portance. It must be capable of reaching whole multitudes with the gospel story, in a limited amount of time. The converts must be well-born, followed up carefully, and they must have conviction as to their role in their country. An historical perspective must be imparted to them.

'Crisis, if the above plan is applied in a Muslim land, cannot be avoided. But neither can a church fail to materialize. Only let the missionary be a pace-setter. As he is gradually forced to leave the land, let him demonstrate to the nascent church how a Christian reacts under persecution. His motto is, "Watch ye, stand fast in the faith, quit you like men, be strong" (1 Corinthians 16:13).'

24

Time to Wake Up

In an extremely perceptive article in *Trinity World Forum* Dr. Edwin L. Frazen, dealing with the subject of mission strategy, draws attention to the major challenges before missions today. He argues that they fall into three categories: theological challenges from within the Christian context, socio-political challenges from outside, and challenges of strategy. His points are so important that we take the liberty of quoting *in extenso*. It is, of course, appreciated that some details may appear irrelevant in the context of assemblies.

Multan Convention 1982: selling Christian literature   (R. W. Orr)

He says, 'Theological confusion and ecumenical pressures present a challenge to the validity of our fundamental doctrines. There are six primary challenges confronting us that come from within the structure of Christianity:

1. *The challenge to the authority of the Bible:* the growing crisis in the acceptance of the inerrancy of the Scriptures. If this continues, it will adversely affect evangelical missions as the theological drift in the ecumenical community has affected missions in the mainline denominations.

2. *The challenge of neo-universalism:* that all men will ultimately be saved. This belief pierces the heart of missionary obedience.

3. *The challenge of syncretism:* combining different religious beliefs into one system – belief in Christ with other religious belief which compromises the uniqueness and finality of redemption through Jesus Christ.

4. *The challenge of contextualization:* attempting to make Christianity culturally relevant. In trying to make the gospel message relevant, more and more Christians are open to political interpretations of the gospel, which, they believe, will solve the grave social problems of the world. In some cases, Biblical theology has been replaced with a theology of liberation.

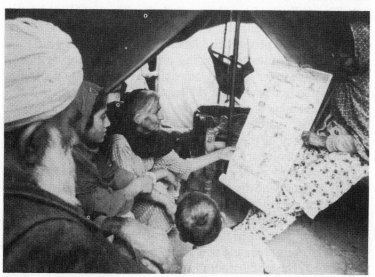

Muslims at literacy class   (Tear Fund)

5. *The challenge of neo-social, or holistic, approach:* placing ministry to physical needs equal to evangelism and preaching or even above them.

6. *The challenge of ecumenical dialogue:* dangers of shifting to a less conservative position. This underscores the urgent need for conservative evangelical theological education on all levels, especially in Third World areas.

'Forces opposing Christianity are getting stronger and more aggressive. We live in an hostile world. It is hostile toward Missions because it is hostile toward God and His Son, the risen Christ. There are a number of socio-political forces that are strong deterrents to evangelical advances toward world evangelization:

1. *The challenge of atheistic ideology.* Never before have there been so many people living in countries controlled by atheistic régimes.

2. *The challenge of non-Christian and anti-Christian religions.* There is a resurgence of these religions, particularly Islām, Buddhism and some tribal religions. Islām is probably the most determined and aggressive enemy of Christianity.

3. *The challenge of world economics.* A serious factor in world evangelization is inflation and the uncertainties of world economics.

4. *The challenge of population explosion.* The world population now stands at 4.5 billion. With an annual increase of 1.73 per cent, 77,850,000 people are added to this planet each year.

'Probably the most demanding challenge before us is that of developing ways for realizing our objective – finishing the task of world evangelization. Some challenges of strategy are:

1. *The challenge of inaccessibility.* About 2.5 billion people are virtually inaccessible to personal witness through traditional methods. Many of these live in countries closed to the physical presence of missionaries.

2. *The challenge of the cities.* Many of the more than 600 million non-Christians who live geographically and culturally near to Christian witness live in large urban areas.

3. *The challenge of insufficient personnel.* Considering furloughs, retirements, and deaths, there are not enough new workers to expand into new areas and new ministries nor to answer the call of the national church for more help.

4. *The challenge of developing national leadership.* Probably the

Multan – Pakistanis preaching and baptising   (R. W. Orr)

greatest need in the Church overseas is for capable national
leaders qualified to lead, well-trained theologically, and convinced
that our Lord's mandate to go into all the world with the gospel
was also given to their church.

5. *The challenge of cultural sensitivity.* How can the church be
authentically Christian and authentically Asian, or Latin, or

African? How much of his culture can a new believer in Christ retain without compromising the gospel?

6. *The challenge of life under totalitarian régimes.* At least one-third of the world's population lives under totalitarianism. Since increasing numbers will live under these systems, it is imperative that the national church be prepared for life in a hostile society.

7. *The challenge of church/mission relationships at home and overseas.* At home, the relationship of the mission to the church must be more than financial. Interaction should provide mutual benefit and assistance in building the body of Christ worldwide. Overseas, the missions need to have discernment to know when the church is mature enough to stand alone. The mission must be willing to work alongside, and under the direction of, the established national church.

8. *The challenge of maintaining standards.* Basic to all its work, a mission must evidence a confession of faith true to the Word of God, maintain a reputation for integrity and stability, have sound and open financial policies and procedures, operate under clearly defined and generally accepted principles and practices, demonstrate good management, and give thoughtful direction to its missionaries overseas.

'These are the challenges to world evangelization. They are specifically related to performance. How we deal with each one determines our effectiveness in evangelizing the world. The lateness of the hour compels us to move forward in the days ahead with aggressive, purposeful strategy.'

Perhaps it should be reiterated that not every detail is relevant in the context of assemblies, but much of what Dr. Frazen says is basically pertinent. These matters are, however, general, and this book deals with the particular rather than the general. In particular those who have gone overseas in fellowship with assemblies believe that they do so looking to the Lord for their direction and for their daily needs and that the strategy of mission is the strategy of the Holy Spirit calling and equipping the Lord's servants for the work He wants them to do. The involvement of the church in mission strategy is primarily 'praying to the Lord of the harvest, that he would send forth labourers into his harvest' (Luke 10:2). Effective prayer must be based on knowledge, the provision of which is one of the major reasons for this series of books.

Tomorrow – Muslim
or Christian?
(D. Frost,
S.I.M. International/
Wiedenest)

The countries referred to in the preceding pages are those in which Islām is almost completely dominant. The list is not complete even in that restricted field; other predominantly Muslim countries have already been covered in *The Restless Middle East* (Volume 1 in this series) and others in which the Islāmic influence is less will be dealt with in other volumes. Enough has probably been said in these pages, however, to give some indication of the size of the problem. Although there are probably 2,000 million in the world under Communist domination and 600 million Roman Catholics, there are nearly 800 million Muslims. By the end of the century, the number of adherents to Islām may well be 1,000 million.

It should be appreciated that Islām is not merely a religion. It is also a culture and a civilization. It is additionally a very strong political force. Islām reveals itself, not merely in the teachings of the Qur'ān or in the practices of its devotees, but also in its various forms of art. It affects life at every level and in every department.

Nor is it without specific purpose. The aim of Communism is to dominate the world, if practicable, by the arguments of dialectical materialism; if necessary, by world revolution and armed conflict. The intention of Roman Catholicism is to achieve recognition of its universal authority and rule, not only in the ecclesiastical sphere but also in the political realm. The objective of Islām is the conversion of the whole world to the teachings of the Prophet and, if possible, by the end of the century.

Islām is on the march and every available weapon will be employed to secure the desired end. An economic instrument lies to hand in the Arab possession of the oil wells. A financial one is found in the astronomical wealth of some of the Muslim countries. The possibility of a united front and its impressive strength lies in the brotherhood of the Arab nations. Military activity, political intrigue, religious zeal may all be employed, but there is no doubt regarding the ultimate intention.

With the increasingly rapid spread of Islām in the west, with Muslim shrines springing up on every side in so-called Christian lands, with Islāmic art and culture presented innocuously on every possible occasion, it is imposible to ignore the comprehensive campaign. Yet many seem totally unaware of the implications, and some seem ignorant even of the beliefs and practices of the Muslim world.

With a realization of the danger in the spread of Islām, and an awareness of the burgeoning population in the Arab countries, there is surely a greater incentive than ever to evangelize the Arab world. Yet the general reaction is the reverse. One often hears the illogical and somewhat fatuous reference to the difficulties of winning Muslims for Christ as though that is an indisputable argument for leaving them alone.

Doors are certainly closing in some countries, but they still remain open in others. Did Christ not die for Arab as well as for

Briton? Is the gospel irrelevant to 800 million people? As Ian Macpherson aptly put it recently, if we do not point them to the Carpenter of Nazareth, they will turn to the camel-driver of Mecca.

Appendix I

Who are the Brethren?

Each volume contains an answer to this question by a different contributor in order to show the measure of spiritual freedom in the application of New Testament church principles.

The brethren is the designation generally given to those Christians who reject all sectarian names, and who gather in the Name of the Lord Jesus Christ *alone*, with the avowed purpose of returning to Scriptural simplicity in church principles and practices. The reception accorded this title by those so designated is mixed. By some there is a reluctant acceptance; by others total rejection. The capitalizing of the 'B' is objectionable to the majority, who would prefer to be known simply as Christians, believers, brethren, members of the Body of Christ, or any other Biblical title belonging to ALL God's people, and not divisive in nature. This preference stems from one of the major tenets of their faith that all God's people in this present church age are members of the Body of Christ and therefore one, and should not be divided into various segments, each with its distinguishing name. Even more objectionable is the misnomer, Plymouth Brethren, given through a mistaken notion that Plymouth, England was the birthplace of a movement of which they are a part.

The history of the Church of God during the past twenty centuries since its inception at Pentecost has been one of recurring manifestations of the Holy Spirit's activity in restoring and revitalizing the testimony. Such times of revival have inevitably followed periods of declension and departure. On some occasions there has been a mighty outpouring of the Spirit's power in the convicting and converting of sinners, and thousands have been swept into the kingdom of God. In the Reformation movement of the sixteenth century, the blessed recovery of the truth of justification by faith was the outstanding feature. In the early part of the nineteenth century there was an evident movement of the Spirit that resulted in the recovery of many precious truths which had been long buried under the accumulated rubble of ecclesiastical tradition and superstition.

This movement of the Spirit appeared almost simultaneously in various places – Dublin in Ireland, Bristol, Plymouth, and London in England, and on the Continent of Europe. At the beginning, those involved were unknown to each other, and for some time there was no direct contact between the various groups. Under the convicting influence of the Spirit of God, godly Christians became deeply concerned regarding the low spiritual state prevailing among professed believers, and about the numerous unscriptural practices in the organized churches with which they were affiliated. Concern led to prayer, and prayer to Bible study, both individual and collective. As a result many neglected truths came to light under the illumination of the Spirit of truth. Among these were: the true nature of the Church as the Body of Christ, the position of the individual believer as a member in that Body, the priesthood of all believers, with a resultant liberty in worship, the sufficiency of the Name of Christ, the ministry of the Spirit, the simplicity of the Lord's Supper, the imminent coming of Christ to the air for His Bride and the Rapture of the Church, the literal, earthly, millennial reign of Christ.

The enrichment these truths brought into the lives of the believers, and the spiritual joy produced led, inevitably, to a deep desire to share them with others, and to meet collectively in such a manner as to be at liberty to preach and practise them in their church fellowship. Thus came into being a true restoration to Scriptural simplicity. Companies of believers began to gather simply in the Name of the Lord Jesus Christ, recognizing the unity of the Body, and receiving all who belonged to Christ.

They owned allegiance to no denomination, took no sectarian name, recognized no human head or earthly headquarters, and sought only to return to the New Testament pattern for the Church. Characterized by a deep concern for the salvation of the lost in the homeland and abroad, these assemblies were soon sending forth gifted evangelists, teachers, and missionaries to carry the glorious evangel of Jesus Christ near and afar. When men and women were brought to a saving knowledge of Jesus Christ through the labours of these servants of Christ, they were instructed in the truths that meant so much to them, and thus companies of believers began to meet as local assemblies in many parts of the world. These assemblies were strictly autonomous, governed solely by elders in the local congregation, and in no way subject to outside legislation or leadership. The link between these assemblies was not an organizational one, but that of fellowship based upon a common salvation (Jude 3), membership in the Body of Christ (1 Cor. 12: 12–13), and the recognition of one Lord, one faith and one baptism (Eph. 4:5).

If this is termed a movement, then it should be designated, not as a brethren movement, but as a movement of the Holy Spirit calling the Church back to its pristine position of Scriptural simplicity. The assemblies of Christian brethren today are not concerned about perpetuating a nineteenth-century movement, but in holding fast to the apostolic principles and practices as enunciated in the New Testament Scriptures. While gratefully acknowledging their indebtedness to those who pioneered the way back to the Scriptural pattern, in situations requiring a decision, the question raised is not, 'What was done in the past by the early brethren?' but 'What saith the Scriptures?'

The assemblies (for so the brethren designate their local gatherings) are firm in their loyalty to 'the faith once for all delivered unto the saints' (Jude 3), including the virgin birth, the impeccable life, the vicarious death, the bodily resurrection, the literal ascension, and the enthronement of Christ as Great High Priest and Advocate of His people. They unreservedly accept the Bible as the inspired, infallible and inerrant Word of God, the sole guide for the faith and practice of the people of God. Much of their preaching and teaching is of an expository nature, with considerable emphasis on prophetic truths. They believe in the total ruin of mankind through the Fall of Adam in Eden, and the futility of all human efforts for salvation. They believe in redemption by the blood of Christ and regeneration by the Holy Spirit, by which alone man is fitted for entrance into the kingdom of God. They believe in salvation on the principle of grace alone, procured through individual faith in Jesus Christ. They believe in the eternal security of the born-again believer, in a heaven for the saved, and a hell for the unrepentant who die in their sins.

These fundamentals of the faith are the common property of all true evangelicals. Not only so, but many of the 'recovered' truths of the nineteenth-century renascence are today being faithfully proclaimed in thousands of denominational and independent churches. This is a cause for heartfelt gratitude to God. Undoubtedly the written and oral ministry of many gifted servants of Christ connected with the assemblies of brethren has contributed to the dissemination of these truths.

Possibly the two characteristics which distinguish the brethren assemblies from many other fundamental, independent church groups are to be found in their views regarding worship and ministry. Collective worship is given priority in importance. There is a complete rejection of liturgical formalism; and strong reservations regarding the appropriateness of designating services for evangelism, prayer, Bible study, etc. as worship meetings. The term is reserved for a service set apart in a definite way for the giving to God of thanksgiving, praise, adoration and homage by the priestly family of believers. In most instances, this is the weekly remembrance feast of the Lord's Supper. Such services are not programmed in any manner, are not conducted by any designated leader, but are left open to the leading of the Spirit.

As to ministry, clerisy is totally rejected. Gifts from the Risen Head of the Church (Eph. 4: 8–13), distributed by the Spirit (1 Cor. 12: 4, 7, 11), are gratefully recognized for evangelism, pastoring and teaching. The human ordination of such is deemed unnecessary and unscriptural. The dividing of the members of the Body of Christ into clergy and laity is likewise believed to be artificial and unscriptural, tending to stifle the development and functioning of these divinely given gifts. Because the title Reverend lends support to this notion of a clergy as distinct from the laity, it is rejected by those who minister among the assemblies. Let it not be thought, however, that these views have robbed the assemblies of brethren of adequate, edifying preaching and teaching. By no means. Rather, it has enriched their ministry, both oral and written. There are few libraries in evangelical circles that do not contain the writings of Anderson, Bellett, Darby, Groves, Grant, Ironside, Kelly, Lincoln, Mackintosh, Newberry, Soltau, Trench, Wigram, Wolston, and many other brethren. This volume, and the others in this series, will contain the names of many honoured missionaries from the assemblies who have laboured for the Lord around the globe.

Because of the emphasis on fellowship rather than on membership in the assemblies of Christian brethren, membership rolls are a rarity. This precludes any accurate information as to their numbers. And, not only are local rolls unavailable, a complete list of all assemblies seeking to follow the New Testament pattern would be impossible to compile. As in Gideon's day, it is not the quantity of professed followers that is important, but rather the quality of dedication to the Lord that counts.

HAROLD MACKAY

Appendix II

Missionary Service Groups

THE ASSEMBLY CONTRIBUTION IN OVERSEAS MISSIONS

As indicated in Appendix I the nineteenth century witnessed the beginning of a number of spontaneous groups aiming, as far as possible, at maintaining the simple and flexible church order of New Testament times. The local churches which were formed became known as assemblies of brethren because of the frequent use of that term in the book of Acts.

Many of the early brethren were also impressed with the obligation to fulfil our Lord's commission to go into all the world and, as early as 1829, one of the early brethren, Anthony Norris Groves, with his wife, two sons and others renounced his lucrative practice as a dentist in Exeter to become a missionary in Baghdād.

Despite privation and sorrow (including the loss of his wife and baby daughter), Groves proved the Lord's sufficiency in every circumstance, not only in Baghdād but also in India, where he subsequently settled to serve the Lord and to which country he also took a band of missionary recruits.

Throughout his overseas service Groves followed God's leading and trusted Him to supply his needs. Others followed his example and in the last century and a half thousands of believers have gone overseas from brethren asemblies, adhering strictly to their understanding of the principles of missionary endeavour recorded in the New Testament.

Anthony Norris Groves 'was completely unfettered by tradition or precedent and regarded the principles and practices of Missionary Societies as having no validity or relevance to himself. It was to the Word of God that he turned for his guidelines' (*A. N. Groves*, by Dr. F. A. Tatford).

Groves had no doubt about the importance of prayer in overseas missionary work and on his return home from India in

September 1852 it is recorded that he made a special plea for prayer at a meeting in Tottenham, London.

As a direct consequence of that plea one J. Van Sommer commenced the *Missionary Reporter* in 1853, two months after Groves' death, and this continued until about 1861. The reason for its cessation is not known.

Van Sommer clearly regarded it to be the responsibility of local churches to stimulate and maintain missionary work in their own neighbourhoods, their country and overseas (*Missionary Reporter*, August 1853, page 9). He wrote 'The Editor would prefer direct communication between churches and individuals and the Lord's servants. But where money is sent he will forward it to the persons named; if no directions are given he will apply it to the best of his judgment' (*Missionary Reporter*, March 1854, page 120).

ECHOES OF SERVICE

In 1871 a circular was sent to various assemblies and individuals suggesting that a missionary periodical be started to publish letters from workers in foreign lands with the intention of stirring up intelligent prayer on their behalf. The new project was well received from its beginning.

With the first edition of *Echoes of Service* in 1872 (then called *The Missionary Echo*) the then Editors, Henry Groves and Dr. J. L. Maclean, defined their role as, 'fellowship in the gospel'. Their primary interest was those who had 'gone forth to other lands simply in His Name to preach the Word on their own responsibility to the Lord. . . .' (*Missionary Echo*, January 1872, page 1). Those early Editors included letters from some serving with missionary societies and from some who served the Lord whilst pursuing their ordinary callings abroad.

With the subsequent rapid increase in the number of missionaries it was inevitable that priority for space in the magazine was given to those who were in full-time service.

From the first issue, those responsible for the magazine made it clear that they were willing to act, not only as Editors of the magazine, but also as treasurers of any funds received for missionaries. The Editors did not declare any Trusts to define their objects and the work of 'Echoes of Service' has continued without any formal constitution or corporate entity. Nonetheless, under the name 'Echoes of Service' it has been recognized in court as a valid charity and is registered as such by the Charity Commissioners in Great Britain under the provisions of the Charities Act, 1960.

The ministry of the Editors has grown out of their own personal exercise before God on the one hand, and the trust placed in them by overseas missionaries, and assemblies and individuals at home on the other.

'Echoes of Service' is not a Missionary Society; the Editors are content to be known as a Missionary Service Group. They do not decide whether a missionary is called of God and whether he has the requisite spiritual qualifications and character to serve the Lord in that way. This is regarded as the responsibility of the local church.

The Editors do not (and cannot) have any authority to direct missionaries as to the place or nature of their service or give any promise of support but they are willing to advise about conditions overseas, about government requirements and to put intended missionaries in touch with workers already serving in the area where they are exercised to serve the Lord.

The number of missionaries to whom the Editors of *Echoes of Service* extended their fellowship continued to grow, as is shown in the addendum to this Appendix. In the early days the Editors were in touch with some serving the Lord in many countries including the U.S.A., Australia and New Zealand. They also included in their fellowship workers with whom they were able to communicate, no matter from what country they were commended.

In 1972 it was decided that as Missionary Service Groups had become well established in the U.S.A., Canada, Australia and New Zealand, each publishing its own list of missionaries and news for prayer, the time had come for the Echoes' *Daily Prayer Guide* not to include the names of such workers unless they were married to a national from the British Isles. Since then this policy has been taken to its logical conclusion and only the names of those commended from the British Isles are now included in the *Daily Prayer Guide*.

There are two regular publications: *Echoes of Service*, published monthly, giving extracts from missionaries' letters and missionary articles to stimulate and encourage interest and prayer; and the *Daily Prayer Guide*, published annually, giving a wealth of personal information about some of those missionaries with whom the Editors communicate.

Whilst the emphasis adopted by each Missionary Service Group differs in some respects, and all except 'Echoes of Service' are incorporated in some way, these factors are prominent in the ministry of each:

1 publishing a list of some missionaries with whom they have fellowship;
2 publishing missionary information;
3 forwarding gifts;
4 caring for the Lord's servants.

All the Missionary Service Groups send gifts for missionaries without any deduction whatever, looking to the Lord for the expenses of their ministry.

NEW ZEALAND TREASURY

When immigrants from assemblies in the British Isles settled as pioneers in New Zealand they brought with them a missionary interest which had been developed in their homeland. When Mr. James Kirk and a party of five others went in 1896 from New Zealand to Argentina and Malaya respectively, interest increased.

The *New Zealand Treasury* magazine for the ministry of the Word of God and reports of the Lord's work was commenced in 1899, the Editor being Mr. C. H. Hinman. Publication of news of the Lord's work in other lands gradually became incorporated, and this side of the journal's usefulness steadily increased as the number of workers multiplied. Owing to the difficulty experienced by Christians and assemblies in rural areas in communicating financially with missionaries overseas, Mr. Hinman was asked repeatedly to forward sums of money. This started a gratuitous service which has steadily grown in scope and usefulness. Successive Editors wisely saw the desirability of having co-treasurers so that this service might be rendered impartially and so that dependable account might be given of their stewardship and their ministry continued under the designation 'Missionary Funds (N.Z.) Incorporated'. The Treasurers have a single aim, and the office exists for the purpose of providing a channel for the remittance of funds and the dissemination of news of work and workers and matters of missionary interest. In no sense do the Treasurers comprise a Mission Board. Their calling and purpose is solely to serve, not to legislate.

A separate list of missionaries commended from New Zealand is compiled and published annually as a free supplement to *The Treasury*.

HOME AND FOREIGN MISSION FUNDS, SCOTLAND

It was in 1876 that the first two assembly missionaries were commended from Scottish assemblies and the number steadily grew. Following the departure of Frederick Stanley Arnot to Central Africa in 1881 brethren in Scotland became increasingly concerned about the care of their missionary brethren and at the suggestion of J. R. Caldwell and Thomas McLaren, 'Home and Foreign Mission Funds' was commenced.

In 1908 a Missionary Council was formed to broaden the base of the Fund, to help and advise missionary candidates from Scotland and to review problems arising on the mission field. The Council has never claimed to be a Selection Board, regarding the responsibility for commendation as proper to the local assemblies.

A monthly newsletter was commenced in 1958, specifically to make known information about Scottish missionaries. It was designed to be used in conjunction with *Echoes' Daily Prayer Guide* in which missionaries commended from Scotland are named.

AUSTRALIAN MISSIONARY TIDINGS

It was in 1910, as a result of the exercise of brethren in Sydney, Australia, that a work was commenced to serve those servants of the Lord from Australia commended to work at home or overseas in a full-time capacity, but with particular emphasis on those serving overseas. The object of those brethren is stated in a foreword in the first issue of *Australian Missionary Tidings*: 'to give information month by month and extracts from letters received from those who have gone forth from Australia and are engaged in the Lord's work in the mission field'. The Editors indicated that they would 'gladly take charge of any sum that might be contributed by those whom the Lord may lead . . . for servants in the field, in the same way as those conducting "Echoes of Service" have done for many years'.

Since that time the title of the magazine has been shortened to *Tidings*. Like the other Missionary Service Groups, 'Australian Missionary Tidings' is not a Missionary Society in any sense and the complete freedom of missionaries, as the Lord's servants answerable only to Him and not to men, is recognized and maintained in practice.

Equally the autonomy of local assemblies is recognized and whilst the brethren responsible for 'Australian Missionary Tidings' are glad to act in co-ordinating activities of assemblies in relation to the missionary enterprise as a whole, each assembly is perfectly free to act before the Lord in deciding whether they avail themselves of the services of 'Australian Missionary Tidings' or not. Like *Echoes of Service, Tidings* gives extracts from missionaries' letters, as well as articles on aspects of overseas missionary work. The magazine from time to time contains a list of those missionaries who have been commended from Australia.

CHRISTIAN MISSIONS IN MANY LANDS, U.S.A.

Early this century a two-page news-sheet of missionary news began to be issued periodically by Mr. L. A. Steen. In 1904 he invited R. J. McLachlan to join him in editing it. *Voices from the Vineyard*, as it was called, was incorporated in 1936, the first president of the corporation being R. J. McLachlan, who continued to hold that office until his death in 1961.

'Christian Missions in Many Lands Ltd.' was formed and incorporated in 1921. The prime movers were Richard Hill, Charles Bellinger, and a few other brethren. The function of 'Christian Missions in Many Lands' has been the legal aspect of assembly missionary work. Governments prefer to deal with a corporation rather than with an individual missionary or assembly. 'Christian Missions in Many Lands' has enjoyed good relations with the United States Government and has assisted in obtaining passports and visas to many mission fields.

In 1925 the Missionary Fund was started by three brethren and the work was carried on by Captain John Barlow, later of Toronto. Later the membership was expanded to include Messrs. P. D. Loizeaux and Howard Gillings, and in 1939 Mr. John Reid was asked to join. The Missionary Fund functioned for 35 years until 1960.

Meanwhile, on 25th January 1938, 'The Fields Inc.' was formed by Messrs. Charles Bellinger, Richard Hill and John Bloore. The first issue of *The Fields* magazine was in February 1938. Until 1971 'Voices from the Vineyard' and 'The Fields' published periodicals and served as transmission agencies to forward gifts to missionaries. 'The Fields' also issued a list of missionaries commended by assemblies in the United States and Canada, beginning in the year 1951. It is called the *Missionary Prayer Handbook*.

In 1971 brethren in the metropolitan area of New York City agreed to unify four missionary agencies under the name 'Christian Missions in Many Lands, Inc.' This involved bringing the two magazines, *Voices from the Vineyard* and *The Fields* under the jurisdiction of 'Christian Missions in Many Lands'. The name of 'Christian Missions in Many Lands Ltd.' was slightly changed to 'Christian Missions in Many Lands Inc.' The Julia Hasse missionary home in Union City, N.J., was also included in this new body. Fred MacKenzie, who was President of 'Fields' at the time, headed the new organization but was called home in 1981.

One magazine called *Missions* is now published 10 times a year without charge.

MISSIONARY SERVICE COMMITTEE
CHRISTIAN MISSIONS IN MANY LANDS (CANADA)

At a meeting in 1940, representatives of assemblies discussed the problem of distributing support for missionaries due to wartime regulations about sending funds from Canada. The following were asked to form a Missionary Service Committee to meet this situation: George Cowan, S. K. Petersen, John Smart, S. F.

Sommacal and E. G. Taylor. The facility that the committee provided proved to be so useful that it has been continued since that time, even though foreign currency control regulations no longer exist.

A sister organization, 'Christian Missions in Many Lands (Canada)' was launched in 1944. From the beginning, the membership of 'C.M.M.L. (Canada)' and the 'Missionary Service Committee' has been interlocking but not identical; both groups have one address and one office staff. 'Missionary Service Committee' accepts funds from donors, issues receipts for income tax purposes, and forwards gifts to missionaries and homeworkers. 'C.M.M.L. (Canada)' represents commended missionaries to government, assures governments both home and abroad that the person is a bona-fide missionary, assists individuals in getting passports and visas, issues Letters of Guarantee when required, and maintains an emergency re-patriation fund for special occasions.

Missionaries commended from Canada are included in the *Missionary Prayer Handbook* issued by 'C.M.M.L. (U.S.A.)' and letters from Canadian missionaries are included in *Missions*, which is sent out without charge.

The Canadian groups are entirely independent of 'C.M.M.L. (U.S.A.)' but work in harmony with the American brethren. A meeting of these missionary service groups from both sides of the border is held annually for discussion of common problems.

OTHER MISSIONARY SERVICE GROUPS

In addition to the Missionary Service Groups named here, other groups have come into being in various parts of the world to support the work of assembly missionaries overseas, although not necessarily carrying out all the functions of those groups previously described in this Appendix and some are guided by somewhat different principles; among such are:

1 'Harvest Fields', Belfast;
2 'Lord's Work Trust', Kilmarnock;
3 'Scriptural Knowledge Institution', Bristol;
4 'Wiedenest Bible School', Germany;
5 'Service Missionaire Evangelique', Geneva, Switzerland;
6 'Comité de Service', Vichy, France.

Addendum to Appendix II

The Assembly Contribution Overseas
1875–1970

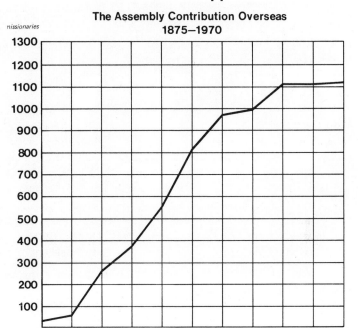

missionaries

1300 1200 1100 1000 900 800 700 600 500 400 300 200 100

year 1875 85 95 1905 15 25 35 45 55 65 70

1972–1982

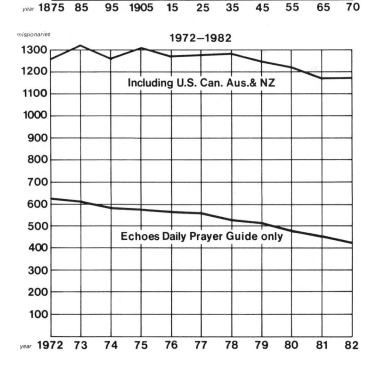

missionaries

1300 1200 1100 1000 900 800 700 600 500 400 300 200 100

Including U.S. Can. Aus.& NZ

Echoes Daily Prayer Guide only

year 1972 73 74 75 76 77 78 79 80 81 82

Missionhaus Bibelschule Wiedenest

Appendix III

Record of Missionaries' Service Since 1872

(For a variety of reasons the dates given may not agree with those shown in the lists issued by missionary service groups or include the whole of an individual's service overseas.)

AFGHANISTAN
Harper, Dr. H. F., 1966
(from and to Pakistan,
from Pakistan,
to Iran), 1971–1973
Harper, Mrs., 1966
(from and to
Pakistan, from
Pakistan, to Iran), 1971–1973

ALGERIA
Arnaud, Mme. V., 1900–1905
Barker, Miss G. G., 1952–1953
Barnes, R. J., 1937–1943
(from Spain)
Barnes, Mrs., 1938–1955
(from Spain)
Blackmore, J. T. C., 1905–1910
Briggen, Mlle. L., 1901–1949
Buckenham, E. T. R., 1952–1957
(to France)
Buckenham, Mrs., 1952–1956
(to France)
Castle, Miss L. E., 1927–1956
Charters, A. H., 1922–1955
(to France)
Charters, Mrs., 1922–1955
(to France)
Clark, Miss C. A., 1921–1945
(See Mrs. T. U. Speare)
Crabtree, Miss E. A., 1924–1958
Daniel, Mlle. M., 1962–1982

Davis, Miss E. M., 1912–1924
(to Italy)
Dobbs, Miss H. O., 1919–1936
Dodds, Miss M. J., 1911–1912
Dudgeon, Miss D. K., 1919–1964
Dudgeon, Miss S. M., 1923–1964
Dufey, J., 1924–1951
Dufey, Mme., 1924–1961
Gieser, Miss M. E., 1911–1915
(from Spain)
Gillard, Miss E. A., 1883–1914
Griffiths, J., 1897–1952
Griffiths, Mrs., 1899–1952
Handford, Miss F., 1894–1897
Hare, Miss V. E., 1912–1914
(See Mrs. H. G. Young)
Harris, Miss I. R., 1954–1981
Hepburn, M E., 1935–1954
Hepburn, Mrs., 1934–1954
Humbert, A., 1919–1921
Humbert, Mrs., 1919–1921
Hunter, J., 1903–1913
Hunter, Mrs., 1911–1913
Lamb, H. G., 1897–1947
Lamb, Mrs., 1899–1949
Marsh, C. R., 1925–1962
(to and from
Chad, to Chad), 1967
Marsh, Mrs., 1925–1963
(to and from
Chad), 1967–1969
Marsh, Miss D. M., 1953–1971
(to France)

Mayor, H. S., 1881–1931
Mayor, Mrs., 1881–1931
Mee, Miss A. P., 1952–1981
(to France)
Merralls, Miss E. M., 1888–1892
Mills, W., 1926–1929
Mills, Mrs., 1912–1946
(to Nigeria)
Moore, A., 1891–1906
Moore, Mrs., 1891–1906
Moore, J., 1933–1954
Moore, Mrs., 1935–1954
Moore, P. M., 1908–1933
(from Spain)
Moore, Mrs., 1908–1912
Müller, Miss A., 1934–1940
Murdoch, Miss L. A. L., 1922–1962
(to France)
O'Conor, Miss L., 1927–1939
(to and from
Nigeria), 1949–1956
Pearse, G., 1880–1882
(from France)
Pearse, Mrs., 1880–1882
(from France)
Pearse, Miss H., 1917–1945
Perkins, F. L., 1950–1976
Perkins, Mrs., 1952–1976
Phillis, C. L., 1936–1946
Pomeroy, H. J., 1902–1922
(to Nigeria)
Pomeroy, Mrs., 1902–1922
(to Nigeria)
Richard, C., 1912–1914
Robb, J., 1915–1922
(to Tunisia)
Robb, Mrs., 1919–1922
(to Tunisia)
Scott, K. W., 1940–1956
Scott, Mrs., 1944–1956
Sears, S. J., 1926–1966
Sears, Mrs., 1926–1966
Shallis, R. H., 1949–1957
(to France)
Shallis, Mrs., 1949–1954
(to France)
Sills, Miss E., 1930–1960
Sinclair, Miss J. A. E. C., 1932–1966

Speare, T. W., 1904–1947
Speare, Mrs., 1904–1940
Speare, Mrs., 1945–1963
(formerly Miss Clark, C. A.)
Squire, Mlle. R., 1911–1944
Steiner, Mlle. M., 1946–1951
Wall, E. A., 1916–1926
Wall, Mrs., 1920–1926
Wicks, Miss F. R. J., 1950–1973
Wordler, Miss A. M. I., 1911–1925
Young, H. G., 1910–1962
Young, Mrs., 1914–1962
(formerly Miss Hare, V. E.)

BANGLADESH
Bourne, Miss R. M., 1969–1971
Game, P. K., 1967–1980
Game, Mrs., 1967–1980
McKenzie, J. S., 1961–1970
McKenzie, Mrs., 1961–1970

CHAD
Baar, M., 1952–1968
Baar, Mrs., 1952–1968
Bouttet, Mlle. C., 1958–1975
Burkhardt, A., 1947–1954
Byard, Miss M., 1971–1977
Clark, N. R., 1973–
Clark, Mrs., 1973–
Cowell, L., 1964–1975
Cowell, Mrs., 1964–1975
Elliott, J. V., 1958–1967, 1977–
Elliott, Mrs., 1958–1967, 1977–
Ford, D., 1965
Ford J., 1949–1952
(to Central Africa)
Ford, Mrs., 1949–1952
(to Central Africa)
Ganz, W., 1936–1952
Ganz., Mrs., 1936–1952
(formerly Mrs. Axtell
see Nigeria)
Gounon, Mlle. D., 1958–
Hewlett I., 1964–1977
Hewlett, Mrs. 1964–1977
King, Miss M., 1958–1974

Lewis, Miss A. M., 1946–1950
MacDougall, Miss J., 1957–
MacLachlan, Miss M., 1934–1939
(see Central Africa)
Mansfield, Miss M., 1969–1974
Marsh, C. R., 1963–1967
(from and to
Algeria, to Chad
1967–1968)
Marsh, Mrs., 1963–1967
(from and to
Algeria)
Metz, J., 1952–1971
Metz, Mrs., 1952–1971
Olley, J. R., 1926–1956
(from Tripoli)
Price, C. H., 1950–1967
Price, Mrs., 1950–1967
Price, R., 1963–1974
Price, Mrs., 1964–1974
Robinson, P. A., 1957–1968
Robinson, Mrs., 1957–1968
Rogers, F. W., 1934–1967
Rogers, Mrs., 1934–1970
Sanders, R., 1965–1979
Sanders, Mrs., 1965–1979
Saxby, R. J., 1959–1974
Saxby, Mrs., 1959–1974
Scott, Miss R., 1972–1980
Shaw, Miss M. W., 1950–1960
(to France)
Stewart, G. J., 1975–1979
Stewart, Mrs., 1975–1979
Taylor, N. J., 1948–1969
Taylor, Mrs., 1948–1969
Wheeler, A. R., 1969–1983
Wheeler, Mrs., 1969–1983

TRIPOLI, LIBYA
Olley, J. R., 1923–1924
(from Tunisia
to Chad)

MOROCCO
Bates, Miss A. L. K., 1948–1957
(from French Guiana)

Beatie, M., 1947–1949
Caroll, Miss R. M., 1958–1965
Chantler, Miss E. A., 1937–1940
Crane, J., 1923
(from Spain)
Crane, Mrs., 1923
(to Spain, later
Mrs. E H. Trenchard)
Dibble, A., 1974–1974
Dibble, Mrs., 1974–1975
Fallaize, A., 1925–1947
Fallaize, Mrs., 1925–1947
Fisk, E. G., 1927–1966
Fisk, Mrs., 1927–1966
Fraser-Smith, C. F., 1939–1940
Fraser-Smith, Mrs., 1939–1940
Frears, T. W., 1938–1983
Frears, Mrs., 1948–1983
Gabriel, C., 1933–1948
Gabriel, Mrs., 1933–1948
Grossholtz, J. J., 1946–1959
Grossholtz, Mrs., 1946–1952
Grossholtz, Mrs. B., 1954–1968
Ksara, M., 1966–1969
Lightbody, Mr. R., 1948–1953
(to Ethiopia)
Lightbody, Mrs., 1948–1953
(to Ethiopia)
Orr, Miss J. S. C., 1948–1969
Ratcliffe, H., 1938–1980
Ratcliffe, Mrs., 1950–1980
Shawner, A., 1974–1975
Shawner, Mrs., 1974–1975
Sietman, J., 1946–1950
Sietman, Mrs., 1946–1950
Taylor, R. C., 1901–1917
Taylor, Mrs., 1901–1917
Whitaker, C., 1961–1969
Whitaker, Mrs., 1961–1969

PAKISTAN
Beckett, R., 1950–1965
Beckett, Mrs., 1950–1965
Blair, C. F., 1953–1958
Blair, Mrs., 1956–1958
Brooks, R., 1970–1982
(to Philippines)

Clark, D. E. C., 1943–1953
 (from and to India)
Clark, Mrs., 1943–1953
 (from and to India)
Cushing, Miss R., 1980
Douglas, I. H., 1948–1953
Douglas, Mrs., 1948–1953
Greig, Miss E. M., 1981
Harper, Dr., H. F., 1954
 (to and from Afghanistan,
  1963–1966; to Afghanistan,
  1966–1971)
Harper, Mrs., 1963–1966
 (to and from Afghanistan,
  to Afghanistan), 1966–1971
Hislop, Miss A. C., 1954–1969,
 1972–1973
Hughes, Miss M. A., 1969
Kerr, S., 1975–1977
McGill, Miss F., 1978–1981
McKenzie, Miss M., 1978–1981
Marsh, P. W., 1951–1966
Marsh, Mrs., 1951–1966
Moore, A. C., 1958–1959
Moore, Mrs., 1959–1961
Moore, Miss E. S., 1968
Orr, R. W., 1951–1983
Orr, Mrs., 1951–1983
Penfold, W. S., 1951–1953
Penfold, Mrs., 1951–1953
Prentice, Miss B. H., 1954–1975
Renvoize, J. A., 1949–1953
Renvoize, Mrs., 1949–1953
Shaw, Miss S. J., 1982
Stewart, Dr. A. G., 1976
Stewart, Mrs., 1977
 (formerly Miss Twamley, R.)
Tarring, Miss S. R., 1969
Twamley, Miss R., 1976–1977
 (See Mrs. A. G. Stewart)

Warren, Miss R. E., 1973–1977
Williamson, E. G., 1950–1955
 (from India to S. Africa)
Williamson, Mrs. 1950–1955
 (from India to S. Africa)

SENEGAL
Bode, G., 1976
Bode, Mrs., 1976
Bramsen, P., 1981
Bramsen, Mrs., 1981
Church, E. D., 1962
Church, Mrs., 1963

SUDAN
Hewstone, A. A., 1913–1916
 (later in Nigeria)
Parks, F., 1913
Parks, Mrs., 1913

TUNISIA
McGavin, E. W., 1909–1919
 (from Italy)
McGavin, Mrs., 1909–1919
 (from Italy)
Olley, J. R., 1919–1923
 (to Tripoli, Libya)
Patching, P. J., 1949–1958
 (to France)
Patching, Mrs., 1949–1958
 (to France)
Robb, J., 1922–1924
 (from Algeria)
Robb, Mrs., 1922–1924
 (from Algeria)
Wasserzug, S., 1896
 (to Israel)

Index

Principal references are in **bold** type; illustrations are indicated by page references in *italics*.

VOLUME 4

...THAT THE WORLD MAY KNOW
that Thou hast sent Me, and hast
loved them, as Thou hast loved Me.

John 17:23